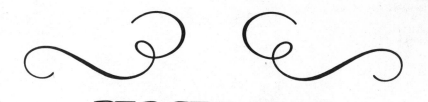

PERCEIVING
THE
ARTS

An Introduction
to the Humanities

DENNIS J. SPORRE

University of North Carolina at Wilmington

PRENTICE-HALL, INC., Englewood Cliffs, N.J. 07632

Library of Congress Cataloging in Publication Data

Sporre, Dennis J
   Perceiving the arts.

   Includes index.
   1. Arts. 2. Perception. 3. Visual perception. I. Title.
NX620.S68 1981   700'.1   80-24855
ISBN 0-13-657031-3

Editorial production, supervision, and
   interior design by Frank Hubert
Manufacturing Buyer: Harry P. Baisley
Cover design by 20/20 Services, Inc.,
   from a concept by Dennis J. Sporre

Previously published under the title
Perceiving the Arts: An Introduction

Printed in the United States of America
10 9 8 7 6 5 4

Prentice-Hall International, Inc., *London*
Prentice-Hall of Australia Pty. Limited, *Sydney*
Prentice-Hall of Canada, Ltd., *Toronto*
Prentice-Hall of India Private Limited, *New Delhi*
Prentice-Hall of Japan, Inc., *Tokyo*
Prentice-Hall of Southeast Asia Pte. Ltd., *Singapore*
Whitehall Books Limited, *Wellington, New Zealand*

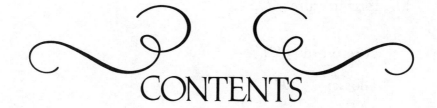

CONTENTS

List of Illustrations

Chapter 1

1.1. Jackson Pollock, *One (Number 31, 1950).*
1.2. Facsimile of an eighteenth-century high chest of drawers.
1.3. 1953 Volkswagen Beetle.
1.4. Jean-Baptiste-Camille Corot, *A View near Volterra.*
1.5. Pablo Picasso, *Guernica.*
1.6. Vincent van Gogh, *The Starry Night.*
1.7. Pablo Picasso, *Girl before a Mirror.*
1.8. Joan Miro, *Painting.*

Chapter 3

3.1. Vincent van Gogh, *The Starry Night.*
3.2. Giovanni Battista Vanni, *The Holy Family with Saint John.*
3.3. Chu Ta, *Lotus.*
3.4. Wood plank and butt.
3.5. Albrecht Dürer, *Lamentation.*
3.6. Daniel Hopfer, *Ceiling Ornament.*
3.7. Thomas Hart Benton, *Cradling Wheat.*
3.8. Charles Sheeler, *Delmonico Building.*
3.9. Hobson Pittman, *Violets No. 1.*
3.10. Nancy McIntyre, *Barbershop Mirror.*
3.11. Joan Miro, *Painting.*
3.12. Three rectangles.
3.13. Jackson Pollock, *One (Number 31, 1950).*

3.14. Basic color spectrum.
3.15. Color spectrum, including composite hues.
3.16. Color wheel.
3.17. Value scale.
3.18. Color-value equivalents.
3.19. Repetition of patterns.
3.20. Pablo Picasso, *Girl before a Mirror.*
3.21. Closed composition.
3.22. Open composition.
3.23. Jean-Baptiste-Camille Corot, *A View near Volterra.*
3.24. Subject-matter continuum.
3.25. Jan Vermeer, *The Girl with a Red Hat.*
3.26. Salvador Dali, *The Persistence of Memory.*
3.27. Pablo Picasso, *Guernica.*
3.28. Vertical composition.
3.29. Horizontal composition.
3.30. Upright-triangular composition.
3.31. Inverted-triangular composition.
3.32. Curved line.
3.33. Broken line.
3.34. Juxtaposition.

Chapter 4

4.1. Roman copy of a Greek statue.
4.2. Roman frieze.
4.3. Giambologna, *Sampson Slaying a Philistine.*

PREFACE

The purpose of this text is to provide a basic, technical, and audience-related reference encompassing all the arts. It is aimed at the individual who has little or no exposure to the arts on a formal basis.

One difficulty in developing an interdisciplinary study such as this is the choice of method of approach. To have meaning a text must have some thread of consistency as it moves from one discipline to another. One possible thread is that of terminology. For example, we speak of the "interrelated arts" because there are terms such as *rhythm* and *form* that occur in all the arts. I find that approach difficult, for although the terms may be identical, meanings and concepts implied by the terms are not. Another approach in interrelating the arts is to treat them in a sociocultural or historical manner. There is a good deal of validity in that approach, as demonstrated by any

number of books on the current market. However, such an approach, fundamentally, is too broad and complex for the purposes of a text such as this.

In trying to provide a respondent-oriented work dealing essentially with the questions of what we can see and what we can hear in works of art, I have chosen to relate the arts in a very cursory fashion by approaching each of them in relation to the perceptual process. In so doing I have utilized and adapted Harry Broudy's formulation of aesthetic response. We can ask four questions about an art or artwork: (1) What is it? (2) How is it put together? (3) How does it stimulate the senses? (4) What does it mean to me? The first three of these questions basically concern cognitive information and are well suited to study. They constitute a workable approach that provides a thread of consistency and a comfortable springboard for a beginner's approach to the arts. However, like any categorical device, it is not foolproof. In some cases, the formula does not fit comfortably and I am guilty of bending corners. Moreover, some elements of some arts defy categorizing. Some overlap categories or seem to fall equally into two. Some, such as the conventionalized forms of music, imply a second category because of the first. In addition, there always is a danger in a work such as this that the necessity of brevity can create its own form of inaccuracy. Definitions of terms are by no means universally agreed upon. Also, the choice of what to include and what to exclude must be arbitrary. This is especially true of the very brief lists of works for study included at the end of each chapter. In using the chronologies and examples that follow Chapter 3–10, the reader should note that dates are approximate and arbitrary. Styles and tendencies do not begin at a given date and end at another; often, periods and styles overlap, and one artist may represent one style at the beginning of his career and another at the end. The attempt here is to provide historical and stylistic references that illustrate the nonstylistic, nonhistorical characteristics described in the text. Any attempt to study individual works or artists, or to define the major historical periods, should be accompanied by additional research. My purpose in providing such lists is to be helpful, not definitive or comprehensive.

There is a great desire and appetite for the arts in our society. Getting the most from an experience with the arts depends essentially on one's skills of perception. Knowing what to see and what to hear in a painting, a play, a building, or a musical composition is one step toward developing discriminating perception. Whether or not the cognitive approach to the aesthetic experience and the presentation of terminology is the first step is a question that is virtually unanswerable. I suggest, however, that before (and perhaps more important than) the development of the ability to discourse on the philosophies of art or its historical periods comes the technical ability to see and hear what is in the individual works. I am not suggesting that philosophy and history do not

contribute to the perceptual experience, but merely that one needs to start at a more basic level. The need to know the difference between polyphony and homophony, between a suite and a concerto, between prints and paintings, is more basic than the need to know the difference between baroque and romantic, iconoclasm and cubism. This text attempts to serve that need only. It is a *brief* introduction. Further development, philosophy, history, *and* value judgments can (and must) come later.

The arts are accessible even to those of limited background. I hope this text will illustrate how much of art can be approached with the use of the cognitive skills we have learned from childhood. However, this step is only the beginning. A lifetime of study and involvement should follow.

An approach such as this is not designed to produce "amateur artists." Mastery of the technical skills basic to aesthetic perception and response does not qualify one as an artist or an art critic. Nowhere in this text will we discuss "good" art or "bad" art, or how one goes about knowing the difference between the two. This study is an introduction designed to teach the basic definitions and processes requisite to informed perception. It starts at ground zero and opens the door.

This book was developed to serve as a text for an interdisciplinary course in aesthetic perception at The Pennsylvania State University. It was designed only as an information sourcebook, and should thus be flexible enough to serve any course that seeks to examine more than one arts discipline. The information contained in these chapters, it seems to me, is required for basic understanding. It also is more easily presented in a text than in a lecture. Students whose background may be expansive can read it rapidly, pausing to fill in the holes in their own background. Students who have had no exposure to the arts can spend the necessary hours memorizing. Classroom time then can be spent on expanded illustration, discussion, or analysis of actual artworks. One's own philosophical bent towards the arts should not be affected by this work. For example, when theories, philosophies, or definitions differ I have tried to provide an overview rather than slavishly following my own or anyone else's viewpoint. So, one possible use of this text might be analogous to the use of a dictionary in a writing course.

Finally, some may find the interviews in Chapter 2 extraneous. Nevertheless, I find it impossible to deal with an introduction to the arts, technical or otherwise, without some consideration for the human beings who are attempting to communicate with us their view of the universe. These interviews attempt to provide in an artist's own words some of the problems, concerns, and procedures that are inherent in the process of communication through the arts.

The photographs in the chapter on landscape artchitecture are the property of Donald Girouard, and I am extremely grateful to him, Ellis Grove, and Warren Smith for their contributions to this text, and to Jane Mease for her assistance in preparing the manuscript.

D.J.S.

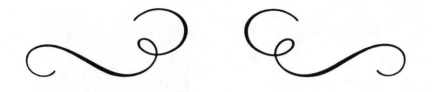

INTRODUCTION

The Arts and Perception

The Human Process

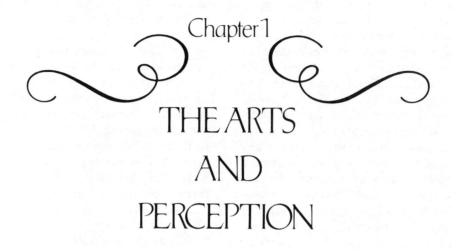

Chapter 1

THE ARTS AND PERCEPTION

THE NATURE OF THE ARTS*

In our passion for categorizing we have sometimes tried to gather the more "humanizing" elements of our civilization into a vague general area called "The Humanities." There is no sharp boundary separating these aspects of life from the sciences, technology, and the social sciences. Still, the curiosity to know the secrets of the natural universe, or to know how something works, or even how people behave en masse, is motivated by a perceptibly different spirit than the one that drives a human being to try to comprehend humankind. In the traditions of formal scholarship—that is to say, in the way universities divide these things—the humanities are thought of as philosophy, literature, the fine arts, and (sometimes) history. But these very often simply constitute a convenient administrative unit. Some of the current studies in these fields turn out to be largely quantitative with computerized data, while over in the microbiology department it may well be that a scientist is far less concerned about the phenomenon he is observing under the microscope than about its meaning for the human race. The humanities (if the term is to have a meaning beyond taxonomy) are marked by a point of view rather than by the names of certain disciplines. It is the point of view that wants to know what humanity is about, what kinds of creatures we are, and how we got to be this way. Are we civilized? What are our hopes and fears? What do we think about and dream about? What do we believe? How do we behave?

The answers to such questions are not likely to be as neat as those demanded by the scientist. The evidence is too scattered. It lies

---

*This section of Chapter 1 was written by Warren S. Smith, and is used with his permission.

in the legends of storytellers and dramatists, in biographies and autobiographies, in the thoughts of the philosophers and the images of the poets. It also lies in the millions of artworks that the human race has left strewn about the planet, from the caves of Lascaux and Altamira to the fleeting images of the latest film festival. The artworks are themselves expressions of the humanities, not—as they are so often presented—merely illustrations of literature or history.

Any definition of a work of art (like any definition of religion or of love) is destined to be inadequate for some people. For me, a work of art is some sight, sound, or movement (or combination)—some sensible manifestation—intended as human expression. This is obviously not a value-laden definition aimed at placing a work of art on a pedestal. It accepts as an artwork whatever is *intended* as an artwork, whether it is a childish effort or a renowned masterpiece. As an expression each artwork carries within itself some evidence of that seeking that characterizes the human condition. Its banality or profundity, its innocence or sophistication, its light-heartedness or solemnity are descriptive, not restrictive, qualities.

Within whatever range the artwork falls, and regardless of whether its creator intended it or not, the artwork has *form:* it occupies space or time, or both. A painting or print or photograph takes its shape on a two-dimensional surface. A piece of sculpture or architecture must occupy three-dimensional space. The sounds of music occupy no space at all but weave their shapes within the duration of time. The performing of a play or an opera or a dance requires both space and time, both visual and auditory elements. So do the film, and, of course, television, though they reduce space to two dimensions, however much the illusion of depth remains.

But the concept of form extends beyond the mere shapes in space and time. Form is concerned not only with the overall structure that contains the work of art, but with the smaller patterns that compose its inner designs as well. It is therefore closely tied to the artist's choice of medium and materials— watercolors or oils, lithography or steel etching, strings or brass or electronic synthesizer, clay or bronze or stone, prose or verse, and so on. The artist's work is a continuous process of making choices, and the only rules he has to guide him are those he imposes on himself. Traditionally the artist has sought both unity and variety. The most admired forms from the past are those in which the separate parts are clear, but not wholly predictable, so that one can say at the same time "Of course!" and "How surprising!"

There are styles and fads in art forms, but unlike advances in technology and the sciences, a new form in the arts never really replaces an old one. Obviously not all styles and forms can survive indefinitely, but a Picasso cannot do to a Rembrandt what an Einstein did to a Newton, nor can the serialism of Schoenberg banish the tonality of Mozart as the evolutionary evidence of Darwin banished the eighteenth-century world of William Paley. The arts, even more than literature, survive by direct impact, and continue to swell the ever-growing reservoir of human manifestations. Times and customs change, the passions that shaped the artist's work disappear, his cherished beliefs become fables, but all of these are preserved in the form of his work. "All the assertions get disproved sooner or later," Bernard Shaw observed, "and so we find the world full of a magnificent debris of artistic fossils, with the matter-of-fact credibility gone clean out of them, but the form still splendid." No doubt one can often read much history or biography in the arts, and no doubt, too, a knowledge of history or of an artist's life can often enhance a work of art, but the response to an artwork is always in the present tense.

Furthermore, a work of art is always a *gestalt:* its form and its content are inseparable. We may pay particular attention to the form today and consider the content more thoroughly tomorrow. But even as we determine to do so we are instantly aware that the two are one. The two concepts are interdependent and inseparable, even though we may attempt verbally to place them in separate paragraphs!

The content of an artwork may include certain subject matter. The sculpture may be a human form, the painting a landscape, the music the description of a storm, the dance a depiction of a fanciful story, the play or film a representation of a family crisis. But in none of these cases will the subject matter be mistaken for the real thing, and in some cases it may be the merest excuse, a framework for the sights, sounds, or movements that the artist has created. Indeed, in many artworks there is no perceptible subject matter at all. Music, for example, quite frequently gets along very well without words, without a descriptive title, without being "about" anything. Very often dance does too. And in more recent years painting, sculpture, and even film have often departed from subject matter. Only the live theatre, it seems, must be tied—however tenuously—to some recognizable activity.

All of this brings us inescapably to the concept of *abstraction.* Every work of art, no matter how literal or representational, is an abstraction, in that it is a thing *apart*—removed from the indiscriminate and chaotic world beyond the picture frame, beyond the pedestal, the stage, the lighted screen, the privileged sound chamber in which the artwork resides. Some works, are, of course, more abstract than others, but abstraction should not be regarded as an attribute only of so-called abstract art but of all art in varying degrees. There comes a point, however, when subject matter seems to disappear altogether and the other arts enter the realm that music and dance have always in some sense occupied—a realm in which recognizable subject matter is not necessarily expected, and therefore not missed. At this point it is proper to speak of an artwork as being *nonobjective,* since there is no longer any evidence of its having been "abstracted" from a recognizable object or activity (Fig. 1.1).

So we must conclude that the content of an artwork necessarily extends beyond mere subject matter. Obviously it must also be closely linked with the arrangement of lines, masses, colors, rhythms, timbres, dynamics —all the elements that, from another viewpoint, we regarded purely as form. But beyond this the content must at last be assumed to be what we get out of the work—or, perhaps more accurately, what the artist has put into it. It may offer us a profoundly emotional or a rigorously intellectual experience. All of the elements come together to affect us in some way. We cannot say exactly in *what* way because there are as many ways as there are artworks. It is not even possible to say that the same artwork will offer the same content to every respondent, for everyone brings to it a different set of experiences and a different level of sophistication. And although there may be no single correct way to respond to an artwork, it would seem worth some effort to discover its true content, to determine what the artist has put into the work that will now communicate with us as respondents.

This is a delicate and sensitive business, involving as it does the ability to sense an artist's *style.* This undefinable quality is a synthesis that carries the same connotation for an artwork that the term *personality* carries for an individual. One style, like one personality, may be easily distinguishable from another, though not easily explainable.

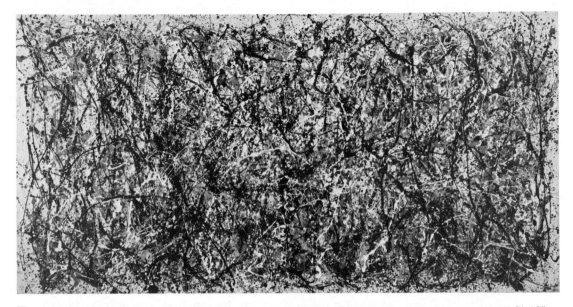

Fig. 1.1.   Jackson Pollock, *One (Number 31, 1950)* (1950). Oil and enamel paint on canvas, 8′ 10″ × 17′ 5⅝″. Collection, The Museum of Modern Art, New York. Gift of Sidney Janis.

An understanding of style comes not from any verbal explanation, but from practice in responding. It is safe to assume that practice is needed, for a complete aesthetic response requires a perception that can make fine distinctions. It also requires a willingness to accept the abstraction of the work in the manner in which the artist has composed it, together with whatever emotional overtones he or she has tried to communicate.

It is, I suppose, impossible to confront a work of art without developing some attitude towards it and placing some personal value on it. Your own response may vary from boredom to adoration to outrage. If your attitude on these matters is firmly fixed—if you have some clear idea of what music *ought* to sound like, what kind of action *ought* to constitute a drama, what a picture *ought* to look like—you will have little trouble in making value judgments. An artwork will be good art to the degree that it fits your preconceptions and bad art to the degree that it does not. These limits were

more clearly set in former times when the church or the court or the "academy" was the accepted arbiter of taste. The advantage of having such guidelines was, however, short-lived, for many of the works we have come to admire the most were created by rebels from the establishments of their times. Nevertheless, for many people certain ideals of beauty and proportion that evolved in earlier centuries are still significant "taste-makers" today, and a study of aesthetics will still probably begin with Aristotle's conception of what is beautiful.

There runs through any discussion of the arts the question of how much we should be influenced by words that are spoken or written about them, and how much by the artwork itself. What part, in other words, should criticism play in our own responses to art? It is easy—and tempting—to say that our responses are to be purely our own, unencumbered by what some "expert" thinks. But it must be remembered that we live in a highly verbal society where *all* our responses tend to be verbalized. Even the respondent who is most outspokenly opposed to art criticism will try to share his own responses with others—and this in itself is an elementary form of art criticism. At its finest, art criticism does not merely set up value systems for what is and what is not acceptable. It also shows us ways to look and listen that may have escaped us, so that whether we agree with the critic's judgment or not, his words have given us an enriched perception of the work.

The value systems in our culture are so pluralistic, not only concerning the arts but concerning politics, religion, morals and manners, that it is not surprising that there are today no universally accepted arbiters of taste. The absence of such arbiters sets us free to accept or reject art experiences as we choose, but it also leaves us in the midst of a plethora of styles (also a plethora of conflicting commentary and criticism) with no guide but our own perception. Many people find this situation so frustrating that they literally beg for guidance. Guidance is, of course, available, but not in the old-fashioned sense of providing a clear-cut scale of esthetic values. Some of the frustrations of living in today's world are unavoidable.

The arts are always a system of relationships, a careful, tenuous equilibrium between one thing and another—so much so that it has often occurred to me that almost any substantive question one can ask of a work of art must be answered initially with "That depends . . ." What should be its size? its complexity? its focal point? its relationship to nature? to society? to the artist? Multiply these questions to infinity, and ask them of any artwork, from an acknowledged masterpiece to a student work in progress. For an answer we must first discover the relationships, both within the work itself and outside itself. "It depends . . ."

Such a relativistic approach to the arts cannot result in giving every artwork a good or bad label, extolling one as a masterpiece and condemning another as a fraud. An enormous amount of nonsense is generated by such questions as "Is it really art?" or "Will it live?" A more proper question would always be, "What can we get out of it at this moment?" If the work engenders some response, there is little point in arguing whether it is "art." Nor is it profitable to concern ourselves too much with the possible response of our grandchildren. History has provided us with no reliable pattern for the survival of art. Moreover, the number of variables involved in forming the taste of our posterity is nearly infinite. If we cannot know what kind of world they will be living in (if indeed the race survives) or what kind of pressures or passions will be driving them, surely we cannot pick their art for them. We cannot even be assured that the great masters, as we judge them, will continue to nourish them. It seems unlikely that Shakespeare, Rembrandt, or Beethoven might one day be passé, but we shall not be alive to defend them.

Actually, to "pick the survivor" is merely an academic game that no one can ever live long enough to win or lose. And it is not entirely healthy to think of art only in terms of the great masters who outlast the centuries. Art is legitimately a day-to-day activity, and it is natural that some of it should turn out to be ephemeral. The pace of living has accelerated so much that it becomes more and more essential to have some symbol of the passing tide held before us, if only for a moment. In a somewhat romantic vein Willa Cather asked, in *The Song of the Lark,* "What was any art but an effort to make a sheath, a mold, in which to imprison for a moment the shining, elusive element which is life itself—life hurrying past us and running away, too strong to stop, too sweet to lose?"

We should be wiser, I believe, to think of the arts more as we think of people. We learn, most of us, at a very early age that an adequate adjustment to the world cannot be made from social responses that simply divide the "good people" from the "bad people." We have learned to be skeptical even of such categories as "the people I like" and "the people I don't like." If we do maintain such divisions, we find individuals constantly moving from one group to the other. Eventually we find human differences too subtle for easy classification, and the web of our relationships becomes too complex for analysis. And we try to move toward more and more sensitive discrimination, so that there are those we can learn from, those we can work with, those good for an evening of light talk, those we can depend on for a little affection, and so on—with perhaps those very few with whom we can sustain a deepening relationship for an entire lifetime. When we have learned this same sensitivity and adjustment to works of art—when we have gone beyond the easy categories of the textbooks and have learned to regard our art relationships as part of our own growth—then we shall have achieved a dimension in living that is as deep and as irreplaceable as friendship.

COHABITING WITH THE ARTS

The difficulty that many individuals have in approaching the arts is caused simply by their lack of familiarity with the arts. That unfamiliarity, perhaps, has been fostered by those individuals, both within the arts and without, who have tried to make the arts elitist enterprises open only to the thoroughly knowledgeable and the truly sophisticated. They have, therefore, attempted to separate the arts from everyday life by making the art gallery, museum, concert hall, theater, and opera house sanctimonious institutions quite apart from our everyday concerns. Nothing could be further from actuality. As has been suggested by the title of this section, the arts, or things aesthetic, are elements of life with which we must deal and to which we must respond in our most ordinary of everyday situations. We cohabit with the arts because the principles of aesthetics permeate our existence, from those high levels of human emotion and human response that we quite rightly and generally associate with the theatre, concert hall, and art gallery right down to the matter of putting on our socks in the morning. The impact of the arts on life is significant, but a full understanding of that significance is possible only if we see the arts not only as elements seminal to great thought, the quality of life, and human understanding, but also as contributors to an effective and successful daily existence.

Very briefly let us examine some of the ways in which aesthetic decisions shape our day-to-day experience. The most obvious aspect of our personality, as seen by those around us, is our dress. We are judged in many ways—by our peers, by our acquaintances, and by our employers—by the way we dress. Our dress projects an image. We hope it is the image we wish to project. Our aesthetic decisions (or lack of them) relative to dress, then, play a vital role in our personal relationships. How does understanding the arts assist us in this area? Quite simply, the principles of composition that govern painting, for example, are the same principles employed by those who design clothing. It is important for us to know, therefore, how the elements of line, form, mass, color, focus, and unity, all of which are aesthetic properties, work together in our clothing to create a picture of ourselves as we go out each day to meet the public. If we are not knowledgeable of how our dress stimulates response in other individuals, then we are at a great disadvantage in trying to accomplish those things we seek to accomplish in life. If our occupation requires us to sell goods to other individuals and our manner of dress is ludicrous or offensive, then that lack of aesthetic knowledge affects our pocketbook.

We also need to understand that the arts, aesthetics, and *design* play an important role in making the world around us a more interesting and habitable place. When elements in our life are developed, essentially they are developed from a design of time and/or space. The design of time and space usually takes into consideration practical matters such as purpose and convention. The term *convention* is one that will be used repeatedly in this text, and it suits our purposes well to begin to discuss it here. A convention is a set of rules or mutually accepted circumstances. For example, that all of our electrical appliances have a standard male connector that we can be relatively assured fits every wall socket in every building in the United States of America is a convention. It is a practical convention to which those who have traveled abroad can testify. In England appliances are sold without connectors because the diversity of wall outlets in that small country is so great that it is impractical for manufacturers to sell appliances with a connector. For our purposes a more appropriate example of a convention might be the keyboard and tuning of a piano. In any case, from these two examples I believe we can imagine clearly the role that conventions play in practical and other circumstances.

To apply the concepts of design and convention to items that have both practical and aesthetic components, examine Fig. 1.2, a facsimile of an eighteenth-century high chest of drawers. The high chest was conceived to fill a practical purpose—to provide for storage of household objects in an easily accessible, yet hidden, place. However, while designing an object to accommodate that practical need, the cabinetmakers felt the additional need to provide an interesting and attractive object. Our experience of this piece of furniture can be enlightening and

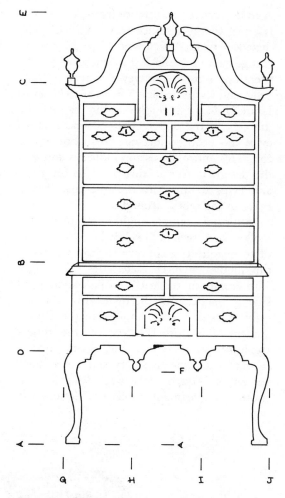

Fig. 1.2. Facsimile of an eighteenth-century high chest of drawers.

challenging if we utilize discrimination and imagination in our perception of its design.

First of all, the design is controlled by a convention that dictates a consistent height for tables and desks. So the lower portion of the chest, from point A to point B, designs space within a height that will harmonize with other furniture in the room. If we look carefully, we also can see that the parts of the high chest are designed with a sophisticated and interesting series of proportional and progressive relationships. The distance from

A to B is twice the distance from A to D and is equal to the distance from B to C. The distances from A to F and C to E bear no recognizable relationship to the previous dimensions but are, however, equal to each other and to the distances from G to H, H to I, and I to J. In addition, the size of the drawers in the upper chest decreases at an even and proportional rate from bottom to top. This entire discussion indicates some of the design factors in this piece of furniture and helps to illustrate the role that design plays in the world around us.

A further example might be the rear of the Volkswagen seen in Fig. 1.3. Here repetition of form reflects a concern for unity, one of the fundamental characteristics of design. The design of the early Volkswagen used strong repetition of the oval with variation only in its size. Later models of the Volkswagen differ from this version and reflect the intrusion of conventions, again, into the world of design. As safety standards called for larger bumpers, the oval design of the motor-compartment hood was flattened in order that a larger bumper could clear it. The size of the rear window was enlarged and squared to accommodate the need for increased rear vision. The intrusion of these conventions changed the design of the Beetle by breaking down the strong unity of the original composition.

One cannot trust to others the matter of making aesthetic decisions in business and personal life. A businessman needs to know whether the design of a sign created to bring individuals into his store from the street or the design of the advertising he uses in the newspaper or on television is well founded. He needs to know whether or not the aesthetic layout of his business establishment is conducive to the clientele he wishes to attract. If he does not, then his only means of assessing the success or failure of the decisions he entrusts to others will be waiting for his bank balance to show a profit or a loss. That is a little late for corrective action. The arts *are* important to us in our daily living; they *do* affect us. Understanding things aesthetic and making aesthetic responses are

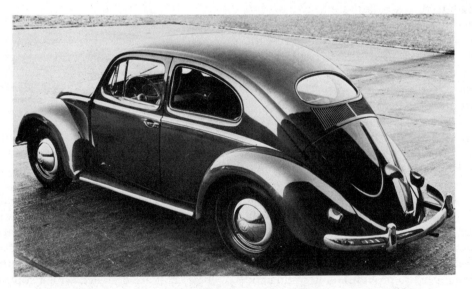

Fig. 1.3.   1953 Volkswagen Beetle. Courtesy of Volkswagen of America.

day-to-day occurrences, and not isolated instances applicable only if one happens to be responding to an artwork.

In addition, as Edwin J. Delattre states when he compares the purpose for studying technical subjects to the purpose for studying the humanities or the arts, "When a person studies the mechanics of internal combustion engines the intended result is that he should be better able to understand, design, build, or repair such engines, and sometimes he should be better able to find employment because of his skills, and thus better his life.... When a person studies the humanities [the arts] the intended result is that he should be better able to understand, design, build, or repair a life—for living is a vocation we have in common despite our differences.

"The humanities provide us with opportunities to become more capable in thought, judgment, communication, appreciation, and action." Delattre goes on to say that these provisions enable us to think more rigorously and to imagine more abundantly. "These activities free us to possibilities that are new, at least to us, and they unbind us from portions of our ignorance about living well.... Without exposure to the cultural ... traditions that are our heritage, we are excluded from a common world that crosses generations."[1] The poet Archibald MacLeish is more succinct: "Without the Arts, how can the university teach the Truth."

AESTHETIC PERCEPTION AND RESPONSE

In this chapter we have examined the nature of the arts and a bit of their relationship to

life. The question of how we go about approaching them, or how we study them, is nearly as complicated. A myriad of methods is available, and so it remains to choose one, for better or for worse, and carry on from there. I have indicated that the purpose herein is to provide a concentrated reference that covers all the arts—a lofty task, indeed. Those who are interested in such a work are, then, assumed to be those whose exposure or background in the arts is limited. So, a method of study must be chosen that can act as a springboard into the arts, as a point of departure from the realm of the familiar into the unknown. Inasmuch as we live in a world of facts and figures, weights and measures, it seems logical to begin a study of the arts by dealing with those characteristics of the arts that lend themselves to the kind of study with which we are familiar. In other words, from a *cognitive* point of view, what can we see and what can we hear in the arts?

To put that question in different terms, how can we sharpen our aesthetic perception? First of all, we must identify those items that can be seen and heard in works of art. Second, we must learn—just as we learn a foreign language—the vocabulary of those items. Third, we must understand why and how what we perceive relates to our potential response. It is, after all, our response to an artwork that interests us. We can *perceive* an object. We *choose* to *respond* to it in aesthetic terms. So, in our study we will concern ourselves with our aesthetic response.

As we indicated earlier, it will be extremely helpful in our examination to utilize a method that allows for consistency of observation as we pass from one art discipline to another. We will ask three questions: (1) What is it? (2) How is it put together? (3) How does it stimulate our senses? We will study these questions in the general context of each of the art disciplines. As we will see,

[1]Edwin J. Delattre, "The Humanities Can Irrigate Deserts," *The Chronicle of Higher Education,* October 11, 1977, p. 32.

these are also the basic questions we can ask of an individual artwork.

When we respond to the question *What is it?* we make a formal response. We recognize that we are perceiving the design of two-dimensional space in a picture, three-dimensional space in a sculpture or the shelter of a piece of architecture, or perhaps the design of time in sound, or of time and space in dance. We also recognize the "form" of the item—for example, a still life, a human figure, a tragedy, a ballet, a concerto, a narrative film, a park, or a residence. It should be noted, however, that the term "form" is a broad one: it can be used as just noted, as noted earlier in the chapter, or in other ways. There are art forms, forms of arts, and forms in art.

When we respond to the question *How is it put together?* we respond to the technical elements of the design. We recognize and respond, for instance, to the fact that the picture has been done in oil, made by a printmaking technique, or created as a watercolor. We also recognize and respond to the elements that constitute the work, the items of composition—line, form, mass, color, repetition, harmony, and the unity that results from all of these. What devices have been employed, and how does each part relate to the others to make a whole? A concerto is composed of melody, harmony, timbre, tone, and more; a tragedy utilizes language, *mise en scène,* exposition, complication, denouement; a ballet has formalized movement, *mise en scène,* line, idea content, and so on.

Moving to the third question, we examine *how the work stimulates our senses*—and why. In other words, how do the particular formal and technical arrangements (whether conscious or unconscious on the part of the artist) elicit a sense response from us? Here we deal with both physical and mental properties. Our response to sculpture, for example, can be physical. We can touch a piece of sculpture and sense its smoothness or its hardness. Mentally, we experience sense responses that stem from what one, for want of better terms, calls the "universal language." When we respond to items composed of upright triangles we grant them the qualities of solidity. When we perceive the colors green and blue we denote them as "cool"; reds and yellows are "warm" colors. Pictures that are predominantly horizontal or composed of broad curves are said to be "soft" or placid. Angular, diagonal, or short, broken lines are said to stimulate a sense of movement. These and other sense responses tend to be universal; most individuals respond in similar fashion to them.

We also can ask a fourth question about a work of art: *What does the artwork mean to me?* For example, if we deal with a painting, we know it is a painting; we know it is a seascape. We also know it has been done in oil with a particular palette. We know how the artist has utilized line and mass, and how he or she has effected balance. In addition, we respond to how all those items stimulate the senses. For example, the artist may have utilized predominantly harsh, broken lines that incite a feeling of movement. We know that the artist has used very intense, saturated colors that give the work a dynamic quality. However, for us *personally* the seascape and the way it is put together may stimulate pleasantly romantic sensations. The causes of this response are strictly internal and subjective. Perhaps at one time in our life we had a romantic encounter on a beach with someone for whom we cared very much. These romantic feelings are brought to the surface whenever we see things that remind us of that situation.

However, we cannot dismiss the question *What does it mean to me?* as a reference to purely subjective and *affective* experience. Meaning in a work of art implies a certain level of communication from artist to respondent. A work of art is a way of looking at the universe that is manifested in a particular medium and *shared with others*. So, the ultimate response, meaning, and experience of an artwork goes beyond the merely personal to encompass an attempt to understand what the communicator may have had in mind. It is not sufficient, for example, merely to regard the disproportionate forms of a Mannerist painting as "strange." *Meaning* implies an understanding of the discomforting circumstances of religion and society that existed during that period. When we understand that, we may understand *why* the paintings of that period appear as they do. We also may sympathize with the agonies of individuals trying to cope with their universe. As a result, the "strangeness" of the artwork may come to mean something entirely different to us personally.

This fourth level of our aesthetic response does not lend itself well to cognitive examination since it stems to a large extent, at least, from our personal background. So, as we proceed in our investigations we will limit ourselves to the first three questions, with only an occasional glance at the fourth.

However, we must understand that the study we undertake (and for which this text is only the beginning) must eventually concentrate itself in that fourth level of response, *What does this work mean to me?* We must also understand fully that achieving any meaningful response at the affective level is contingent upon the ability to respond fully at the cognitive level and involves an attempt to understand the *meaning* that the *artist* has tried to impart in the artwork.

STYLE IN THE ARTS

A work of art or an art form is a way of looking at the universe that is manifested in a particular medium and shared with others.

That summation indicates concisely what the aesthetic experience is all about. Artists are human beings trying to cope with the cosmos and needing to share their insights and feelings with others. The manner in which they express themselves constitutes their style. *Style,* then, is the composite use of the devices and characteristics applicable to their medium of expression. As we noted earlier in the chapter, style is tantamount to the personality of an artwork, and can be defined rather simply. However, applying its connotations to a body of artworks calls for breadth and depth of knowledge. Style is that body of characteristics that identifies an artwork with an individual, a historical period, a "school" of artists, or a nation. Applying the term means assimilating materials and, inductively, drawing conclusions.

Therefore, determining the style of any artwork requires analysis of how the artist has utilized the characteristics applicable to his medium. If his usage is similar to others', we might conclude that they exemplify the same style. For example, Bach and Handel typify the *baroque* style in music; Haydn and Mozart, the *classical*. Listening to works by these composers quickly leads to the conclusion that the ornate melodic developments of Bach are like those of Handel, and quite different from those of Mozart and Haydn, whose clearly articulated motifs and structures are likewise different from Bach and Handel, and so on. The precision and symmetry of the Parthenon compared with the ornate opulence of the Palace of Versailles suggest that in line and form the architects of these buildings treated their medium differently. Yet the design of the Parthenon is obviously a visual companion, stylistically, of Mozart and Haydn, whereas Versailles reflects a similar approach to design to that of Bach and Handel.

We can take our examination one step further and play a game of stylistic analysis with

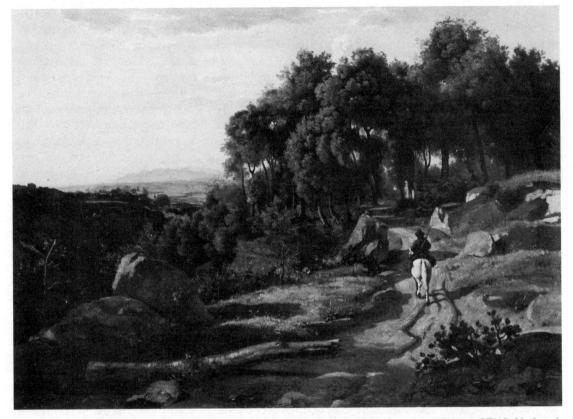

Fig. 1.4.   Jean-Baptiste-Camille Corot, *A View near Volterra* (1838). Canvas, 27⅜″ × 37½″. National Gallery of Art, Washington, D.C. Chester Dale Collection.

four paintings. The first three of these paintings were done by three different artists; the fourth, by one of those three. By stylistic analysis we will determine the painter of the fourth painting. Inasmuch as we have not yet dealt with definitions in composition, my analysis will be as nontechnical as possible. I will use three characteristics only: *line, palette,* and *brush stroke.*

The first painting (Fig. 1.4) is Corot's *A View Near Volterra.* We can see that Corot has used curvilinear line primarily, and that line (which creates the edges of the forms or shapes in the painting) is somewhat softened. That is, many of the forms—the rocks, trees, clouds, and so on—do not have crisp, clear

edges. Color areas tend to blend with each other, giving the painting a softened, almost fuzzy or out-of-focus appearance. That comfortable effect is heightened by Corot's use of *palette.* Palette, as we will note later, encompasses the total use of color and contrast, and since our illustrations are black and white we can deal with only one aspect of palette, and that is *value contrast.* As with his use of line, Corot maintains a subtle value contrast—that is, a subtle relationship of blacks to whites. His movement from light to dark is very gradual, and he avoids stark contrasts. He employs a full range of black, grays, and white, but does so without calling attention to their positioning. His *brush*

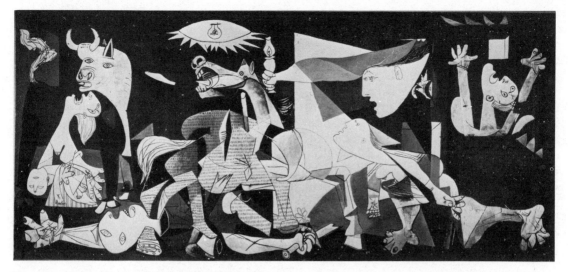

Fig. 1.5. Pablo Picasso, *Guernica* (1937, May–early June). Oil on canvas 11′ 5½″ × 25′ 5¾″. On extended loan to The Museum of Modern Art, New York, from the artist's estate.

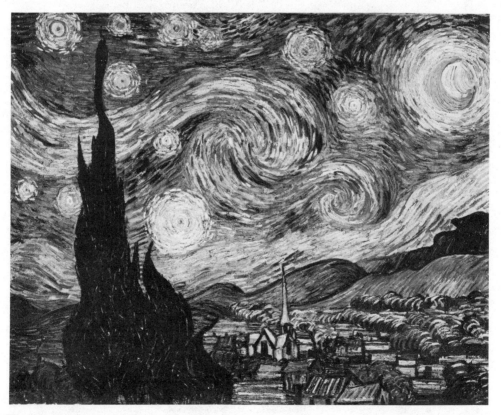

Fig. 1.6. Vincent van Gogh, *The Starry Night* (1889). Oil on canvas 29″ × 36¼″. Collection, The Museum of Modern Art, New York. Acquired through the Lillie P. Bliss Bequest.

stroke is somewhat apparent. That is, if we look carefully we can see brush marks, individual strokes where paint has been applied. Even though the objects in the painting are lifelike, Corot has not made any pretensions about the fact that his picture has been painted. We can tell that the foliage was executed by stippling—that is, by dabbing the brush to the canvas as one would dot an "i" with a pencil. Likewise, we can see throughout the painting marks made by the brush. The overall effect of the painting is one of realism, but we can see in every area the spontaneity with which it was executed.

The second painting (Fig. 1.5) is Picasso's *Guernica.* We hardly need be an expert to tell that this painting is by a different painter—or certainly in a different style than the previous one. Picasso has joined curved lines and straight lines, placing them in such relationships that they create a great sense of movement and discomfort. The edges of color areas and forms are sharp and distinct; nothing here is soft or fuzzy. Likewise, the value contrasts are stark and extreme. Areas of the highest value—that is, white—are forced against areas of the lowest value—black. In fact, the range of tonalities is far less broad

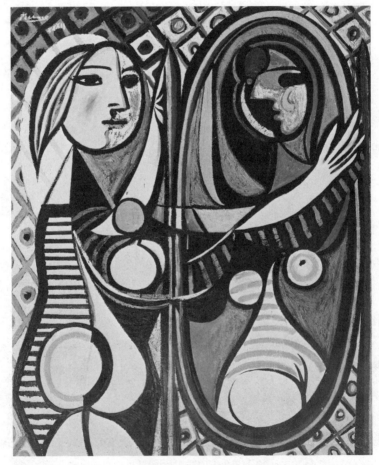

Fig. 1.7. Exercise painting. See Fig. 3.20 (p. 55) for identification.

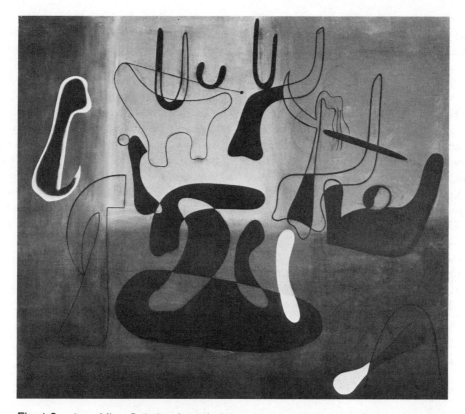

Fig. 1.8. Joan Miro, *Painting* (1933). Oil on canvas 68½" × 77¼". Collection, The Museum of Modern Art, New York. Gift of the Advisory Committee.

than in the previous work. The mid or medium (gray) tones are there, but they play a very minor role in the effect of the palette. Our examination of palette does not suffer here, because the work is executed only in blacks, whites, and grays. The starkness of the work is also reinforced by brush stroke, which is noteworthy in its near *absence*. Tonal areas are flat, and no trace of brush exists.

The third painting (Fig. 1.6) is van Gogh's *The Starry Night*. Use of line is highly active although uniformly curvilinear. Forms and color areas have both hard and soft edges, and van Gogh, as does Picasso, uses outlining to strengthen his images and reduce their

reality. The overall effect of line is a sweeping and undulating movement, highly dynamic and yet far removed from the starkness of the Picasso. On the other hand, van Gogh's curvilinearity and softened edges are quite different in effect from the relaxed quality of the Corot. Van Gogh's value contrasts are very broad, but moderate. He ranges from darks through medium grays to white, all virtually equal in importance. Even when movement from one area to another is across a hard edge to a highly contrasting value, the result is moderate: not soft, not stark. It is, however, brush stroke that gives the painting its unique personality. We can see thousands of individual brush marks where the artist applied paint to canvas. The nervous, almost frenetic use of brush stroke makes the painting come alive.

Now that we have examined three paintings in different styles and by different artists, can you determine which of the three painted Fig. 1.7? First, examine the use of line. Form and color edges are hard. Outlining is used. Curved and straight lines are *juxtapositioned* against each other. The effect is active and stark. By comparison, use of line is not like Corot, a bit like van Gogh, and very much like Picasso. Next, examine palette. Darks, grays, and whites are used broadly. However, the principal utilization is of strong contrast—the darkest darks against the whitest whites. This is not like Corot, a bit like van Gogh, and most like Picasso. Finally, brush stroke is generally unobtrusive. Tonal areas mostly are flat. This is definitely not a van Gogh and probably not a Corot. Three votes out of three go to Picasso, and the style is so distinctive that you probably had no difficulty deciding, even without my analysis. However, could you have been so certain if asked whether Picasso painted Fig. 1.8? A work by another "cubist" painter would pose even greater difficulty. So some differences in style are obvious; some are unclear. Distinguishing the work of one artist from another who designs in a similar fashion becomes even more difficult. However, the analytical process we just completed is indicative of how we can approach artworks in order to determine *how* they exemplify a given style, or what style they reflect if we do not already know it.

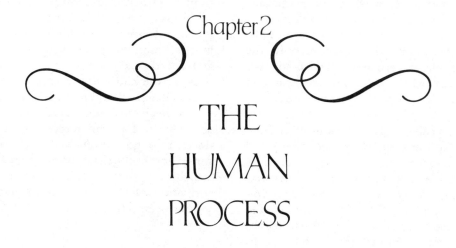

Chapter 2

THE
HUMAN
PROCESS

The arts are human communication, and any attempt at understanding must also accommodate an understanding of the human process involved in the creation of an artwork. That is not to say that one must understand the biography of the artist, but one must understand that there are mental processes, anguishes, and decisions that occur while the artist is approaching his artwork and while he is executing it. In order to convey a sense of the human process in the arts, we include several interviews in this chapter.

First, a critic discusses his role in the aesthetic process. He gives some controversial opinions on what skills and background a critic needs, and how he approaches the same performance relative to *his* differing readership. He expands upon his relationship to art, to artists, to the role of art, and to the public, and finally gives his opinion of what the arts need to do to fulfill *their* role in society.

Next, a painter describes the elusive quality of development and achievement. He wonders about the nature of growth as an artist, the need to survive, and the relation between the two. Within that relationship of growth and survival a delicate balance sometimes exists between communicating what the artist feels and what he knows will sell. There also exists a problem of wishing to speak in visual language to a mass audience who cannot speak or understand that language. Yet the need to communicate persists. Finally, the painter discusses how an artwork is developed, what makes an appropriate subject, and how the medium in which he works relates to the final product.

A musician discusses the framework of balance among the various artists who contribute to a musical presentation, the composer, the conductor, the players. Like the painter's, the musician's work is the result of a developmental process. However, creation

of a score and interpretation and performance of it require different talents and procedures. Yet music needs to be communicated, and the audience as a whole plays a
role in that process for the musician. In addition, because music occupies time only, the
art itself places certain constraints on the
artist—what he can or cannot communicate
and what goals he may set for himself.

Finally, a theatre director faces some of
the same problems that the musician does:
usually, he must use other performers and
his own creativity to shape a work not of his
own creation. The director, in my interview
with him, speculates on his role as a collaborator, yet leader. The factor of human to
human response in the live theatre brings the
audience into a more forceful role in the
communicative process, and direct control
of audience response becomes a part of the
director's concern.

I do not wish to imply that the individuals
selected for the interviews are in any way
typical artists or that the mental or physical
processes involved in their approach to art
reflect a majority or certain percentage of artists. However, by listening to the artist describe his own approach to his art we are able
to see and to understand more clearly something of that important human process. I
have tried to select individuals who have
achieved some substantial success, who are
recognized outside of their local areas, and
who are respected by their peers. I also have
tried to select individuals who are reasonably
articulate in order to provide an interesting
and enlightening interview. But it has to be
recognized that these individuals are responding as individuals. Other artists in the
discipline may work in similar fashion and
experience similar emotions, or may work
and feel quite differently.

This chapter is different from the rest of
the textbook. However, its content is an essential part of informed response to the arts.

Earlier I argued that technical information
was the first step toward full aesthetic response. That is true. However, aesthetic response is not a sterile or isolated curiosity; it
is an involvement in the human condition, in
human communication. So it seems to me,
at least, that along with basic information
must go the knowledge that information as-
sists us in understanding and communicating
with other *people,* who have chosen the arts
as a vehicle for communication. An introduction to how *individuals* cope with the
forces and problems of creating artworks to
which we respond places the technical information of the following chapters in its
proper perspective.

the critic and criticism

Interview with Philip Radcliffe

Educated at The University of Sheffield and
Cambridge University in England, Philip
Radcliffe is Head of Communications at the University of Manchester, England. He is also a critic of music and theatre for the *Sunday Times*
and the *Daily Mail,* two of the national newspapers in England. He also has written for the
London Times Literary Supplement and the
Manchester Guardian.

**What do you feel are the particular
tools or skills that are requisite to
functioning as an arts critic?** I think the
problem is, as you get into the professional
work as a critic, it's all too easy to be a critic
of anything at any time at a drop of the hat.
You do develop the professional skills, almost, of hack journalism. I think that is
fairly inevitable. You just have to keep them
under control. The skills required I find very
difficult to identify because basically my
view is that it just so happens that one is
fortunate enough to be paid to do this work.

I still consider myself very fortunate that people will pay me to go to the theatre to express an opinion, or go to a concert to express an opinion, and provide me, free of charge, the very best tickets. In addition, they actually pay me for doing so. It really is remarkable. The skills clearly have to be largely professional journalistic skills, in the sense that you have to be able to work within the disciplines of time: you may have to write a notice within a half-hour of leaving the event. You have to be able and prepared to work within the disciplines of space: the newspaper only allows you so much space, and you have to work within it. You have to be prepared to work within the disciplines of style: you must have a clear idea of the audience for which you are writing, depending on the newspaper for which you are writing. You have to be able professionally to combine these skills with a critical faculty, which is very indefinable, and an experience which produces judgment values which may be taken to be reasonable. So you are basing your judgment on something or other—probably a wide experience of having seen good performances and bad performances before. You have to have the facility to express yourself, to communicate your interest, enthusiasm, disappointment, or whatever, to the reader. So it is very much a combination of skills and interests which take some time, I think, to come together.

Does the preparation or methodology differ relative to one's approach to a concert or play, depending on the kind of review one writes? That is, is there a difference between a newspaper critic and one who writes for a scholarly journal that only comes out quarterly, for example? My own experience of this is immediate, in the sense I might well be covering the same event for two quite different newspapers, the *Daily Mail* and the *Sunday*

Times. There you are working within different time scales, different wordage, and to a different readership. Therefore, it is different. In one case I am writing for a popular newspaper, and writing for an audience who well may not be particularly interested in the first place in a symphony concert, who may never go near a concert hall. But what I want to do is to write a piece which they can read with interest and understanding, and perhaps sense the enjoyment and enthusiasm of the event. I have a kind of missionary zeal, I must confess, that I hope that maybe they might be encouraged to put their nose inside a concert hall for the first time ever, and maybe find a new level of pleasure. The notice has to be written within a very short word span and within a very short time scale. With the *Sunday Times* one is writing in a different medium altogether, in the sense that one is writing for a quality newspaper with a very high educational level in its readership. The review appears in the actual arts-review section of the paper, which is separate from the business section and general news section of the magazine. The person who is reading you there is likely to be much better informed and has chosen in the first place to read the *Sunday Times*; that classifies him to an extent. That person has chosen to read the arts-review section and within that section has chosen to read your criticism. Therefore, it is a much more specialized audience. You have more time to write because the deadline is further away, and you generally get more space to write what you want to write. I think one of the main considerations is that nothing is ever complete and nothing is ever totally satisfactory. So the constraints of space and time often lead you to be unable to say the things you would like to say, maybe even to mention people you feel deserve to be mentioned, and similarly may lead you to say things which on further reflection you might not have said. Such reviewing is very much a product of the moment.

Your experience has been in the performing arts. Do you see a difference between your approach or task and that of a critic of the visual arts? I'm tempted to say yes, perhaps because I have not really had the experience of covering the visual arts. Therefore, something you haven't done you tend to think of as different. I suspect it may not be that much different, although there again, what you need to have is knowledge gained by experience. I spend a lot of time looking at paintings as a personal pleasure in various parts of the world, and so I might be able to have a go at some visual-arts criticism, I suppose. However, nobody has ever asked me to do it. I think that what I would say which may be helpful is that there is a vast difference, I find, between writing criticism of music and writing criticism of theatre. Music is much more difficult to describe to a reader. To communicate sound through words is not that easy. Whereas, with a play you start with a common language: you describe a story as well as a performance. Also, in the music field, almost by definition the level of performance is in a sense much less variable than the level of performance in the theatre. Most often one is listening to music that is well-established "classical music." Of course, one hears new works and has to assess those, but by and large one hears a standard repertoire and one hears constantly performers of international repute. Therefore, the demands on the music critic are much more keenly felt than the demands on the theatre critic.

Do you see any kind of special purpose behind the role of the arts critic? I personally think that it is very important for a critic to keep in perspective his own position in the total context of the performing arts—or the visual arts, for that matter. There is a quotation which says "One man in the arena is worth one hundred critics," and I would certainly go along with that. I think every critic should have that hanging over his or her desk. It's too easy to exaggerate your own importances as a critic. You have a lot of opportunities because, since you are writing for a newspaper often with a large readership, you are given a very privileged position to express what, after all, is only your opinion. Therefore, I think you want to be sure that at the very least you are being fair to the artist. That's the way I would like to be known. I think sometimes the critic can be constructively critical so that the artists themselves would find some enlightenment there, and may be able to build that into subsequent performances. That would be very encouraging. One should be critical and constructive. It is too easy, and too often done throughout the world, for newspaper critics to be destructive and smart. Often, it seems to me, editors even demand it in the sense that the critic who is destructive and smart is often highly readable or highly amusing. It is easy to score off somebody else. It boosts circulation, and newspapers like to boost circulation, of course. I think, therefore, it is up to the individual critic to decide how far he wants to go along that line. My own view would be that I would not want to work in that situation. Indeed, I would go so far as to say that sometimes today I would choose not to write—indeed, I do choose not to write, occasionally—some totally destructive notices because it seems to me it is not doing any good to anybody, and is really wasting precious space in my newspapers. If I am writing in the newspaper, there are a dozen other critics in other parts of the world who are not able to get anything into the newspaper that particular week. So I think one should use judgment and one should try to be fair. I would always like to be able to face up to the people I criticize and defend, if necessary, my view and hopefully get their agreement that it was reasonable at the time.

Do you commune in art circles and among artists, or do you feel a need to remain separate from them, personally, in order to be objective? Well, I think a bit of both in my own case. I live a normal, rounded life, I would like to think, because I do spend a lot of my time in this sense working in theaters and concert halls and whatnot. Inevitably, of course, I see a lot of artists and musicians, and talk with them. I think this builds up a general background of knowingness. I think, also, that any critic worth his salt really hopes that the people he is sitting in judgment upon not exactly value his opinion, but at least trust his opinion. I think that you need to have, for your own self-preservation, a credibility. Therefore, it's important to know as much as you can about the topic, even though you are judging a particular performance on a particular night and no more than that.

You spoke earlier of missionary zeal. Do you ever feel in conflict with yourself in your role of a critic as opposed to an apologist for the arts? My missionary zeal relates to the context of one particular paper—that is, the context of writing for a paper with a general readership rather than a readership you know is already committed to an interest in the arts. That zeal would not lead me to give false judgment on any performance or event. I would express my opinion and would not change that opinion simply because it did not convince people that they ought to go to see it. That would be counter-productive, and would spoil the missionary zeal when I really wanted to exploit it. I think my concern is really to better the arts and to make a contribution to the furtherance of the arts. One of the exciting

things, really, would be the thought that one just might communicate to somebody who hasn't had that experience the possibilities held for them in terms of lasting pleasure in such things as paintings, music, and theatre. I think if a critic can do that while at the same time being constructively critical of what's happening, then I think that is a reasonable way to spend part of one's time.

From your point of view, what do the arts need to do to fulfill their role in society? I find this very difficult because in the end the public is going to make up their own minds. I think what worries me to an extent, and links it to my missionary-zeal feeling, is that the arts are not so easily communicated in terms of the use of television. When you think about it, it is very rare for people to see through such a medium as television—although it is ideal for the job—the work of the artist or the workings of a musician. What I am trying to say, really, is that I would like to see the arts made more accessible to a wider public, because I suspect that as long as the arts seem to be a kind of elitist, intellectual preserve there are a lot of people who are missing a lot of pleasure. Anything the arts can do—I don't know what the answer is, really—to disassociate themselves from this mystique that they are terribly special things for terribly special people, the better. How you do it I don't know. Sometimes I think it works by, if you like, cheating slightly. Certainly, at home I know we had a very popular exhibition at an art gallery; it was an exhibition of Hollywood costumes from the movie houses in Hollywood, costumes worn in various movies by distinguished actors. That attracted people into the museum, into the art gallery, for the first time; many people had never been there before. If by chance a few of those, then, see enough while they're there to want to come again and look at the other things in the art gallery, then that's good. I think that's an idea: that one offers a temptation for people to come in who otherwise wouldn't come in. In any case I would like to see this mystique broken down.

the painter

Interview with Richard Mayhew

Richard Mayhew is a painter who delights in multimedia. He has received, among other awards, a John Hay Whitney Fellowship, an Ingram Merril Foundation Grant, a Ford Foundation Purchase Award, a Tiffany Foundation Grant, and the Benjamin Altman Award of the National Academy of Design in 1970.

His list of exhibitions includes the American Academy of Arts and Letters, Brooklyn Museum, Chicago Institute, Gallery of Modern Art, Museum of Modern Art, and the Whitney Museum.

He has taught art at Pratt Institute, Smith College, Hunter College, and the Pennsylvania State University.

What do you strive to achieve and what do you feel you accomplish in your art? Many of us in exchanges with each other constantly review that kind of question—that is, what are we striving for? For myself, and in these discussions, a lot of different attitudes come out. There wasn't an intent involved in the beginning, when I started as an artist. There was a need to create, which now I can evaluate on the basis of a need for survival. As the years went by there was more dependence on the area of multimedia as I got involved with theatre and music. The various challenges through the years continued to build; in the beginning it was just a matter of mirroring or reflecting objects and the challenge of mastering technique. In the course of time it kept

building, because new challenges kept coming up, such as the use of color, the understanding of space, and the science of the art itself. There is a continuation through the years; nothing was ever solved, because it kept building with new challenges developing. As a youngster I started to paint a pond in my back yard. Philosophically, it must have dropped a pebble in the pond, and the ripples have been going out since then. The development from that beginning point to where I am now is unbelievable, I guess. That identity in itself is like something on the other side of the mountain, or of thinking of Rembrandt or someone else in a particular field and striving to compete at that level. One would never feel that one could achieve it.

Do you feel that there is a conscious effort on your part to communicate something to a respondent? Again, this is a question debated in conversation with other artists. Is one painting for an audience or painting for himself? I guess many artists paint for an audience out of survival, in terms of protecting their creative existence, because it is very difficult to survive as an artist, composer, or whatever. There isn't a subsidy for that kind of function in our society. So there are many artists who compromise their values on the basis of catering to a particular public which is not necessarily reflective of their image or impression, and so there is a prostitution of their art somewhere along the way in doing that. I haven't compromised my particular values because there is a dedication to a constant challenge of science in the art. In the course of this how does one communicate with the public? I found myself being involved with a lot of art programs within the various communities in making the community aware of the arts. There is a problem in that the public is not educated to the degree to comprehend what the artists are doing. There is difficulty there. There is a need to communicate, and there is certainly a joy if someone understands and appreciates what one does. But to directly appeal to a particular public is difficult because what you are doing is unique, and if you compromise for a dictation of, let us say, the art market or a general public, you stagnate in development.

But how important is it to you that a respondent receive whatever message you may feel, as an individual artist, you have put into a work? There is a certain satisfaction that the artist is making a contribution in his society. Now, again, there is the commitment to what one is doing and the feeling that one has an influence in subliminal contributions to persons' development. If you are a dedicated artist there is a profound element in your work which is very strong, and anyone exposed to it is influenced by it. There are those who are very deliberate in their control over it, using subject matter and the manipulation of the science to control the viewer where there is a popular subject matter, and also manipulating them in control of the geometry or physics of the composition.

What are the most challenging aspects that you find in the media within which you work, specifically? That is a very difficult question because everything about it is extremely difficult yet extremely enjoyable. Nothing ever seems to be resolved if one is a dedicated artist. If one is just a technician he masters technique, media, procedure, and image. As a result, it's just a performance which has determined what the end result would be. If one is really freely involved with the experimental, creative process, there is no mastering the media, the direction, or the future. It's always that elusive area. Actors walk out on the stage and there

is a moment of truth. They know their lines well, and if they go out and perform like a puppet, they do it in a very sterile way. Painting is the same thing: when you are painting a painting, in the course of that painting there is a whole new moment of truth. If that is predetermined and controlled, it is limited. Many of us do stagnate: even though we may remain technicians, we cease to make a contribution.

In your own personal work do you find any particular ways in which ideas come to you for a particular work? Everything being visualized, that one sees or comes in contact with, is potential subject matter. So it is impossible ever to paint all the things you want to paint, to meet all the challenges you would like to meet; there is never enough time; life is just too short to do it, especially if there is complete dedication to it. It is constantly elusive: it's like in a dream, trying to hold on to a door knob, and you can't quite get the grip of it, and it always keeps changing and moving. When you do open the door there is another one beyond it that you have to open.

Once you do decide on a subject or a treatment, do you conceive of the total painting before you begin, or is it a developmental thing as you work? In the early stages I was working directly from subject matter as a landscape painter; I was apprenticed, very young, to an illustrator and Hudson Valley painter. At the time I didn't realize the value of it. When I started painting, the fascination of the medium came from picking up color from blobs on a palette and transferring it over to the canvas. Pictures came out of the end of the brush. It was unbelievable fascination—magic. One does not have control over it. No matter how well you plan that image, it evolves and changes because of an intuitive extension which you cannot predetermine. Many writers talk about the world beyond, that marvel of consciousness that they have planned, that keeps changing.

the musician

Interview with Robert Hull

Robert Hull has had a long and successful career as conductor, performer, composer, and teacher. He earned bachelor's and master's degrees from Eastman School of Music and a Ph.D. degree from Cornell University. He has been director and conductor of the Fort Worth Symphony Orchestra and conductor of the Fort Worth Ballet Company, as well as guest conductor of many orchestras around the country, including the Rochester Philharmonic, Buffalo Philharmonic, and Phoenix, Flagstaff, and Tucson symphony orchestras. Listed in *Who's Who in America,* Dr. Hull also has been Dean of Fine Arts at Texas Christian University and the University of Arizona. He has made recordings in New York City for the Concert Hall Society and the Handel Society and in Los Angeles for Columbia Records.

What do you feel are the relationships among the composer, conductor, and individual musician relative to the creation and interpretation of a musical work? Let me respond as I envision what the conductor's (or interpreter's) relationship should be to the composer when he is conducting an orchestral work. I think it is incumbent upon the conductor to know as much as possible about the composer and his music, the circumstances of its creation, first performance, things of that nature, before he even begins to study the work intensively. It is important, therefore, for him to transmit that kind of knowledge to the musicians of the orchestra, so it, in turn, can with him transmit coherent and cohesive interpreta-

tion for the benefit of the audience. I think the relationship we have to remember is that the creative artist is the composer, and the conductor and individual musician in a sense exist to serve him. Without him, in other words, there would be no performance. So I would rate in order of importance, first the composer, possibly second the individual musician, and third the conductor, even though I happen to prefer conducting as a method of performance rather than violin or viola playing, which I also have done.

As a composer, what events or occurrences trigger your conceptualization of a work? I can't really claim to be a composer, although for a period of about ten years earlier in my life I spent some time in compositional activities. Almost anything could trigger the conceptualization of a work, although most of the time my ideas came from some kind of philosophic or inner urge, rather than being triggered by some outside or natural occurrence—for example, a dream sequence, thinking about relationships between people, or idealizing a perfect performance of a work which you would like to create. These are some of the ways it happens. Of course, it happens another way: an idea occurs to you, a portion of the tune or a fragment of a tune occurs to you, as far as I'm concerned, for no particular reason. You examine that; you try it out; you work with it; you stretch it; you pound it; you turn it upside down, forwards and backwards, and decide you have something you can work with. From there, depending on the kind of material you have and the idea, you let it grow into what you hope will be some kind of final form.

Do you conceptualize a work in its entirety, or does it grow as you work on it? Well, I think I inadvertently answered this earlier. For the most part, at least with me, the conception begins with a small germ and, usually, grows organically from that point until it is a completed work. I don't think it is possible in a temporal art form such as music to conceive a thing in its entirety unless it is a very small song form.

As a conductor or performer, how do you go about your preparation for a concert? As a performer, meaning a violinist or violist, of course I spend a considerable number of hours in various slow and painful practices just to make sure that I have solved all the technical problems and that whatever technique I have is at the command of the interpretive artist. Obviously, before I engage in that kind of practice I play through the work several times at near concert speed to see whether it serves the purpose, whether I can cope with it. Obviously, also in the matter of preparation, I must go back to make sure I understand the work, how it fits into the scheme of things in its era, in its composer's life, whether or not he had any extramusical motives for composing it, or any extramusical ideas that he wanted to convey through the composition. Once I have ascertained all this, and once I have been able to make the work one of my own (meaning I feel comfortable with it, I believe in it, and I want to share it with somebody else), then I set about the very painful technical development of the means to interpret it properly. As far as the conductor is concerned, I do somewhat the same process, but my preparation here, of course, is a matter not necessarily of making music but of studying the score, making sure I understand all of its harmonic, contrapuntal, and melodic implications, and where the counter-melodies are at every stage of the game. I must know where I want my rubatos, what it is that is being expressed, and how I am going to react to it as a conductor. I have to be aware, of course, of

what all the instruments are doing every step of the way, and yet I have to prepare an overall concept of how I want them balanced one against the other. You do that in terms of your understanding in terms of the style of the period in which the composer was doing his work. You also try to understand, in terms of the capability of your performing organization, whether or not the work fits it, whether or not the organization will be able to give a reasonable accounting of itself when it plays the work, and therefore whether you are able to give a reasonably accurate and a reasonably faithful interpretation to the audience. This requires many hours of painful study and slow study, and for the most part it should be quiet study. From time to time, if there is a recording in existence of the work I am preparing and if the interpretation of the recording is relatively close to my conceptualization of the work, I may listen to the recording a few times, just so it will help me hear the work, visualize it, as it were, so that it makes it a little easier for me to keep the whole thing in mind, and a little easier to memorize it.

Is it important to you that the audience respond in a particular manner to your artwork? This is a difficult one to answer. At the moment I am not performing publicly or conducting publicly enough to recall with any degree of certainty exactly how I react each time I do a performance. I must say that for the most part I believe I know when I have done something well, and that therefore the audience's immediate reaction may not be that important to me. But I share with all artists and with all people a desire sometime to get my message across and, if you will, to please. In that respect it is important, and particularly the communicative artist, the performing artist, must know that some of his ideas are reaching the public. Therefore, it is terribly important that at least we get some reaction; I believe it is more important to get a reaction than it is to make absolutely sure that we get a positive and pleasing reaction, or the reaction of those that are pleased by the work. Nothing is more stultifying and deadly than no reaction at all.

What do you feel are the major attributes and limitations of the musician as a communicative artist? Let me put it another way around. Instead of saying major attributes and limitations, maybe I should say major advantages and disadvantages for the musician or communicative artist. The major advantage, of course, probably lies in the fact that the musician is dealing with symbols which are ineffable, which means that they may connote certain kinds of basic meanings, but they do not denote anything specific. That gives, I believe, the musician a much greater latitude than the painter, for example, the sculptor, or the playwright, or even the opera composer, where there are some ideas that are denoted and narrative in character which may be transmitted with the music. The music itself—since it tends to be universal, as it were, and can mean so many things to so many people—gives the musician a considerable advantage and leeway in the use of his materials. The limitations, of course, are that it is very difficult for the musician to communicate a specific denotive idea—that is, to be delimiting in the definition of the symbols that he is using. For example, I would not agree with the late Richard Strauss, who claimed that by purely musical means he could convey to the audience how much water was in a tumbler full of water. He might be able to convey to the audience the idea that he had a body of water which was in turmoil or which was quite placid or which was freely flowing. But to be able to convey to the audience where that body of water was, how much water was in

it, the precise size, what part of the hemisphere it was, what the color of the day was, is something that I think is beyond the normal communicative processes of music, unless we insist upon reading more into music than actually exists. I make this last remark because, obviously, many of the impressionists in music believe that is possible, and we frequently (the musician and the composer frequently, and/or the music critic more likely than the other two) will borrow the vocabulary from the artist and talk about various kinds of color in music. This doesn't mean to say that by purely musical means you can paint a picture greener than another picture. I don't think this is possible. On the other hand you can give the feeling of lightness, effervescence, looking forward, striving, an ongoing feeling which one might in one way or another associate with the idea of spring, *ergo,* green. But I don't believe you can go beyond that.

As a musician, composer, conductor, or performer, what specific ends do you try to accomplish through your art? It probably would sound a little egotistical or self-centered if I would say that there are so many things in music that I enjoy, and to such a degree, that I have a kind of burning desire to share that feeling and enjoyment with other people. I suppose you might say, in the last analysis, it is a kind of missionary zeal to convert others to the point where they can get the same kind of enjoyment, although maybe in a slightly different way, but some of the same kind of enjoyment out of the same kind of music that I have been privileged to know and to understand. In connection with that, I might say here something that you know very well—that frequently the average person, in meeting a composer or artist, will say "Well, I don't know anything about music or art, but I know what I like." I frequently try to counter by saying "I agree with part of your statement, but I wonder if you don't really mean that you don't know anything about music and you like what you know." I think it is characteristic of man to be a little standoffish or tend to be a little suspicious of what he does not understand. And if we are not willing to keep on with the process of learning after our high-school days and to make it a lifelong experience, it is quite likely that all the most recent developments in various art forms, which take a little understanding and a little exposure to get used to, may eventually outstrip our ability to respond to them and to appreciate them. And this is why I think it is more nearly accurate to say about the person who doesn't know much about art that he has a tendency to end up liking what he knows. Anyhow, it is just for this reason that I am involved one way or another in teaching and lecturing and writing and administering: hoping I can widen the circle of appreciation for the people who come into contact with me. I suppose I am not trying necessarily to impose my taste on somebody else, but simply to say "Look, I enjoyed this particular work and let me share that enjoyment with you; I hope you get some of the same ecstatic or uplifted feeling from it that I did." If one can accomplish this in a few cases in his life, then I think one's life in his art or whatever he is doing has been worthwhile.

the theatre director

Interview with Richard Edelman

Richard Edelman's background in the theatre is lifelong and extremely broad. While his current concentration is exclusively in directing, he has worked as an actor since childhood, when he appeared in WPA theatre projects and radio shows in New York City. Later, in Europe he appeared on the stage and in films.

Educated at St. John's College in Annapolis, Maryland, he has pursued advanced work at Columbia University in New York and the Sorbonne in Paris. As a director he has been affiliated with New York's Neighborhood Playhouse, Living Theatre, and England's Mermaid Theatre. He also has been affiliated with many summer theatres, including the Green Mansions Camp. His directing credits, however, go far beyond legitimate English-language theatre. He has staged operas for such organizations as New York's North Shore Friends of Opera, the Mozart Opera Festival of the Brooklyn Academy, and the Buffalo Symphony, and has been involved in cross-cultural theatre, directing in French and Italian both in the United States and in Europe.

What is the relationship of the director to the playwright in the development of the theatrical artwork? Are you an artist, an interpreter, or something in between? I think no one can be just an impartial deliverer of the play as written. We fool ourselves if that is the case. In having read the play, without any attempt to add anything, we do add something, because it goes through our consciousness; it goes through our sensibilities; it goes through the specifics of our image-making process, and there is no way of avoiding that. I think that people who say that they are simply there just to do what the author wants are fooling themselves. It is impossible. The more you try to be absolutely honest and available to the author, the more likely you are to create something that is more different and unique. When I do a production, I have certain very clear ideas of what I think should happen to it. But I feel that almost every idea I have is based on what I read in the text and what I know about the particular theatre of a historical period and what the playwright's resources were. As a director, what I really want to find out is what conventions did he have in mind, what was he basing it on. Sometimes, as a director, you have to add a dimension when you enter into a collaboration, whether the writer is there or not. If the writer is dead or not available you almost owe it to him to develop a dimension that he has not. Had you been around and worked with him as one does with a live author with whom you are collaborating, then you are making an input. There is no question about it. Somebody like Kazan made enormous inputs into the works of Tennessee Williams that did not appear in the originals of the scripts.

In this regard, how inviolable do you as a director regard the script with which you are working, especially of an author who is not available for collaboration? I tell you that this is a quirk of mine. I find it a challenge to cut as little as possible, a challenge that I want to meet. I want to find ways of making it work. I find that is the interesting challenge. I am not even sure that is an artistic challenge. Very frequently it is to my own and the play's disadvantage that I am motivated to say "Now that line has to work some way" instead of just saying "Well, we can't handle that line; let's just cut it or let's just substitute something." Translations add another dimension, and very frequently cloud the issue. I try to find out, again, what the author really wanted. I think very frequently something like Shakespeare gets cut, because people don't take the time to find out, directors and actors, just how brilliantly constructed his plays are. Sometimes they are layed out in a triptych. You know there are three sections, even though there are five acts. He makes the statement once, then he makes it a slightly different way, then he makes it some kind of resolution the third time. That is a structure that we do not understand in the theatre because we are much more interested in the direct

narrative line. However, today I think we are a little better off; the changes of the '50s and especially of the '60s made us more open to that kind of theatrical experience. We will accept it more, but very frequently as thinkers we are not able to cut through to see what his structure is, and I think that is what a director should be about. And very frequently that doesn't happen. The director simply will cut or find a palatable coating for the pill. You put the play into ante-bellum Charleston because it is going to work there. Well, maybe that is sensible, or maybe it isn't. I have seen very splendid and really good productions where they have been put into other eras or where they have been modernized. More often than not, though, these are just ways of making Shakespeare palatable, meaning watering it down, meaning that they haven't really gone to the trouble to find out what the guts of that experience are.

How do you as a director view the relationships of all of the parts of a production—that is, actors, designers, and so forth? Do you see the production as a joint venture or are you like a musical conductor—that is, a dictator? I have been told that when I was young I was a dictator; I don't remember it. I have been told by actors that I have since worked with, again, that I was impossible at that point. I see myself, and I think I have always seen myself, as a collaborative director. I think it is a collaboration and I think one of the difficulties that we have is with the director who really does have very clear images of what he wants. Then he has to find people who are just going to give him what he wants, and that takes enormous organizational skills and strength, character, or extraordinarily self-centered potency. I find that I prefer to work with ideas that other people are contributing, and somehow fashion them into a joint world. The director, I think, is largely responsible for the completeness of the world that is presented on the stage at that moment. He has to find the reality of that given world—that is, the completeness of the reality, moment to moment throughout the play—the style of the piece, the form of the piece, and the life of the piece. So I see myself essentially as collaborator. I think that happens as one gets older. I think that is a function of one's maturing and having perhaps less energy and a little more humility concerning what one is doing—and a little more respect for the efforts of the people that one is working with. I find I modify more and more what are my original conceptions so that it is not simply a question of incorporating what somebody else has done, but incorporating what I have done into what somebody else has done. I find myself essentially a collaborative worker with the playwright if he is alive and immediately available. Or if he is dead, then I feel I have a certain commitment to find out what he had in mind.

How does the audience fit into your development of the production? Is "communication" important? The whole notion of communication is a bugaboo in the theatre, particularly for actors. Young actors, particularly, misunderstand this; they think that means that they have to show it and tell it to the audience, which is not the actors' work. The actors' work is to find the life in that particular world and if they do it fully and completely, any audience that is attentive will be able to find what has to be seen and understood. An audience sees and understands what it wants to, and not what you want it to. It is a communal experience: the audience is a commu-

nity, if you like, and the actors are the other part of that community—the actors and all the support elements that go into putting the actors on the stage. It is a completed circle at that time, and I don't think a play really exists until it is in the moment of performance, and until it is experienced by the audience, which gives something back to the actors.

So are you saying, then, that when you make choices relative to what you are going to do in the production—what the set is going to look like, or the particular kind of movements that the actors are going to use—these choices are based on something other than how you want something to go across to the audience or how to get them to respond in a particular way? Or don't you care how they respond? I care how they respond, very definitely. I think the director has to be aware of a given audience. Particularly in this day and age it might be good to say there is no such thing as a vast audience. We no longer have the great popular audiences that they had in the nineteenth and early twentieth centuries. So I think you have to know which audience you are going for, and I think that in some sense that has to be considered. You have to know which language, as it were, you are talking in when you are directing and acting and designing. Sometimes it is a little difficult. I would do a given play in different ways depending on what the audience was and what my expectations of that audience were. I don't mean I play it down to them. That is not what I am saying. I am saying that I try to find that legal binder that makes it possible for life to go on between the two—to create that union.

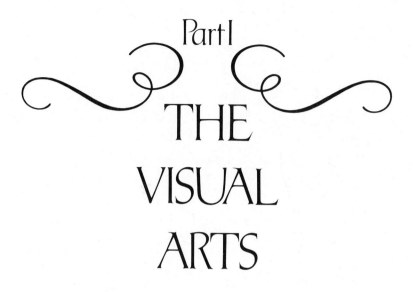

Part I
THE
VISUAL
ARTS

Pictures: Painting, Printmaking,
and Photography

Sculpture

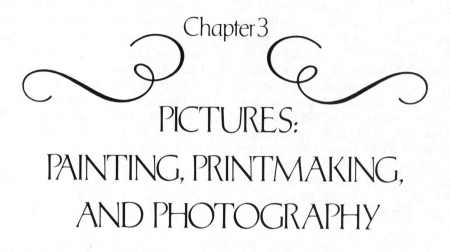

Chapter 3

PICTURES:
PAINTING, PRINTMAKING,
AND PHOTOGRAPHY

WHAT IS IT?

Paintings, photographs, and prints are pictures, differing only in the technique of their execution. They constitute design of two-dimensional space. Our initial level of response to all three is to subject matter. A picture might be a landscape, seascape, portrait, religious picture, nonobjective (non-representational) or abstract picture, still life, or something else. So this level of our response is a rather simple and straight-forward matter of observation, although subject matter can be a significant factor in the meaning of a work.

HOW IS IT PUT TOGETHER?

Medium

Our technical level of response is more complex. First of all, our response to how a

work is put together is to the medium by which the work was executed.

Paintings and Drawings

Paintings and drawings are executed through use of (1) oils, (2) watercolors, (3) tempera, (4) acrylics, (5) fresco, (6) gouache, (7) ink, (8) pastels, and (9) pencils, to name just a few of the more obvious. An artist may combine these media, and may use some other media. Each medium has its own characteristics, and to a great extent dictates what the artist can or cannot achieve as an end result.

Oils are perhaps the most popular of the painting media, and have been since their development near the beginning of the fifteenth century. Their popularity stems principally from the great variety of opportunity they give the painter. Oils offer a tremendous range of color possibilities; they can be reworked; they present many options for textural manipulation; and, above all, perhaps, they are durable. If we compare two oils, van Gogh's *The Starry Night* (Fig. 3.1) and Giovanni Vanni's *Holy Family with Saint John* (Fig. 3.2), the medium shows its importance to the final effect of the works. Vanni creates light and shade in the Baroque tradition, and his chiaroscuro (pronounced key·ahr´·uh·skū´·rō) depends upon the capacity of the medium to blend smoothly among color areas. Van Gogh, on the other hand, requires a medium that will stand up to form obvious brush strokes. Vanni demands the paint to be flesh and cloth. Van Gogh demands the paint to be paint, and to call attention to itself.

Watercolor is a broad category that includes any color medium that uses water as a thinner. However, the term has traditionally referred to a transparent paint usually applied to paper. Since watercolors are transparent, an artist must be very careful to control them. If he overlaps one area of color with another, the overlap will show as a third area combining the previous hues. On the other hand, their transparency gives watercolors a delicacy that cannot be produced in any other medium.

Tempera is an opaque-watercolor medium whose use spans recorded history. It was employed by the ancient Egyptians, and is

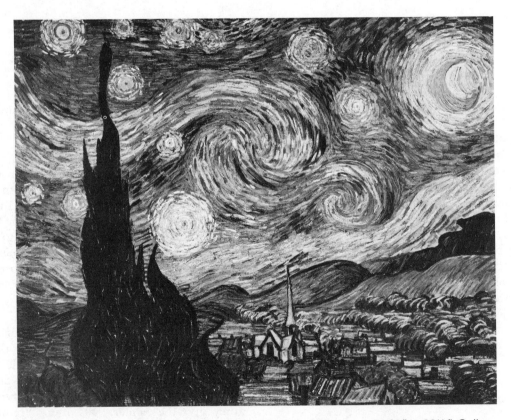

Fig. 3.1. Vincent van Gogh, *The Starry Night* (1889). Oil on canvas, 29″ × 36¼″. Collection, The Museum of Modern Art, New York. Acquired through the Lillie P. Bliss Bequest.

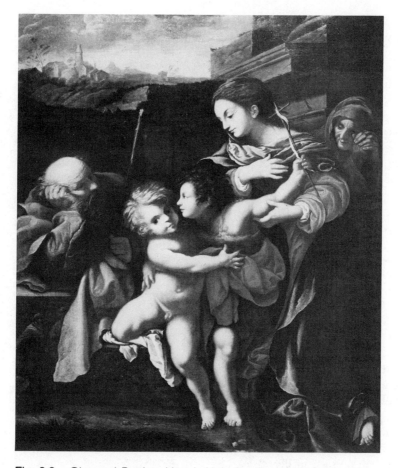

Fig. 3.2.   Giovanni Battista Vanni, *Holy Family with St. John*. Oil on canvas 70″ × 58″. Museum of Art, The Pennsylvania State University.

still used today by such familiar painters as Andrew Wyeth. Tempera refers to ground pigments and their color binders such as gum or glue, but is best known in its egg tempera form. It is a fast-drying medium that virtually eliminates brush stroke and gives extremely sharp and precise detail. Colors in tempera paintings appear almost gemlike in their clarity and brilliance.

Acrylics, in contrast with tempera, are modern, synthetic products. Most acrylics are water-soluble (that is, they dissolve in water), and the binding agent for the pigment is an acrylic polymer. Acrylics are flexible media offering the artist a wide range of possibilities both in color and technique. An acrylic paint can be either opaque or transparent, depending upon dilution. It is fast-drying, thin, and resistant to cracking under temperature and humidity extremes. It is perhaps less permanent than some other media, but adheres to a wider variety of surfaces. It will not darken or yellow with age, as does oil, and dries more rapidly than oil.

Fresco is a wall-painting *technique* in which pigments suspended in water are applied to fresh, wet plaster. Michelangelo's Sistine Chapel frescoes are, of course, the best-known examples of this technique. Since the end result becomes part *of* the plaster wall rather than being painted *on* it, fresco provides a long-lasting work. However, it is an extremely difficult process, and once the pigments are applied, no changes can be made without replastering the entire section of the wall.

Gouache is watercolor medium in which gum is added to ground opaque colors mixed with water. Transparent watercolors can be made into gouache by adding Chinese white to them. Chinese white is a special, white, water-soluble paint. The final product, in addition to being water-soluble, is opaque.

Ink as a painting medium has many of the same characteristics as transparent watercolor. It is difficult to control, yet its effects are nearly impossible to achieve in any other medium. Because it must be worked quickly and freely, it has a spontaneous and appealing quality, as can be seen in Fig. 3.3

Drawing media such as ink, when applied with a pen (as opposed to a brush), pastels (crayon or chalk), and pencils all create their effect through build-up of line. Each has its own characteristics, but all are relatively inflexible in their handling of color and color areas (see Fig. 3.9).

Prints

Prints are executed by means of the techniques of (1) woodcut and wood engraving, (2) intaglio, (3) lithography, or (4) serigraphy. Because the printmaker's techniques are unfamiliar to most of us, we need to spend some time in further explanation.

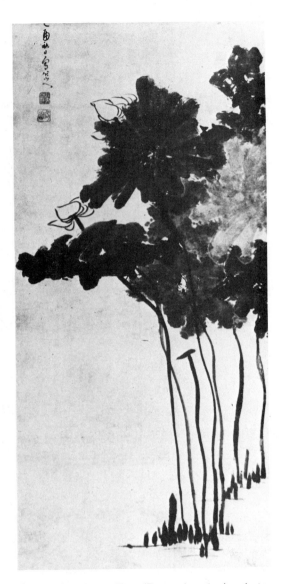

Fig. 3.3. Chu Ta (Pa-ta-shan-jen), *Lotus* (1705). Brush and ink, 61½" × 28". Museum of Art, The Pennsylvania State University.

To begin with, however, we need to ask, What is a print? A print is a hand-produced picture that has been transferred from a printing surface to a piece of paper. The artist personally prepares the printing surface and personally directs the printing process. Each step in the production of a print is accomplished by hand. In some cases a press is used, as we shall see, but it is always operated by hand. The uniqueness and value of a print lies in the fact that the block or surface from which the print is made usually is destroyed after the desired number of prints has been made. In contrast, a reproduction is not an original. It is a *copy* of an original painting or other artwork, reproduced usually by a photographic process. As a copy, the reproduction does not bear the handiwork of the artist. In purchasing prints we must be sure that we are buying an actual print (which has value as an artwork) and not a reproduction (which lacks such value) disguised by obscure or misleading advertising. The surest sign of an original print is the signature of the artist—*in pencil. The artist signs each and every print.*

We need also to note that on every print is a number. On some prints the number may appear as a fraction—for example, "36/100." The denominator indicates how many prints were produced from the plate or block. This number is called the *issue number,* or *edition number.* The numerator indicates where in the series the individual print was produced. If only a single number appears, such as "500," it simply indicates the total number of prints in the series; it is also called the issue number. Printmakers are turning to the practice of eliminating the former kind of numbering because there is a misconception that the relationship of the numerator to the issue total has a bearing on a print's value. The numerator is an item of curiosity only; it has nothing to do with a print's value, monetarily or qualitatively. The issue number does have some value in comparing, for example, an issue of 25 with one of 500, and usually is reflected in the price of a print. However, the edition number is not the sole factor in determining the value of a print.

The quality of the print and the reputation of the artist are more important considerations.

Woodcuts and Wood Engravings.   Woodcuts and wood engravings are the oldest of the printmaking techniques. A woodcut is cut into the plank of the grain, and a wood engraving is cut into the butt of the grain (Fig. 3.4). The image to be transferred to the paper is left after the artist removes unwanted wood from the block. This process, which is called *relief printing,* since the image protrudes (in relief) from the block, produces a picture that is reversed from the image carved by the artist. This is a characteristic of all printmaking media. Figure 3.5 illustrates the linear essence of the woodcut and shows the precision and delicacy possible in this medium in the hands of a master.

Intaglio.   The intaglio process is the opposite of relief printing. The ink is transferred to the paper not from raised areas but rather from grooves cut into a metal plate. *Line engraving, etching, aquatint,* and *drypoint* are some of the methods of intaglio.

LINE ENGRAVING involves cutting grooves into the metal plate with special sharp tools.

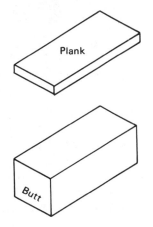

Fig. 3.4.   Wood plank and butt.

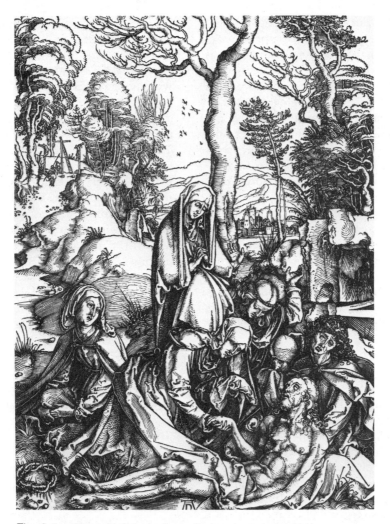

Fig. 3.5. Albrecht Dürer, *Lamentation* (c. 1497–1500). Woodcut, 15½″ × 11¼″. Museum of Art, The Pennsylvania State University. Gift of the Friends of the Museum of Art.

It requires great muscular control because the pressure must be continuous and constant if the grooves are to produce the desired image. The print resulting from the line–engraving process is very sharp and precise. This form of intaglio is the most difficult and demanding on the artist.

ETCHINGS are less demanding. In this process the artist removes the surface of the plate by exposing it to an acid bath. First the plate is covered with a thin waxlike substance called a *ground*. Then the artist scratches away the ground to produce the desired lines. The plate is then immersed in the acid, which burns away the exposed areas of the plate. The longer a plate is left in the acid, the deeper the resulting etches will be; the deeper the etch, the darker the final image. So, artists wishing to produce lines or areas of differing darkness must clean and re-cover the plate and rescratch those lines that they desire to be more deeply cut. They can accomplish this task easily since the ground is very thin and the earlier lines can be seen through it. The desired number of repetitions of the process yield a plate that will produce a print with the desired differences in light and dark lines. All the details of Fig. 3.6 consist of individual lines, either single or in combination. The lighter lines required less time in the acid than the darker ones. Because of the precision and clarity of the lines, it would be difficult to determine, without knowing in advance, whether this print is an etching or an engraving. Drypoint, on the other hand, produces lines with less sharp edges.

AQUATINT is a difficult process to explain, and therefore to understand, without an actual print to which to refer. The intaglio methods noted thus far consist of various means of cutting lines into a metal plate. On occasion, however, an artist may wish to create large areas of subdued tonality. Such shadowlike areas cannot be produced effectively with lines. Therefore, the artist dusts the plate with a resin substance. The plate is then heated, which affixes the resin, and put into the acid bath. The result is a plate whose surface is rough in texture, like sandpaper, and a print whose tonal areas reflect that texture.

DRYPOINT is a technique in which the sur-

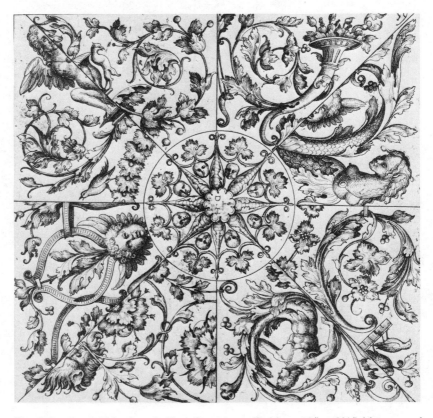

Fig. 3.6.   Daniel Hopfer, *Ceiling Ornament.* Etching, 10″ × 8¾″. Museum of Art, The Pennsylvania State University.

face of the metal plate is scratched with a needle. Unlike the line engraving, which results in a clean, sharp line, the drypoint technique leaves a furrow on either side of the groove. The resulting line is somewhat fuzzy.

Once the plate is prepared, whether by line engraving, etching, aquatint, drypoint, or a combination of methods, the artist is ready for the printing process. The plate is placed in a press and a special dampened paper is laid over it. Padding is placed on the paper and then a roller is passed over, forcing the plate and the paper together with great pressure. The ink, which has been carefully applied to the plate and left only in the grooves, is transferred as the paper is forced into the grooves by the roller of the press. Even if no ink had been applied to the plate, the paper would still receive an image. This *embossing* effect is the mark of an intaglio process; the three-dimensional *platemark* is very obvious.

Lithography. Lithography (the term's literal meaning is "stone writing") is based on the principle that water and grease do not mix. To create a lithograph, an artist begins with a stone, usually limestone, and grinds one side until it is absolutely smooth. He then draws

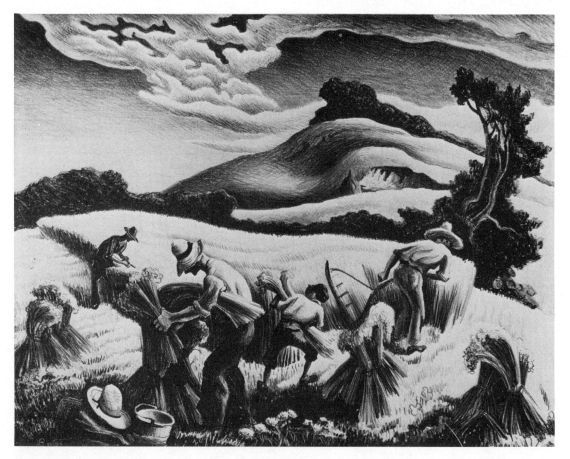

Fig. 3.7. Thomas Hart Benton, *Cradling Wheat* (1938). Lithograph, 9½″ × 12″. Museum of Art, The Pennsylvania State University. Gift of Carolyn Wose Hull.

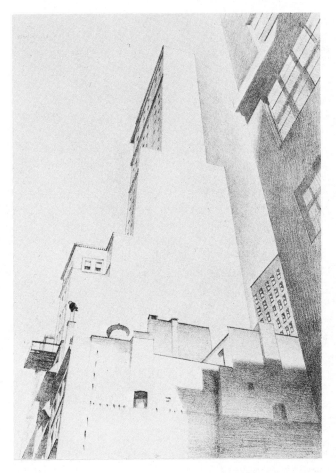

Fig. 3.8. Charles Sheeler, *Delmonico Building* (1926). Lithograph, 10″ × 7⅛″. Museum of Art, The Pennsylvania State University.

an image on the stone with a greasy substance. He can vary the darkness of the final image by the amount of grease he uses: the more grease applied, the darker the image will be. After the artist has drawn the image he treats the stone with gum arabic and nitric acid and then rinses it with water. This bath fixes the greasy areas to the surface of the stone. The next step is baffling to most people. When the artist removes the stone from the bath he wipes it clean! However, the water, gum, and acid have impressed the grease on the stone, and when the stone is wetted it absorbs water (limestone being porous) only in those areas that were not previously greased. Finally, a grease-based ink is applied to the stone. *It,* in turn, will not adhere to the water-soaked areas. As a result the stone, with ink adhering only to the areas on which the artist has drawn, can be placed in a press and the image transferred to the waiting paper. In both Fig. 3.7 and Fig. 3.8 we can see the characteristic most attributable to the medium of lithography— a crayon-drawing appearance. Since the lithographer usually draws with a crayonlike

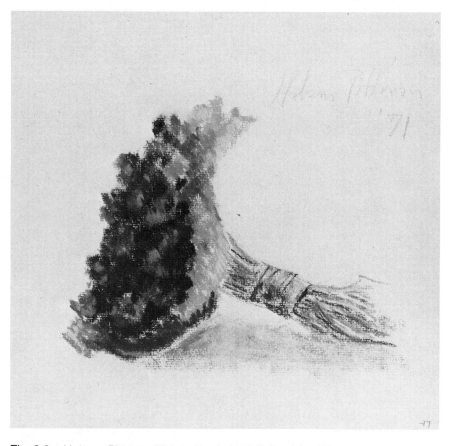

Fig. 3.9. Hobson Pittman, *Violets No. 1.* (1971). Pastel, 9½″ × 10¼″. Museum of Art, The Pennsylvania State University.

material on the stone, the final print has exactly that quality. Compare these prints with Fig. 3.9, a pastel drawing, and the point is clear.

Serigraphy. The serigraphic process employs a stencil to produce its image. The most familiar type of serigraphy is the silkscreen process. Silkscreens are made from a wooden frame covered with a finely meshed fabric such as silk. The stencil is placed in the frame and ink is applied. By means of a rubber instrument called a squeegee the ink is forced through the openings of the stencil, through the screen, and onto the paper below. This technique allows the printmaker to achieve large, flat, uniform color areas. We can see this smooth uniformity of color areas in Fig. 3.10. Here the artist has, through successive applications of ink, built up a complex composition with highly verisimilar (lifelike) detail.

Looking over Figs. 3.5–3.10, we can see how the images of the various prints reflect recognizable differences in technique. Again, it is not always possible to discern the technique used in executing a print, and some prints reflect a combination of techniques.

However, in seeking the method of execution we add another layer of potential response to a work to those we shall note momentarily.

Photography

To many individuals photography is not an art at all; it is merely a matter of personal record executed with equipment of varying degrees of expense and sophistication. Certainly, photography as a matter of pictorial record, or even as *photojournalism,* may lack the qualities we believe are requisite to art. A photograph of a baseball player sliding into second base or of Aunt Mable cooking hamburgers at the family reunion may trigger expressive responses for us, but it is doubtful that the photographers had aesthetic communication or particular artistic design in mind when they snapped the shutter. On the other hand, a carefully composed and sensitively designed and executed photograph can contain every attribute of human expression possible in any art form.

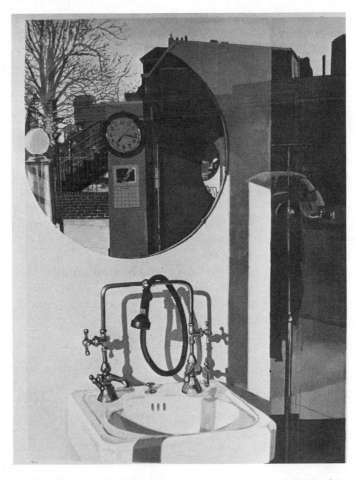

Fig. 3.10. Nancy McIntyre, *Barbershop Mirror* (1976). Silk-screen, 26½" × 19". Museum of Art, The Pennsylvania State University.

It is obvious that in producing a multiple exposure or a nonobjective picture photographers are not merely reproducing nature. However, even photos that are high in *verisimilitude* can be carefully arranged with the use of the elements of composition that we will discuss in the following section. Nevertheless, we balk at calling photography an *art* because the transferral of image from the mind of the artist to his picture appears to be a matter of mechanization rather than the hand process that is used even by the printmaker.

Ansel Adams sees the photographer as an interpretative artist; he likens the photographic negative to the musical score, and the print to a performance. In other words, despite all the choices the artist may make in committing an image to film, they are only the beginning of the artistic process. The photographer still has the choice of *size, texture,* and *value contrast* or *tonality*. A photo of the grain of a piece of wood has an enormous range of aesthetic possibilities depending upon how the artist employs and combines these three elements.

Consequently, the question "Is it art?" may have a cogent application to photography. However, the quality of our aesthetic repayment from the photographic experience is higher if we view photography in the same vein as we do the other arts—as a visualization manifested through a technique and resulting in an aesthetic response or communication.

Composition

Our discussions of how any artwork is put together eventually result in a discussion of how it is composed. The elements of *composition* are basic to all the arts, and we shall return to them time and time again as we proceed.

Line. To most of us a line is a thin mark such as this: _____. We find that denotation in art as well. In Fig. 3.11 we find amorphous shapes. Some of these shapes are like cartoon figures; that is, they are identifiable from the background because of their *outline*. In these instances line identifies form and illustrates the first sentence of this paragraph. However, the other shapes in Fig. 3.11 also exemplify line. These shapes appear black or white against the background. If we put our finger on the edge of these shapes, we have identified a second meaning of line—the boundary between areas of color and between shapes or forms. (We noted this use of line in our discussion of style in Chapter 1.) There is one further aspect of line, which is implied rather than physical. The three rectangles in Fig. 3.12 create a horizontal "line" that extends across the design. There is no physical line between the tops of the forms, but their spatial arrangement creates one by implication. A similar use of line occurs in Fig. 3.1, where we can see a definite linear movement from the upper left border through a series of swirls to the right border. That "line" is quite clear although it is composed not of a form edge or outline but of a carefully developed relationship of numerous color areas. This treatment of line is also seen in Fig. 3.13, although here it is much more subtle and sophisticated. By dripping paint onto his canvas (a task not as easily executed, simplistic, or accidental as it might appear) the artist was able to subordinate form, in the sense of recognizable and distinct areas, and thereby *focal areas,* to a dynamic network of complex lines. The effect of this technique of execution has a very strong relationship to the actual force and speed with which the pigment was applied.

Line is used by an artist to control our vision, to create unity and emotional value, and ultimately to develop meaning. In pursuing those ends, and by employing the three aspects of line noted earlier, the artist finds that line has two characteristics: it is curved or it is straight. Whether it is expressed as an

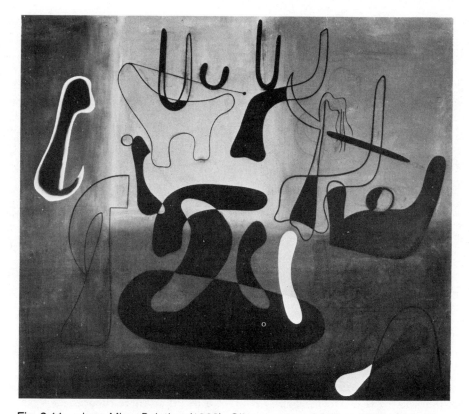

Fig. 3.11.   Joan Miro, *Painting* (1933). Oil on canvas, 68½″ × 77¼″. Collection, The Museum of Modern Art, New York. Gift of the Advisory Committee.

outline, an area edge, or by implication, and whether it is simple or in combination, a line is some derivative of the qualities of straightness or curvedness. It is interesting to speculate, as some do, whether line can also

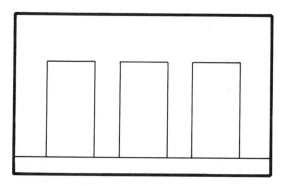

Fig. 3.12.   Three rectangles.

be thick or thin. Certainly that quality is helpful in describing some works of art. Those who deny line that quality, however, have a point difficult to refute in asking, If line can be thick or thin, at what point does it cease to be a line and become a form?

As we will discover, and will have to reiterate, definitions can be problematic. We, of course, are attempting to deal with the perception of artworks by noting what we can look for and what we call it. But we must remember that while this approach is important, all the terms it employs are highly related and serve only to make it more convenient for us to talk about an artwork. More important than complete agreement on definitions is the ability to apply the concepts they represent to the artwork. How has the

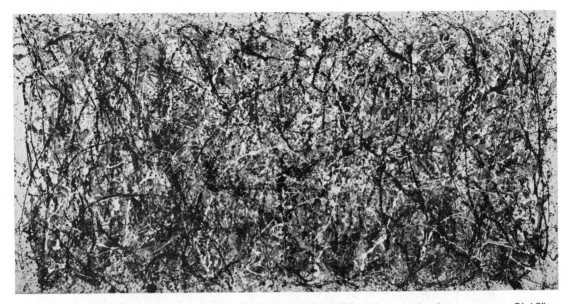

Fig. 3.13.   Jackson Pollock, *One (Number 31, 1950)* (1950). Oil and enamel paint on canvas, 8′ 10″ × 17′ 5⅝″. Collection, The Museum of Modern Art, New York. Gift of Sidney Janis.

artist utilized line? Does it make his composition active or passive? Are her forms sharp or fuzzy? Is the photograph in focus or not?

Form.   Form and line are closely related both in definition and in effect. Form is the *shape* of an object within the composition, and *shape* often is used as a synonym for form. Literally, form is that space described by line. A building is a form. So is a tree. We perceive them as buildings or trees, and we also perceive their individual details because of the line by which they are composed; form cannot be separated from line in two-dimensional design. If this sounds a bit complex, it is. This complexity is the reason why an artwork is unique in the universe. Regardless of how hard we try, we cannot reduce its essences into words. If we could, the *Mona Lisa* would exist not as a picture of an intriguing woman but as a framed photograph of descriptive words.

Color.   Color is a complex phenomenon, and no less than three theories exist as to its nature. It is not important for our purposes to understand these theories or how they differ. But knowing they exist helps us understand why some sources use different terms to describe the same color characteristics and other sources use the same terms to describe different characteristics. Although the treatment that follows may not be entirely satisfactory to those who learned color theory from one or another of these sources, I think it is a fair way to introduce color to those whose knowledge of color terminology is for response and communication rather than for creation of an artwork.

To begin, color characteristics differ depending upon whether we are discussing color in light or color in pigment. For example, in light the primary hues (those hues that cannot be achieved by mixing other hues) are red, *green,* and blue; in pigment they are red, *yellow,* and blue. If we mix equal proportions of yellow and blue pigments we will have green. Since green can be achieved by mixing, it cannot be a primary—in pigment. However, no matter how hard we try, we cannot mix any hues that will achieve green light. Inasmuch as our response to artworks most often deals with colored pigment, the discussion that follows concerns color in pigment. We will not discuss color in light.

HUE. Hue is the spectrum notation of color; a hue is a specific pure color with a measurable wavelength. The visible range of the color spectrum extends from violet on one end to red on the other. The color spectrum consists of the three primaries blue, yellow, and red and three additional hues that are direct derivatives of them—green, orange, and violet. These six hues are the basic hues of the spectrum, and each has a specific, measurable wavelength (Fig. 3.14). In all there are (depending upon which theory one follows) from ten to twenty-four perceivably different hues, including these

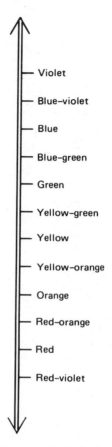

Fig. 3.15.   Color spectrum, including composite hues.

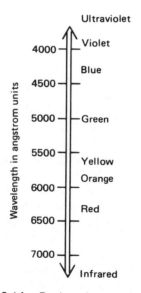

Fig. 3.14.   Basic color spectrum.

six. These perceptible hues are the composite hues of the color spectrum.

For the sake of clarity and illustration let us assume that there are twelve basic hues. Arranged in a series, they would look like Fig. 3.15. However, since combinations of these hues are possible beyond the straight-line configuration of the spectrum, it is helpful to visualize color by turning the color spectrum into a color wheel (Fig. 3.16). With this visualization we now can discuss what an artist can do to and with color. First, an artist can take the primary hues of the spectrum, mix them two at a time in varying proportions, and create the other hues of the

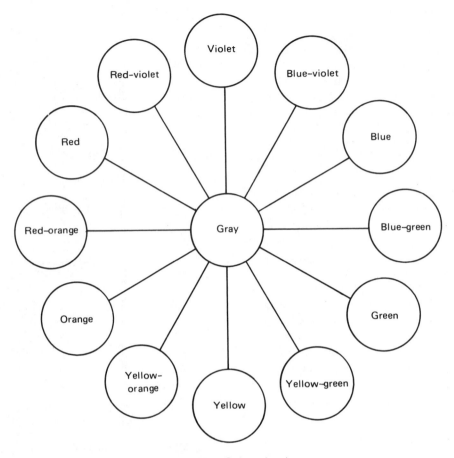

Fig. 3.16. Color wheel.

spectrum. For example, red and yellow in equal proportions make orange, a *secondary hue*. Varying the proportions—adding more red or more yellow—makes yellow-orange or red-orange, which are *tertiary hues*. Yellow and blue make green, and also blue-green and yellow-green; red and blue give us violet, blue-violet, and red-violet. First, therefore, an artist can vary hue.

VALUE. In discussing photography we noted in passing the concept of value contrast—the relationship of blacks to whites and grays. The range of possibilities from black to white forms the *value scale,* which has black at one end, white at the other, and medium gray in the middle. The perceivable tones between black and white are designated light or dark (Fig. 3.17).

The application of the effects of value on color is treated in different ways by different sources. Providing an overview is difficult. However, it appears most helpful if we approach the subject less from a theoretical point of view and more from a practical one. That is, what can painters do to change color in order to create a painting that gives the effect they desire? As we indicated, they may mix primaries to create secondary and tertiary hues. They thereby change hue. Every

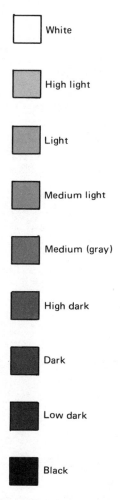

White

High light

Light

Medium light

Medium (gray)

High dark

Dark

Low dark

Black

Fig. 3.17. Value scale.

hue has its own value; that is, in its "pure" state each hue falls somewhere on the value scale in Fig. 3.18. An artist may change the value of a hue by *raising* or *lowering* it. For example, there are nine different values of red.

In practical terms the application of this concept causes different sources to travel different roads. How does one change a hue to a different value on the value scale? Many authorities propose that value is changed by adding white or black. White raises value;

black lowers it. However, the actual mixing of paints to achieve different values is not quite that simple. For example, if we take primary red, whose value is medium dark, and add various amounts of pure white, the changes that occur are perceivably different from the changes that occur when medium gray, medium-light gray, light gray, and high-light gray are added to the same pure red. Identical ranges of color do not result from the two processes. Let's take it from another direction. Suppose we wish to create a gray-pink color for our painting. We take primary red and add white. The result is pink. To subdue the pink we add just a bit of black. What we have just done seems impossible, because we have both raised and lowered the value of our original red—at the same time. Of course, it is not impossible at all. We have merely raised our red to a lighter value by adding light gray (black and white).

There is a broad range of color possibilities between high-light gray and pure white, or between a pure hue and white, which does not fall on the traditional value scale. That range of possibilities is described by the term *saturation*. A saturated hue is a pure hue. An unsaturated hue is a hue to which some quantity of white alone has been added. Unsaturated hues, such as pink, are known as *tints*. What is not entirely clear is whether saturation is part of or separate from value—that is, whether the two terms should be considered as separate properties of color change or whether value includes saturation. More on this momentarily.

We can easily see that some colors are brighter than others. As we noted, the perceivable difference in brightness between primary yellow and primary blue is due to their difference in value. However, it is possible to have a *bright* yellow and a *dull* yellow. The difference in brightness between the two may be a matter of value, as we just

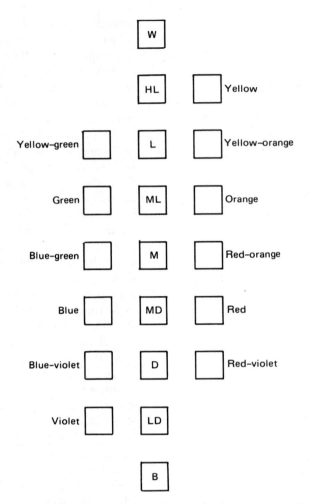

Fig. 3.18. Color-value equivalents.

observed—a pure yellow versus a grayed yellow. It also may be a matter of surface *brilliance,* or reflectance, a factor of considerable importance to all visual artists. A highly reflective surface creates a brighter color, and therefore a different response from the observer, than does a surface of lesser reflection, although all other color factors may be the same. This is the difference among high-gloss, semigloss, and flat paints, for example. Probably surface reflectance is more a property of texture than of color.

However, the term *brilliance* is often used to describe not only surface gloss but also characteristics synonomous with value. Some sources also use brilliance as a synonym for saturation, while still others use saturation as a synonym for an additional color-change possibility, *intensity.*

INTENSITY. Intensity is the degree of purity of a hue. It also is sometimes called *chroma.* Returning to the color wheel (Fig. 3.16), we note that movement around the wheel creates a change in hue. Movement *across* the wheel creates a change in intensity. If we add green to red we alter its intensity. When, as in this case, hues are directly opposite each other on the color wheel (that is, when they are *complementary*) such mixing has the practical effect of *graying* the original hue. Therefore, since graying a hue is a *value* change, one occasionally finds intensity and value used interchangeably. Some sources use the terms independently but state that changing a color's value *automatically* changes its intensity. It is well to ponder the implications of these concepts. There is a difference between graying a hue by using its complement and graying a hue by adding black (or gray derived from black and white). A gray derived from complementaries, because it *has color*, is far livelier than a gray derived from black and white, which are not colors.

All this discussion and divergence may be academic, but it illustrates the problem of attempting to describe complex phenomena.

The point to be made here is not that definitions are illogical, hopeless, or incomprehensible, but rather that one can use proper descriptive terminology as an aid to understanding what is happening in a work of art. If one is aware of divergences in theory and usage regarding a given term, he can phrase his response in such a way or in such a context as to make his own observations even clearer. Some individuals never will admit to the viability of someone else's usage if it in any way differs from their own. But divergences are not necessarily matters of correct or incorrect. Often they are simply attempts to describe the indescribable so as to promote a clearer interchange of understanding and experience. The difficulties I have noted regarding color terminology essentially stem from differences in theory and the application of theory to practice. Attempts to create color wheels, three-dimensional color models, and all-inclusive

terminology are man's attempts to explain a marvelously complex natural phenomenon —color perception—that we still do not comprehend in its entirety.

The composite, or overall, use of color by the artist is termed *palette*. An artist's palette can be broad, restricted, or somewhere in between, depending upon whether the artist has utilized the full range of the color spectrum and/or whether he or she explores the full range of *tonalities*—brights and dulls, lights and darks.

Mass.   Only three-dimensional objects have mass—that is, take up space and have density. However, two-dimensional objects give the illusion of mass, *relative* only to the other objects in the picture.

Texture.   The texture of a picture is its apparent roughness or smoothness. Texture ranges from the smoothness of a glossy photo to the three-dimensionality of *impasto*, a painting technique wherein pigment is applied thickly with a palette knife to raise areas from the canvas. The texture of a picture may be anywhere within these two extremes. Texture may be illusory in that the surface of a picture may be absolutely flat but the image gives the impression of three-dimensionality. So the term can be applied to the pictorial arts either literally or figuratively.

Repetition.   Probably the essence of any design is repetition: how the basic elements in the picture are repeated or alternated. In discussing repetition let's consider three terms: rhythm, harmony, and variation.

RHYTHM results from the spatial relationships among the objects of a composition. One may say that the relationships are regular or irregular. If the relationships among the objects are equal, the rhythm is regular

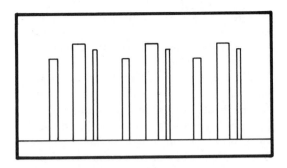

Fig. 3.19. Repetition of patterns.

(Fig. 3.12). If not, the rhythm is irregular. However, one must examine the composition as a whole to discern if patterns of relationships exist and whether or not the *patterns* are regular, as they are in Fig. 3.19.

HARMONY is the logic of the repetition. Harmonious relationships are those whose components appear to join naturally and comfortably. If the artist employs forms, colors, or other elements that appear incongruous, illogical, or "out of sync" with each other, then we could use a musical term and say the resulting picture is dissonant; its constituents simply do not go together naturally.

VARIATION is the relationship of repeated items to each other; it is similar to theme and variation in music. How does an artist take a basic element in the composition and use it again with slight or major changes? The artist of Fig. 3.20 has taken two geometric forms, the diamond and the oval, and created a complex painting via repetition. The diamond with a circle at its center is repeated over and over to form the background. Variation occurs in the treatment of color. Similarly, the oval of the mirror is repeated with variations in the composition of the girl. The circular motif is also repeated throughout the painting, with variations in color and size—similar to the repetition and

variation in the design of the Volkswagen noted in Fig. 1.3.

Balance. The concept of balance is very important. It is not difficult to look at a composition and almost intuitively respond that it does or does not appear balanced. Most individuals have this "second sense." However, *how* artists achieve balance in their pictures is the object of our concern.

SYMMETRY. The most mechanical method of achieving balance is *symmetry,* the balancing of like forms, mass, and colors on opposite sides of the centerline of the picture. Symmetry is so precise that we can measure it. Pictures employing symmetry tend to be stable, stolid, and without much sense of motion. They are also, probably for that very reason, quite rare. Many works approach symmetry, but nearly all retreat from placing mirror images on opposite sides of the centerline, as do Figs. 3.12, 3.21, and 3.22, all of which are symmetrical. This, however, is not the case in architecture, as we shall see in Chapter 10.

ASYMMETRICAL BALANCE is achieved by careful placement of unlike items. It is sometimes referred to as psychological balance. It might seem that asymmetrical balance is a matter of opinion. However, intrinsic response to what is balanced or unbalanced is relatively uniform among individuals, regardless of their aesthetic training. Every painting illustrated in this chapter is asymmetrical. Comparative discussion as to *how* balance has been achieved would be a useful exercise, especially if colors were to be considered. Often color is used to balance line and form. Since some hues, such as yellow, have a great attraction for the eye, they can balance tremendous mass and activity on one side of a painting, by being placed on the other side.

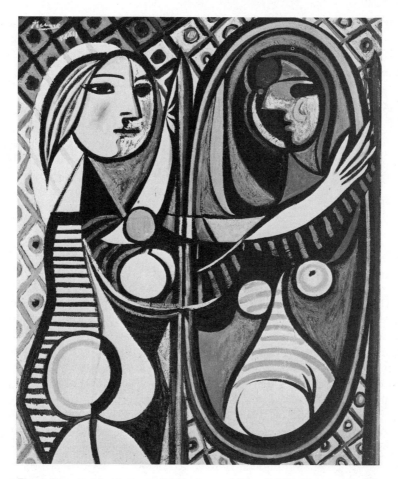

Fig. 3.20.   Pablo Picasso, *Girl before a Mirror* (1932, March 14). Oil on canvas, 64 × 51¼". Collection, The Museum of Modern Art, New York. Gift of Mrs. Simon Guggenheim.

Unity.   The culminating element of composition, since it involves all the other elements, is unity. In some way or another all the elements of a picture must work together to form a complete whole. Perhaps unity is more easily illustrated by examples that lack it. We all have seen pictures that seem not to "hang together," or that appear to be two pictures placed within the same frame. In these cases the artist has failed in his or her use of composition. Every element we have discussed in this section should be utilized in such a manner that it works with all the other elements to give us a picture that is unified. Our discussion of how an artist has employed compositional devices is not complete until we discern how the composition works as a totality.

With regard to unity one also must consider whether or not the artist allows the composition to *escape the frame.* People occasionally speak of *closed composition,* or composition in which use of line and form always directs the eye into the painting (Fig.

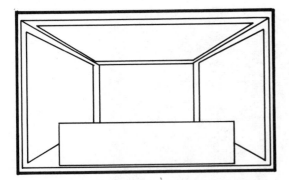

Fig. 3.21. Closed composition (composition kept within the frame).

3.21), as unified and *open composition,* in which the eye is allowed to wander off the canvas, or *escape the frame* (Fig. 3.22), as disunified. Such is not the case. Keeping the artwork within the frame is a stylistic device that has an important bearing on the artwork's meaning. For example, painting in the classical style is predominantly kept within the frame. This illustrates a concern for the self-containment of the artwork and for precise structuring. On the other hand, baroque design tends to force the eye to escape the frame. Here the device has philosophical intent, suggesting the world or universe outside or the individual's place in an overwhelming cosmos. So, unity can be

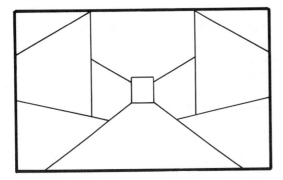

Fig. 3.22. Open composition (composition allowed to escape the frame).

achieved by keeping the composition closed, but it is not necessarily lacking when the opposite state exists.

Other Elements

Perspective. Perspective is a tool by which the artist indicates the spatial relationships of objects in a picture. It is based on the phenomenon of *foreshortening,* which causes objects further away from us to appear smaller. If we examine a painting that has some degree of verisimilitude, we can identify, through perspective, the spatial relationship between the objects in the foreground and the objects in the background. We also can discern whether that relationship is rational—that is, whether or not the relationships of the objects appear as we see them in life. For example, paintings executed prior to the Italian Renaissance (when mechanical procedures for rendering perspective were developed) look rather strange to us because while background objects are painted smaller than foreground objects the positioning does not appear rational. So their composition strikes us as being rather primitive.

LINEAR PERSPECTIVE. Two types of perspective may be used. The first, *linear* perspective, is characterized by the phenomenon of standing on railroad tracks and watching the two rails apparently come together at the horizon. It uses *line* to achieve the sense of distance. In Fig. 3.23 the road recedes from foreground to background and becomes narrower as it does so. We perceive that recession, which denotes distance, through the artist's use of line.

AERIAL PERSPECTIVE indicates distance through the use of light and atmosphere. For example, mountains in the background of a picture are made to appear distant by being painted in less detail; they are "hazy." In the

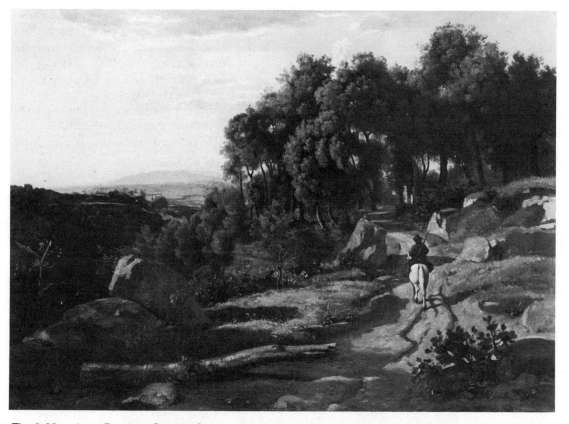

Fig. 3.23.   Jean-Baptiste-Camille Corot, *A View near Volterra* (1838). Canvas, 27⅜″ × 37½″. National Gallery of Art, Washington, D.C. Chester Dale Collection.

upper left of Fig. 3.2 a castle appears at a great distance. We know it is distant because it is smaller and, more important, because it is indistinct.

Focal Area.   When we look at a picture for the first time our eye moves around it, pausing briefly at those areas that seem to be of greatest visual appeal. These are *focal areas*. A painting may have a single focal area to which our eye is drawn immediately, and from which it will stray only with conscious effort. Or it may have an infinite number of focal points. We describe a picture of the latter type as "busy"; that is, the eye bounces at

will from one point to another on the picture, without any attraction at all.

Focal areas are achieved in a number of ways—through confluence of line, by encirclement, or by color, to name just a few. To draw attention to a particular point in the picture the artist may make all line lead to that point. She may place the focal object or area in the center of a ring of objects, or she may give the object a color that demands our attention more than the other colors in the picture. Again, for example, bright yellows attract our eye more readily than dark blues. The artist uses focal areas, of whatever number or variety, as her control over what

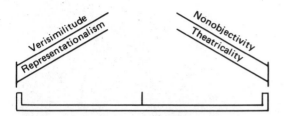

Fig. 3.24. Subject-matter continuum.

we see and when we see it when we glance at a picture for the first time.

Subject Matter. We can regard treatment of subject matter as ranging from verisimil-

itude, or representationalism, to nonobjectivity (Fig. 3.24). We will use this continuum again in later chapters, substituting the term *theatricality* for nonobjectivity. Between the two ends of this continuum are the "isms" we all are familiar with in the art world: realism, impressionism, expressionism, cubism, fauvism, and so forth. Each denotes a particular method of treatment of subject matter.

Chiaroscuro. *Chiaroscuro* (sometimes called *modeling*), whose meaning in Italian is "light and shade," is the device used by artists to

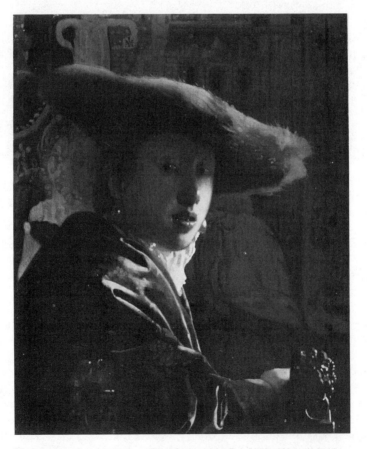

Fig. 3.25. Jan Vermeer, *The Girl with a Red Hat*. Wood, 9⅛″ × 7⅛″. National Gallery of Art, Washington, D.C. Andrew Mellon Collection.

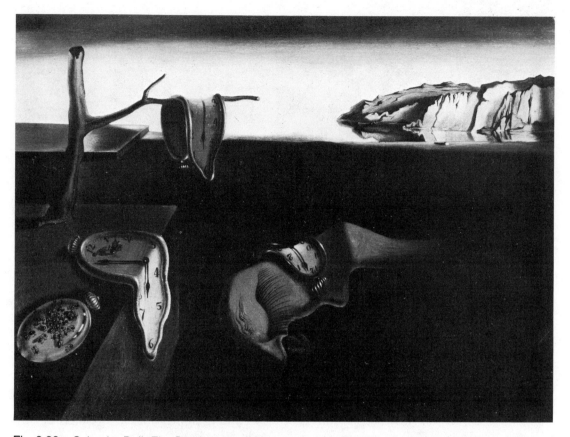

Fig. 3.26. Salvador Dali, *The Persistence of Memory* (1931). Oil on canvas, 9½ × 13″. Collection, The Museum of Modern Art, New York. Given anonymously.

make their forms appear *plastic*—that is, three-dimensional. Artists may spend long periods of time observing and sketching objects from life. The problem of making two-dimensional objects appear three-dimensional rests entirely on the artist's ability to effectively render highlight and shadow. Without them all forms are two-dimensional in appearance.

Use of chiaroscuro gives a picture much of its character. For example the dynamic and dramatic treatment of light and shade in Fig. 3.25 give this painting a quality quite different from what would have resulted had the artist chosen to give full, flat, front light to the face. The highlights, falling as they

do, create not only a dramatic effect but also a compositional triangle extending from shoulder to cheek, down to the hand, and then across the sleeve and back to the shoulder. Consider the substantial change in character of Fig. 3.2 had highlight and shadow been executed in a different manner. Finally, the treatment of chiaroscuro in a highly verisimilar fashion in Fig. 3.26 helps give that painting its strangely real yet dreamlike appearance.

In contrast, works that do not employ chiaroscuro have a two-dimensional quality. This can be seen to a large extent in Fig. 3.1 and also Figs. 3.2 and 3.27.

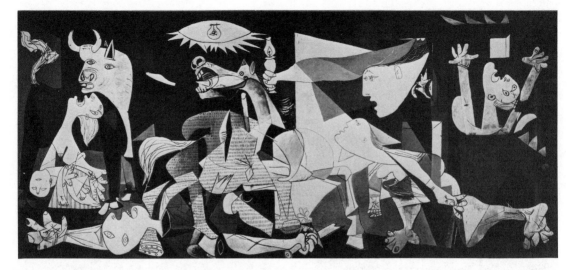

Fig. 3.27.   Pablo Picasso, *Guernica* (1937, May–early June). Oil on canvas, 11′ 5½″ × 25′ 5¾″.   On extended loan to The Museum of Modern Art, New York, from the artist's estate.

HOW DOES IT STIMULATE THE SENSES?

Our discussion of the ways in which pictures stimulate our senses must be in terms of mental images. We do not touch pictures, and so we cannot feel their roughness or their smoothness, their coolness or their warmth. We cannot hear pictures and we cannot smell them. So, when we conclude that a picture affects our senses in a particular way we are responding in terms of visual stimuli that are transposed into mental images of our senses of touch, taste, sound, and so forth.

Color.   The colors of an artist's palette are referred to as warm or cool depending upon which end of the color spectrum they fall. Reds, oranges, and yellows are said to be warm colors. Those are the colors of the sun, and therefore call to mind our primary source of heat. So they carry strong implications of warmth. Colors falling on the opposite end of the spectrum—blues and greens—are cool colors because they imply shade, or lack of light and warmth. Here we have, as we will notice frequently, a stimulation that is mental but has a physical basis. Tonality and color contrast also affect our senses, by creating impressions of liveliness or subdued relaxation.

Chiaroscuro.   Many of the sense-affecting stimuli work in concert and cannot be separated from each other. We already have noted some of the effects of chiaroscuro, but one more will serve well. One of the most interesting effects to observe in a picture is the treatment of flesh. Some flesh is treated harshly, and appears like stone. Other flesh appears soft and true to life. Our response to whatever treatment has been given is very tactile—we want to touch, or we believe we know what we would feel if we touched. Chiaroscuro is essential in an artist's achieving those effects. Harsh shadows and strong contrasts create one set of responses; diffused shadows and subdued contrasts create another.

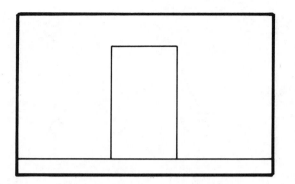

Fig. 3.28.   Vertical composition.

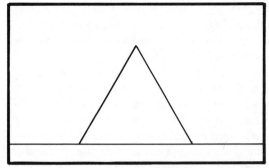

Fig. 3.30.   Upright-triangular composition.

Dynamics.   Pictures, although they are static (they do not move), can effectively stimulate a sense of movement and activity. They also can create a sense of stable solidity. The artist stimulates these sensations by using certain accepted universal symbols. A painting that is principally vertical in its use of forms tends to elicit a sense of grandeur (Fig. 3.28). A picture that is horizontal tends to elicit a sense of placidity (Fig. 3.29). The triangle, which is a most interesting form in engineering because of its structural qualities, is also interesting in art because of its psychological qualities. If we place a triangle so that its base forms the bottom of a picture, we give the respondent a definite sense of solidity and immovability (Fig. 3.30). If that triangle

were a pyramid sitting on a level plane, a great deal of effort would be required to tip it over. However, if we invert the triangle so that it balances on its apex, a sensation of extreme instability results (Fig. 3.31). We can feel quite clearly the specific sensations stimulated by these rather simple geometric forms in Figs. 3.28–3.31.

Trompe l'oeil.   This aspect of response is illustrated by Figs. 3.28 and 3.29. *Trompe l'oeil,* or "trick of the eye," gives the artist a varied set of stimuli by which to affect our sensory response. Although not designed as trick, Figs. 3.28 and 3.29 illustrate the basis for the deception. The rectangular form in 3.28 appears narrower than that of 3.29, even

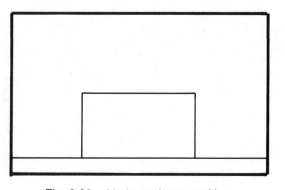

Fig. 3.29.   Horizontal composition.

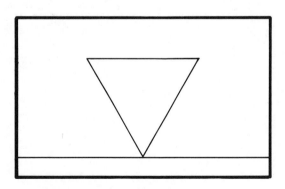

Fig. 3.31.   Inverted-triangular composition.

though both are identical in size. Our eye is tricked because of the change in relationship of the object to the rest of the design. Occasionally this device forms the core of a painting; at other times it is used to enhance a work's appeal. For example, in executing linear perspective an artist knows that all objects drawn with parallel sides recede to a vanishing point. Some artists make subtle changes in the placement of the vanishing point with the effect that the picture, while appearing verisimilar, gives the impression of rotating forward at the top. Its kinesthetic appeal is thereby much more dynamic.

Line. The use of line also effects sense response. Figure 3.32 illustrates how curved line can elicit a sense of ease and relaxation. On the other hand, the broken line in Fig. 3.33 creates a much more dynamic and violent sensation. We can also feel that the upright triangle in Fig. 3.30, although solid and stable, is more dynamic than the horizontal rectangle of Fig. 3.29 because it uses diagonal line, which tends to stimulate a sense of movement. Precision of linear execution also can create sharply defined forms or soft, fuzzy images.

Juxtaposition. We also can receive sense stimuli from the results of an artist's jux-

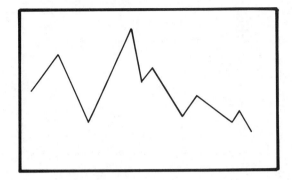

Fig. 3.33. Broken line.

taposing. Juxtaposing curved and straight lines results in linear dissonance or consonance. Figure 3.34 illustrates the juxtaposing of inharmonious forms, which creates instability. Careful use of this device can stimulate some very interesting and specific sense responses, as the artist has done in Fig. 3.20.

Subject Matter. The method of treatment of subject matter, which, of course, involves any or all of the characteristics we have discussed, is a powerful device for effecting both sensory responses and more intense, subjective responses. The relative use of verisimilitude or nonobjectivity seems to be the most noticeable stimulant of individual re-

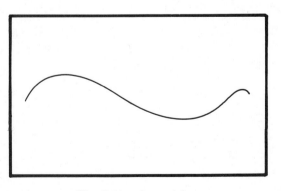

Fig. 3.32. Curved line.

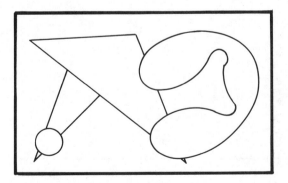

Fig. 3.34. Juxtaposition.

sponse. It would seem logical for individuals to respond objectively and intellectually to nonobjective pictures, since the subject matter should be neutral, with no inherent expressive stimuli. However, no other aspect of a picture seems to create so extreme a *subjective* response (especially a negative one) as nonobjectivity. When asked whether they feel more comfortable with the treatment of subject matter in Fig. 3.2 or that in Fig. 3.13, most individuals choose the former, even though the latter is a product of our age, our society, our world. Why is this so? Does the contemporary work tell us something about ourselves that we do not wish to hear?

So, the viewer's response seems to depend on how directly the subject matter is communicated. For example, an artist may wish to communicate his idea of the agonies of hell. To do so he may utilize verisimilitude, nonobjectivity, or some point in between. If he chooses nonobjectivity, he might use broken line and warm, saturated colors. However, our reactions to his presentation of hell would commence only after we read the title of the picture, since the nonobjective treatment of the subject would give us little or no clue to its identity. On the other hand, a highly representational portrayal of a mass execution might depict human bodies writhing and dangling, with distorted, pain-ridden, and screaming faces. That method of communication would stimulate us very directly, perhaps causing us to imagine, among other things, the sound of the screaming.

Does the more direct appeal to our senses cause a more profound response? Or does the stimulation provided by the unfamiliar cause us to think more deeply and respond more fully, since our imagination is left free to wander? The answers to these questions are worth considering as we perceive artworks whose keys to response are not immediately obvious.

CHRONOLOGY OF SELECTED MAJOR PERIODS, STYLES, AND EXAMPLES FOR STUDY IN WESTERN ART

PAINTING

Prehistory–c. 4000 B.C.
paleolithic and neolithic cave paintings

c. 4000 B.C.–c. 1000 B.C.
Ancient Egypt
tomb paintings

c. 3000 B.C.–c. 500 B.C.
Ancient Mesopotamia, Persia, Crete, and Mycenae
wall and vase paintings

c. 1200 B.C.–c. 300 B.C.
Ancient Greece
vase paintings

c. 500 B.C.–c. 300 A.D.
Rome and Hellenistic Greece
vase and wall paintings

c. 300–1500
Early Christian and Byzantine Art
catacomb and wall paintings
manuscript illustration
mosaics

c. 400–c. 900
The Middle Ages
manuscript illustration

c. 900–c. 1200
Romanesque Europe
manuscript illustration

c. 1200–c. 1400
Gothic Art
manuscript illustration
Duccio: *Majestas Altarpiece*
Martini: *Madonna in Majesty; Virgin of Paris*
Cimabue: *Madonna Enthroned*
Giotto: *Death of St. Francis; Joachim and Anna at the Beautiful Gate*

c. 1400–c. 1500
Flanders
  Martorel: *St. George and the Dragon*
  Pol de Limbourg: *Les Très Riches Heures du Duc De Berri*
  Jan van Eyck: *The Arnolfini Marriage*
  Roger van der Weyden: *Deposition*
  Jerome Bosch: *Temptation of St. Anthony*
Italy (early Renaissance)
  Fra Angelico: *Annunciation*
  Fra Lippo Lippi: *Adoration*
  Botticelli: *Spring*
  Ghirlandajo: *Old Man and Boy*
  Perugino: *Christ Delivering the Keys to St. Peter*
The Reformation
  Schongauer: *Annunciation*
  Dürer: *The Four Horsemen of the Apocalypse; The Four Apostles*
  Baldung Grien: *Three Ages of Man*

c. 1480–c. 1550
High Renaissance
  Leonardo da Vinci: *The Last Supper; Mona Lisa*
  Michelangelo: *Sistine Chapel Frescoes*
  Raphael: *Sistine Madonna; Madonna of the Chair; The School of Athens*
  Bellini: *Portrait of Doge Loredano*
  Giorgione: *Fête Champêtre; Sleeping Venus*
  Titian: *Bacchus and Ariadne; The Young Englishman*

c. 1510–c. 1570
Mannerism
  Bronzino: *Portrait of a Young Man*
  Parmigianino: *The Madonna with the Long Neck*
  Tintoretto: *The Last Supper*
  El Greco: *The Nativity; View of Toledo*
  Clouet: *Francis I*
  Brueghel the Elder: *The Wedding Dance*

c. 1570–c. 1700
Baroque Art
  Domenichino: *The Last Communion of St. Jerome*
  Caravaggio: *Bacchus; Death of the Virgin*
  Velasquez: *Portrait of Philip IV; Las Meniñas*

Rubens: *Descent from the Cross; Judgment of Paris; The Garden of Love*
Van Dyck: *Portrait of Charles I of England*
Poussin: *Orpheus and Eurydice; Funeral of Phocian*
Lorrain: *Embarkation of the Queen of Sheba*
Hals: *Malle Bobbe*
Rembrandt: *The Night Watch; Man with the Golden Helmet*
van Ruysdael: *The Jewish Cemetery; Wheat Fields*
Vermeer: *Officer and Laughing Girl*

c. 1700–c. 1800
Rococo Art
  Watteau: *Embarkation for Cythera; Giles*
  Boucher: *Toilet of Venus*
  Chardin: *Boy with Teetotum; Still Life*
  Canaletto: *Grand Canal*
  Fragonard: *The Romance of Young Love: Storming the Citadel*
Social Criticism
  Hogarth: *The Rake's Progress* series; *The Harlot's Progress* series
Portraiture
  Gainsborough: *The Honorable Frances Duncombe*
  Reynolds: *Sarah Siddons as the Tragic Muse*
  Copley: *Nathanial Hurd*
  Stuart: *George Washington*
Neoclassicism
  David: *The Oath of the Horatii*

c. 1800–c. 1905
Classicism
  Ingres: *Odalisque*
Romanticism
  Goya: *Executions of the Third of May, 1808*
  Gros: *Napoleon Among the Plague-stricken at Jaffa*
  Gericault: *The Raft of the "Medusa"*
  Delacroix: *Massacre at Scio*
  Constable: *Hampstead Heath with a Rainbow*
  Turner: *The Slave Ship; Valley of Aosta*
Realism
  Millet: *The Sower*

Courbet: *My Studio*
Manet: *Luncheon on the Grass*
Daumier: *The Third-Class Carriage*
Naturalism
Corot: *View of Genoa*
Impressionism
Manet: *Execution of Maximilian*
Monet: *Regatta at Argenteuil*
Renoir: *Luncheon of the Boating Party*
Degas: *Dancers Practicing at the Bar*
Postimpressionism
Seurat: *Sunday Afternoon on the Island of the Grande-Jatte*
van Gogh: *Church at Auvers*
Cézanne: *Mont Sainte-Victoire* (1904–6)
Gaugin: *L'Appel*

c. 1900–

Fauvism
Matisse: *The Green Stripe; The Young Sailor*
Rouault: *Mr. X*
Cubism
Picasso: *L'Arlesienne*
Braque: *Le Pauquet de Fabac*
Futurism
Severini: *Armored Train*
Machine Art
Léger: *Elément Mécanique*
De Stijl
Mondrian: *Composition with Blue and White; Composition in White, Black, and Red*
Expressionism
Kandinsky: *Improvisation; Interior*
Klee: *Actor's Mask*

Surrealism
Dali: *The Persistence of Memory*
Abstract Expressionism
De Kooning: *Woman and Bicycle*

PRINTMAKING

Anonymous: *S.S. Christopher, Margaret and Barbara*, woodcut, c. 1420–30
Albrecht Dürer: *St. Michael and the Dragon*, woodcut, c. 1497–98; *Adam and Eve*, copper engraving, 1504
Francisco Goya: *He Died without any Aid*, etching, aquatint, and drypoint, nineteenth century
James McNeill Whistler: *The Storm*, drypoint
Edouard Manet: *Berthe Morisot*, chalk lithograph, 1872
Georges Rouault: *Christ*, colored aquatint etching, 1935
Sam Francis: *Tokyo Mon Amour*, lithograph, 1963
Frank Kupka: *Vegetables*, silkscreen

PHOTOGRAPHY

Matthew Brady: *Wounded Soldiers*, 1863
Charles M. Currier: *The Bicycle Messengers, Seated*, 1900
Lewis W. Hine: *Fresh Air for the Baby*, 1907
Arnold Genthe: *Watching the Approach*, 1906
Alvin L. Coburn: *The Octopus*, 1912
Edward Weston: *Church Door, Hornitos*, 1930
Dorothea Lange: *White Angel Breadline*, 1933
Robert Frank: *Trolley*, 1958
Dean Brown: *California Cows*, 1969

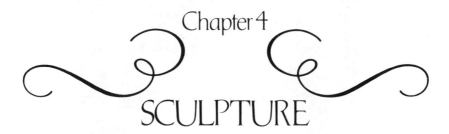

Chapter 4

SCULPTURE

WHAT IS IT?

Sculpture is the design of three-dimensional space. It may take the form of whatever it seeks to represent, from pure, or nonobjective form to lifelike depiction of the human being or any other entity. Occasionally one hears the claim that sculpture has the capacity to be whatever it says it is. That, of course, is not fully accurate. Even a sculptural work by Duane Hanson or John DeAndrea cannot *be* what it depicts. Hanson and DeAndrea use plastics to render the human form so realistically that the viewer must approach the artwork and examine it closely in order to determine that it is not a real human. Every art form employs some degree of abstraction, and so it is with sculpture.

HOW IS IT PUT TOGETHER?

Sculpture may be *statuary* or *relief*. Statuary works are freestanding and fully three-dimensional. We can walk around them and examine them on all sides (Fig. 4.1). A work that can be viewed from only one side—that is, one that projects from a background, is said to be *in relief* (Fig. 4.2). A sculptor's choice of statuary or relief as a mode of expression dictates to a large extent what he or she can and cannot do, both aesthetically and practically.

Statuary. Painters, printmakers, and photographers have virtually unlimited choice of subject matter and compositional arrangements. A sculptor choosing to execute a work of statuary finds considerable difficulty in dealing with such subjects as clouds, oceans, and panoramic landscapes. Statuary, therefore, is limited to rather small numbers of objects grouped in the same plane. That is, since sculpture occupies real space, the use of perspective, for example, to increase spatial relationships poses certain obvious problems. In addition, since statuary is freestanding and three-dimensional, sculptors must concern themselves with the practicalities of engineering and gravity. They cannot, for

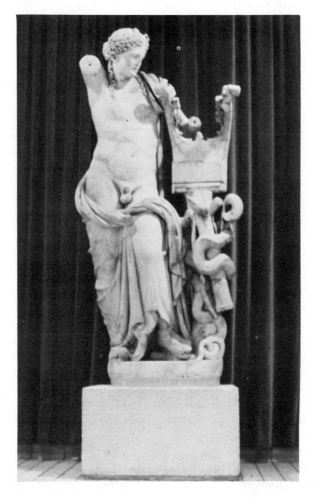

Fig. 4.1. Roman copy of a Greek statue. The British Museum, London.

example, create a work with great mass at the top unless they can find a way (within the bounds of acceptable composition) to keep the statue from falling over. After we have viewed numerous statuary works we begin to note the small animals, branches, tree stumps, rocks, and other devices that have been employed to give practical stability to a work.

Relief. On the other hand, the sculptor who creates a work in relief, does not have quite so many restrictions. Since his work is attached to a background, he has freer choice of subjects, and need not worry about their positions or supports. Clouds, seas, and perspective landscapes are within the relief sculptor's reach, since his work needs only to be viewed from one side.

Methods of Execution

In general, sculpture is either *carved, built,* or *cast.* In addition, *found* objects are becoming increasingly evident as works of sculpture.

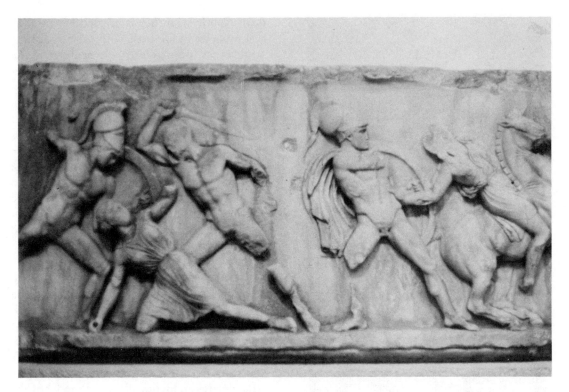

Fig. 4.2.   Roman frieze. The British Museum, London.

Carved.   Carved works are said to be *subtractive*. That is, the sculptor begins with a large block, usually wood or stone, and cuts away (subtracts) the unwanted material. In previous eras, and to some extent today, sculptors had to work with whatever materials were at hand. Wood carvings emanated from forested regions, soapstone carvings sprang forth from the Eskimos, and great works of marble descended to us from the regions surrounding the quarries of the Mediterranean. Anything that can yield to the carver's tools can be formed into a work of sculpture. However, stone, with its promise of immortality, has proven to be the most popular material.

Three types of rock hold potential for the carver. *Igneous* rocks, of which granite is an example, are very hard and potentially long-lasting. However, they are difficult to carve and therefore suffer in popularity. *Sedimentary* rocks such as limestone are relatively long-lasting, easy to carve, and polishable. Beautifully smooth and lustrous surfaces are possible with sedimentary rocks. *Metamorphic* rocks, including marble, seem to be the sculptor's ideal. They are long-lasting, are "a pleasure to carve," and exist in a broad range of colors. Whatever the artist's choice, one requirement must be met: the material to be carved, whether wood, stone, or a bar of soap, must be free of flaws.

A sculptor who sets about to carve a work does not begin simply by imagining a *Samson Slaying a Philistine* (Fig. 4.3) and then attacking the stone. He first creates a model usually smaller than the intended sculpture. The model is made of clay, plaster, or wax and is completed in precise detail—a miniature of the final product.

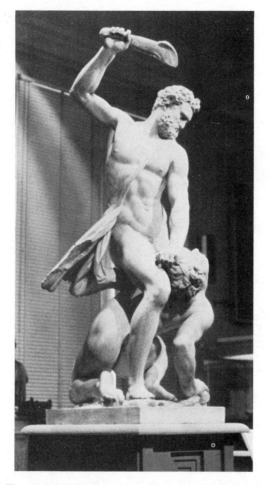

Fig. **4.3.** Giambologna, *Sampson Slaying a Philistine* (c. 1562). Courtesy, The Victoria and Albert Museum, London.

Once the likeness of the model has been enlarged and transferred, the artist begins to rough out the actual image ("knocking away the waste material," as Michelangelo put it). In this step of the sculpting process the artist carves to within two or three inches of what is to be the finished area, using specific tools designed for the purpose. Then, using a different set of carving tools, he or she carefully takes the material down to the precise detail. Finishing work and polishing follow.

Built. Built sculpture is created by an *additive* process. In contrast with carving from a large block of material, the sculptor starts with raw material and *adds* element to element until the work is finished. The materials employed in this process can be plastics, metals such as aluminum or steel, terra cottas (clay), epoxy resins, or wood. Many times materials are combined. For example, the final effect of the terra–cotta sculpture in Fig. 4.4 came originally from the paint applied to the clay. It is not uncommon for sculptors to combine methods as well. For example, built sections of metal or plastic may be combined with carved sections of stone.

Cast. Any material that can be transformed from a plastic, molten, or fluid state into a solid state can be molded or *cast* into a work of sculpture. Of course, the material must hold together permanently in its solid state. The creation of a piece of cast sculpture always involves the use of a mold. First, the artist creates an identically sized model of the intended sculpture. This is called a *positive*. He then covers the positive with a material, such as plaster of paris, that when hardened and removed will retain the surface configurations of the positive. This form is called a *negative,* and becomes the mold for the actual sculpture. The molten or fluid material is poured into the negative and allowed to solidify. When the mold is removed the work of sculpture emerges. Surface polishing, if desired, brings the work to its final form. Figures 4.5, 4.6, 4.7, and 4.13 all show the degrees of complexity and variety achievable through casting.

Very often sculpture is cast so that it is hollow. This method, of course, is less expensive, since it requires less material. It also results in a work that is less prone to crack, since it is less susceptible to expansion and contraction resulting from changes in temperature. Finally, hollow sculpture is, natur-

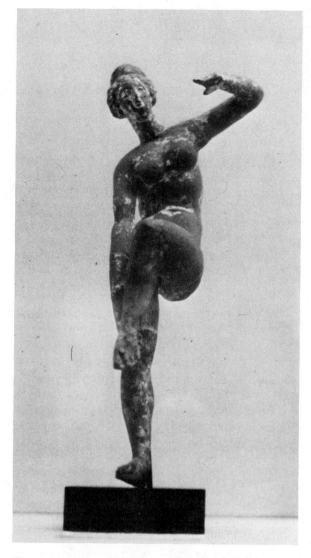

Fig. 4.4. *Aphrodite Undoing Her Sandal* (Palermo, second century B.C.). Terra cotta, approx. 8″ high. The British Museum, London.

ally, lighter and thus more easily shipped and handled.

Found.   This category of sculpture is exactly what its name implies. Very often natural objects, man-made or otherwise, are discov- ered that for some reason have taken on characteristics that stimulate aesthetic re- sponse. They become *objets d'art* not because an artist put them together (although an ar- tist may combine found objects to create a work), but because an artist chose to take

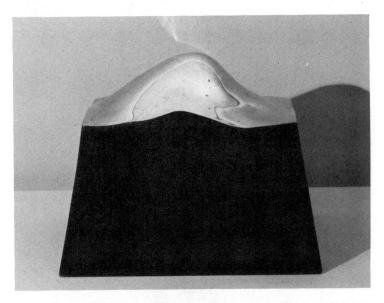

Fig. 4.5.   Ronald J. Bennet, *Landscape #3*. Cast bronze, 8″ high ×
10″ wide × 7″ deep. Museum of Art, The Pennsylvania State University. Gift of the Class of 1975.

them from their original surroundings and hold them up to the rest of us as vehicles for aesthetic communication. In other words, an "artist" decided that such an object said something aesthetically. As a result, he or she *chose* to present it in that vein. That the work was not created "from scratch" is moot.

Composition

Composition in sculpture comprises the same elements as composition in the pictorial arts—mass, line, form, balance, repetition, color, proportion, and unity. Sculptors' uses of these elements are significantly different, however, since they work in three dimensions.

Mass.   Unlike a picture, a sculpture has literal mass. It takes up three-dimensional *space,* and its materials have *density.* Mass in pictures is *relative* mass: the mass of forms in

a picture has application principally in *relation to* other forms within the same picture. In sculpture, however, mass is literal and consists of actual volume and density. So, the mass of a sculpture that is twenty feet high, eight feet wide, and six feet deep, but made of balsa wood, would seem less than a sculpture ten feet high, four feet wide, and three feet deep, made of lead. Space and density must both be considered. What if the material of a statue is disguised to look and feel like a different material? We will discuss this question later in the chapter, when we look at how a sculpture affects our senses.

Line and Form.   As we stated in the last chapter, line and form are highly related. We can separate them (with some difficulty) when we discuss pictures, since in two dimensions an artist uses line to define form. In painting, line is a construction tool. Without using line artists cannot reveal their forms, and when

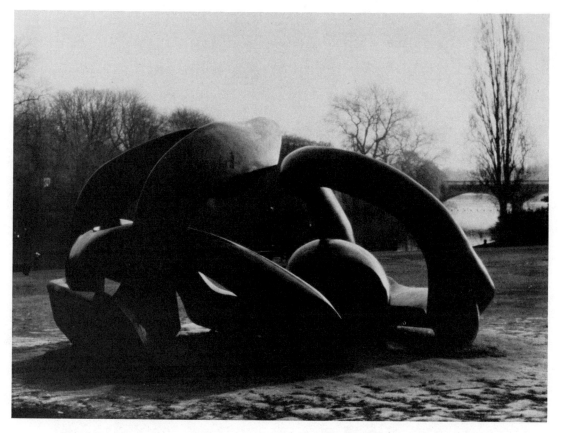

Fig. 4.6. Henry Moore, *Hill Arches* (1973). The Serpentine, Hyde Park, London.

we analyze a painting line is perhaps more important to us than the actual form it reveals. However, in sculpture the case is nearly reversed. It is the form that draws our interest, and when we discuss line in sculpture we do so in terms of how it is revealed in form.

When we view a sculpture its elements direct our eye from one point to another, just as focal points do, via line and color, in a picture. In some works the eye is directed through the piece and then off into space. Such sculptures have an *open* form. In Figs. 4.1 and 4.4 the eye is directed outward from the work in the same fashion as composition that escapes the frame in painting. If, on the other hand, the eye is directed continually

back into the form, we say the form is *closed*. If we allow our eye to follow the linear detail of Fig. 4.8, we find that we are continually led back into the work. This is similar to composition kept within the frame in painting and to closed forms in music, which we will discuss in Chapter 5. Often it is difficult to fit a work precisely into one or the other of these categories. For example, in Fig. 4.3 there are elements of closed composition and, as indicated by the fabric flying to the left, open composition as well.

Obviously, not all sculptures are completely solid; they may have openings. We call any such holes in a sculpture *negative space,* and we can discuss this characteristic in

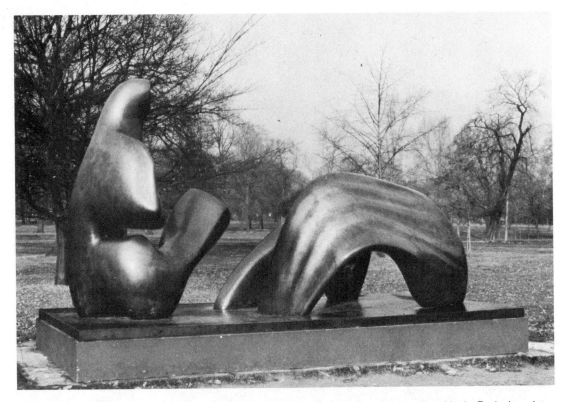

Fig. 4.7. Henry Moore, *Three Piece Reclining Figure* (1975). The Serpentine, Hyde Park, London.

terms of its role in the overall composition. In some works negative space is inconsequential; in others it is quite significant. It is up to us to decide which, and how it contributes to the overall piece. In Figs. 4.6 and 4.7 negative space plays a significant role. In the former it might be argued that negative space is as instrumental to the overall concept of the work as is the metal form. On the other hand, in Fig. 4.1 negative space is clearly incidental.

Proportion. Proportion is the relationship of forms. Just as we have a seemingly innate sense of balance, so we have a feeling of proportion. That feeling tells us that each form in the sculpture is in proper relationship to the others. However, as any student of art history will tell us, proportion—or the ideal of relationships—has varied from one civilization or culture to another. For example, such a seemingly obviously proportioned entity as the human body has varied greatly in its proportions as sculptors over the centuries have depicted it. Study the differences in proportion in the human body among Michelangelo's *David,* a medieval figure of Christ, an ancient Greek statue of a human, and examples of primitive African sculpture. Each depicts the human form, but each utilizes differing proportions. This difference in proportion helps transmit the message the artist wishes to communicate about his or her subject matter.

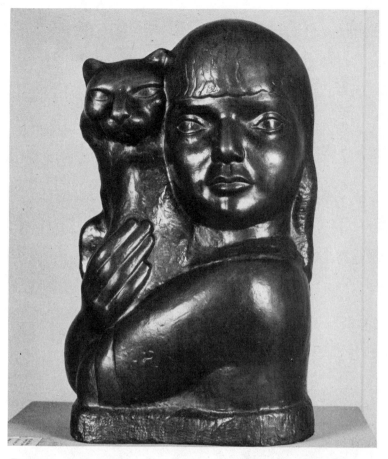

Fig. 4.8.   William Zorach, *Child with Cat* (1926). Bronze, 17½″ × 10″ × 7½″. Museum of Art, The Pennsylvania State University.

Repetition.   Rhythm, harmony, and variation constitute repetition in sculpture, as they did in the pictorial arts. However, in sculpture we must look more carefully and closely to determine how the artist has employed these elements. If we reduce a sculpture to its components of line and form, we begin to see how (as in music) rhythmic patterns—regular and irregular—occur. In Fig. 4.2, for example, a regular rhythmic pattern is established in space as the eye moves from figure to figure and from leg to

leg of the figures. We also can see whether the components are consonant or dissonant. For instance, in Fig. 4.2 a sense of dynamics, that is, action or movement, is created by the dissonance that results from juxtaposing the strong triangles of the stances and groupings with the *biomorphic* lines of the human body. On the other hand, unity of the curves in Fig. 4.9 provides us with a consonant series of relationships. Finally, we can see how line and form are used in theme and variation. We noted the repetition of triangles in Fig.

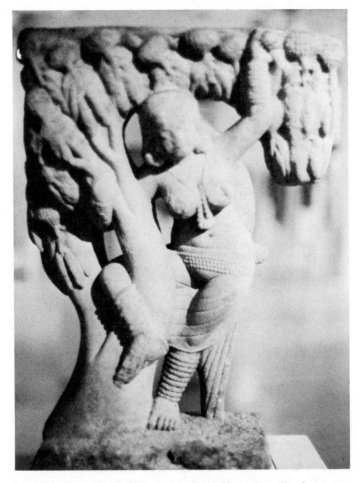

Fig. 4.9. *Tree Spirit (Bracket Figure)* (Central India, first century A.D.). The British Museum, London.

4.2. In contrast, the sculptor of Fig. 4.8 varies his motif, the oval, as the eye moves from the child's face to the upper arm, the hand, and finally the cat's face.

Articulation. Basic to the concept of repetition is the manner by which we move from one element to the next. That manner of movement is called *articulation,* and it applies to sculpture, painting, photography, and all the other arts. As an example, let us step outside the arts to consider human speech.

Sentences, phrases, and individual words are nothing more than sound syllables (vowels) articulated (that is, joined together) by consonants. We understand what someone says to us because that individual articulates as he or she speaks. Let us put the five vowel sounds side by side: Eh—EE—Ah—O—OO. As yet we do not have a sentence. Articulate those vowels with consonants, and we have meaning: "Say, she must go too." The nature of an artwork depends on how the artist has repeated, varied, harmonized, and related its parts and how he has articulated the movement from one part to another—that is, how he indicates where one stops and the other begins.

Color. Perhaps color does not seem particularly important to us as we think of sculpture. We tend to see ancient sculpture as white and modern sculpture as natural wood or rusty iron. It may therefore prove shocking to some of us to find out that the Statue of Liberty is green! Color is as important to the sculptor as it is to the painter. In some cases the material itself may be chosen because of its color; in others, such as terra cottas (Fig. 4.4), the sculpture may be painted. The lifelike sculptures of Duane Hanson depend on color for their effect. They are so lifelike that one easily could confuse them with real persons. Finally, still other materials may be chosen or treated so that nature will provide the final color through oxidation or weathering.

Other Factors

Texture. Texture, the roughness or smoothness of a surface, is a tangible characteristic of sculpture. Sculpture is unique in that we can perceive its texture through our sense of touch. Sculptors go to great lengths to achieve the texture they desire for their works. In fact, much of a sculptor's technical mastery manifests itself in that final ability to impart a surface to the work. We will examine texture more fully in our discussion of sense responses.

Focal Area. Sculptors, like painters or any other visual artists, must concern themselves

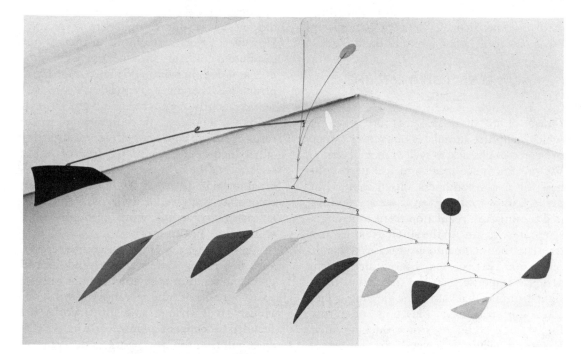

Fig. 4.10. Alexander Calder, *Spring Blossoms* (1965). Painted metal and heavy wire, extends to 52″ × 102″. Museum of Art, The Pennsylvania State University. Gift of the Class of 1965.

with drawing the respondent's eye to those areas of their work that are central to what they wish to communicate. They also must provide the means by which the eye can move around the work. However, their task is much more complicated, because they deal in three dimensions and they have little control over the direction from which the viewer will first perceive the piece; the entire 360-degree view contributes to the total message communicated by the work.

The devices of convergence of line, encirclement, and color work for sculptors as they do for painters. The encircling line of the tree and body parts in Fig. 4.9 causes us, however we proceed to scan the work, to focus ultimately on the torso of this sensuous fertility figure. One further device is available—movement. Sculptors have the option of placing moving objects in their work. Such an object immediately becomes a focal point of the sculpture. A mobile (Fig. 4.10) presents many ephemeral patterns of focus as it turns at the whim of the breezes.

HOW DOES IT STIMULATE THE SENSES?

Texture. Our discussion of the ways in which sculpture stimulates our senses can be presented in physical as well as mental terms. We can touch sculpture and feel its roughness or its smoothness, its coolness or perhaps its warmth. Even if we are prohibited by museum regulation from touching a sculpture, we can see the surface texture and translate the image into an imaginary tactile sensation. That is a much more direct form of sense response than the translation from sight to mind that occurs in viewing a picture. Unfortunately, museums often are forced to prohibit us from touching their sculptures. There is a very practical set of reasons behind that prohibition. Repeated touching of anything, whether it be stone,

metal, or plastic, wears the surface. Even the oils from our fingers may deteriorate the surface. Certainly touching causes problems for the museum in keeping sculptures clean. Nevertheless, any work of sculpture cries out to be touched. Figure 4.11, for example, has a surface texture that is nearly irresistible. The sensuousness of this large representation of nature has a complex appeal to our senses, and its surface textures are a vitally important part of this appeal. Undoubtedly the first and most compelling response that any of us has to a sculpture is to touch it. When we can do so our sense responses are repaid many times over. Therefore, the surface that the artist has imparted to a sculpture is probably the most important stimulant of our aesthetic response to it.

Color. As we indicated earlier, we usually do not think of color as significant in our response to a sculpture, at least not as significant as in our response to a picture. However, color in sculpture stimulates our response by utilizing the same universal symbols as it does in paintings, photographs, and prints. Reds, oranges, and yellows stimulate sensations of warmth; blues and greens, sensations of coolness. In sculpture color can result from the conscious choice of the artist, either in the selection of material or in the selection of the pigment with which the material is painted. Or, as we indicated earlier, color may result from the artist's choice to let nature color the work through wind, water, sun, and so forth.

This weathering effect, of course, creates very interesting patterns, but in addition it gives the sculpture the attribute not only of space but also of time, because the work obviously will change as nature works her wonders. A copper sculpture early in its existence will be a different work, a different set of stimuli, than it will be five, ten, or twenty years hence. This is not entirely accidental;

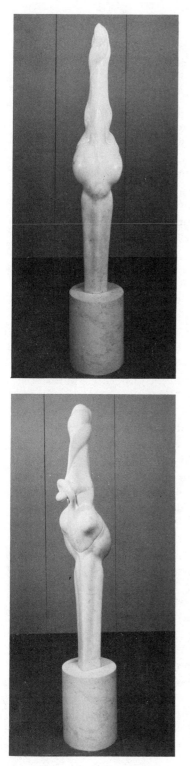
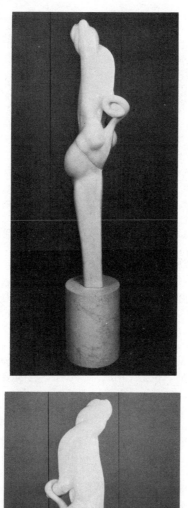
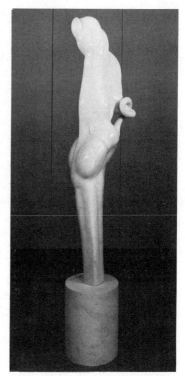

Fig. 4.11. Philip Grausman, *Anthurium* (1971–73). Marble. Museum of Art, The Pennsylvania State University. Acquired with matching funds from the National Endowment for the Arts and from alumni and friends of The Pennsylvania State University.

the artist chooses copper, knowing what weathering will do to it. He obviously cannot predict the exact nature of the weathering or the exact hues of the sculpture at any given time in the future, but such predictability is irrelevant.

In this regard it is interesting to note how our response to a work of art may be shaped by the effects of age on it. There is a great deal of charm and character in ancient objects. When I visited Hampton Court, the palace of Henry VIII, outside of London, a great deal of restoration was in progress. In the inner court only half the walls had been cleaned. To me the clean walls looked new, bright, and *sterile!* They appeared as they must have when they witnessed the dramas of English history. However, the grimy, soot-stained walls were much more appealing. They looked old—and historic. So it might be when we view a weathered wooden statue from the Middle Ages. Our response can be enhanced or diminished by the weathering of centuries—even though the artist may not have intended the work to appeal through the effects of nature on it.

Dynamics.   An artist's use of line, form, and juxtaposition impart to a sculpture varying characteristics of motion or activity in the same sense that it does to a painting (see Figs. 4.2 and 4.7). The activity of a sculpture, however, tends to be heightened because of its three-dimensionality. In addition, we experience a certain sense of dynamics as we walk around it. Although we are moving and not the sculpture, we perceive and respond to what seems to be movement in the work itself. The progression shown in Fig. 4.11 illustrates clearly how a work of sculpture changes as we view it from different vantage points.

Line and Form.   Line and form can, of course, work apart from dynamics. Figures 4.4 and

4.9 are both symbols of fertility. However, even though both exhibit full development of the breast, the former is the more sensuous because each area of the body is treated with greater softness of line. (Of course, *what* one finds to be sensuous may be a result more of convention than of treatment. Certainly, convention leads to treatment. Our modern conception of glamour, illustrated in the tall, leggy, and slender fashion model, contrasts sharply with that of the High Renaissance or baroque, in which corpulence was considered sexually appealing.)

Mass.   Since sculpture has mass—that is, takes up space and has density—our senses respond to the weight or the size of a work. Egyptian sculpture, which is solid, stable, and oversized (see Fig. 4.12), has mass and proportion as well as line and form that make it appear heavier than a non-Egyptian work of basically the same size and material, such as Fig. 4.3. Moreover, the very same treatment of texture, verisimilitude, and subject would elicit a completely different sense response if the work were three feet tall than if it were thirty feet tall.

Early in the chapter we mentioned the possibility of an artist's *disguising the material* from which the work is made. Marble polished to appear like skin or wood polished to look like fabric can change the appearance of mass of a sculpture and significantly affect our response to it.

We also must consider the purpose of disguising material. For example, does the detailing of the sculpture reflect a formal concern for design, or does it reflect a concern for the greatest verisimilitude? Examine the cloth represented in Figs. 4.1 and 4.9. In both cases the sculptor has disguised the material by making stone appear to be cloth. In Fig. 4.1 the cloth is detailed to reflect reality. It drapes as real cloth would drape, and as a result its effect in the composition depends

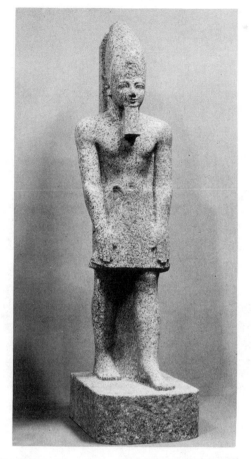

Fig. 4.12. Egyptian statuary. The Metropolitan Museum of Art. Gift of Edward S. Harkness, 1914.

We might also consider whether or not a sculpture appears conscious of its own weight. For example, a work that has been carved from a huge block of stone, sitting squarely on the ground, and has a natural, undisguised texture and very little definition in terms of line would give us a strong impression of being *conscious of its own weight.* In contrast, a large sculpture of a human form positioned with all weight on one foot and possessing a skinlike texture would appear totally *unconscious of its own weight* (Fig. 4.4).

Lighting and Environment. One final factor that significantly influences our sense response to a sculpture, a factor that we very often do not consider and that is outside the control of the artist unless he or she personally supervises every exhibition in which the work is displayed, is that of *lighting and environment.* As we will note in the chapter on theatre, light plays a seminal role in our perception of and thereby our response to three-dimensional objects. The direction and number of sources of light striking a three-dimensional work can change the entire composition of that work. In Fig. 4.13 we can see very graphically how the shifting of light from the front to the rear changes the work from a three-dimensional entity into a silhouetted, two-dimensional one. Whether the work is displayed outdoors or indoors, the method of lighting affects the overall presentation of the work. Diffuse room lighting allows us to see all aspects of a sculpture without external influence. However, if the work is placed in a darkened room and illuminated from particular directions by spotlights, it becomes much more dramatic and our response is affected accordingly.

Where and how a work is exhibited also contributes to our response. A sculpture can create a far different response if placed in a

upon the subtlety of line characteristic of draped cloth. However, in Fig. 4.9 the sculptor has depicted cloth in such a way that its effect in the design is not dependent upon how cloth drapes, but rather upon the decorative function of line as the sculptor wishes to use it. Real cloth cannot drape as the sculptor has depicted it. Nor, probably, did the sculptor care. His main concern here was for decoration, for using line (that looks like cloth) to emphasize the rhythm of the work.

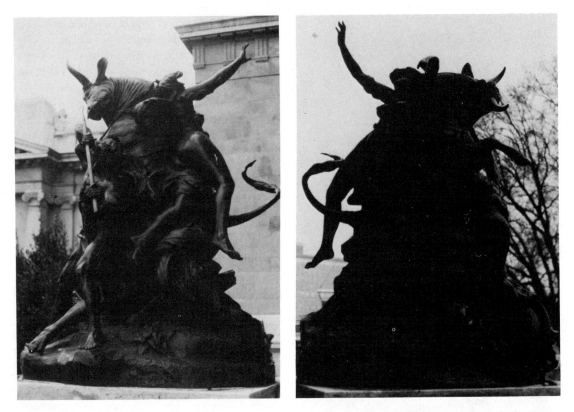

Fig. 4.13. Sir Charles Lawes-Witteronge, *Dirce* (1906). The Tate Gallery, London. *Left,* three-dimensionality through lighting; *right,* two-dimensionality through absence of lighting.

carefully designed environment that screens our vision from distracting or competing visual stimuli than if exhibited among other works amid the bustle of a public park. Even a background formed by the corner and ceiling of the museum, as in Fig. 4.10, might affect our response.

CHRONOLOGY OF SELECTED MAJOR PERIODS, STYLES, AND EXAMPLES FOR STUDY IN WESTERN SCULPTURE

Prehistory to c. 4000 B.C.
paleolithic and neolithic carvings
African masks and carvings

c. 4000 B.C.–c. 1000 B.C.
Ancient Egypt
   tomb and temple sculptures

c. 3000 B.C.–c. 500 B.C.
Ancient Mesopotamia, Persia, Crete, and Mycenae
   Tell Asmar sculptures
   Assyrian relief sculpture
   carved figurines

c. 1200 B.C.–c. 300 B.C.
Ancient Greece
   The Horses of Heracles
   Nike of Delos
   Artemision Zeus
   Polycleitus: *Lance Bearer*

Myron: *Discus Thrower*
Praxiteles: *Cnidian Aphrodite*

c. 500 B.C.–c. 300 A.D.
Rome and Hellenistic Greece
Winged Victory of Samothrace
Dying Gaul
Laocoön Group (Rhodes)
Etruscan Warrior
portrait sculpture

c. 400–c. 900
The Middle Ages
Celtic and Germanic ornaments

c. 300–c. 1500
Early Christian and Byzantine Sculpture
sarcophagus sculpture
altarpiece carvings

c. 900–c. 1200
Romanesque Europe
Bronze doors of Hildesheim Cathedral
relief sculpture
Last Judgment tympanum, Autun
Cathedral

c. 1200–c. 1400
Gothic Sculpture
sculptures of Chartres Cathedral

c. 1400–c. 1500
Flanders
Claus Sluter: *The Well of Moses*
Italy (early Renaissance)
Donatello: *David; The Gattamelata*

c. 1480–c. 1550
High Renaissance
Michelangelo: *Pietà; David*

c. 1510–c. 1570
Mannerism
Giovanni da Bologna: *Mercury*
Goujon: *Fountain of the Innocents*

c. 1570–c. 1700
Baroque Sculpture
Bernini: *Apollo and Daphne; Ecstasy of St.
Theresa*
Salvi: *Trevi Fountain*, Rome

c. 1700–c. 1800
Rococo Sculpture
Guenther: *Pietà*

c. 1800–c. 1900
Neoclassicism
Cortot: *Triumph*
Maillol: *Night*
Eclecticism
Rodin: *Balzac*

c. 1900–
Zorach: *Affection*
Epstein: *Madonna and Child*
Lipchitz: *Seated Figure*
Brancusi: *Bird in Space*
Gabo: *Linear Construction*
Moore: *Reclining Figure*
Roszak: *Fire-bird*
Calder: *7 Red, 7 Black, 1 White*

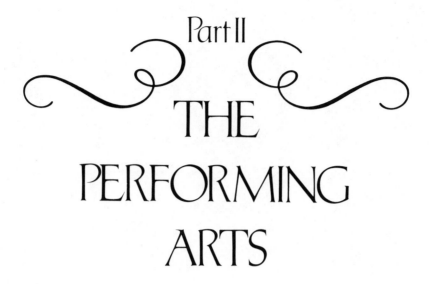

Part II

THE PERFORMING ARTS

Music and Opera

Theatre

Film

Dance

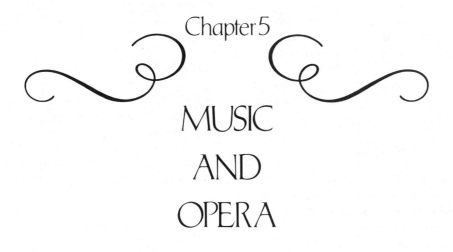

Chapter 5

MUSIC
AND
OPERA

Music often has been described as the purest of the art forms because it is free from the physical restrictions of space that adhere to the other arts. However, the freedom enjoyed by the composer becomes a constraint for the respondent, because music is an art of time and sound that places significant responsibility in the hands (or the ears) of the listener. That consideration is especially critical for the respondent trying to learn and apply musical terminology, because he or she has only a fleeting moment to capture many of the characteristics of music. A painting or a sculpture stands still for us; it does not change or disappear, despite the length of time it takes us to find or apply some new characteristic. Such is not the case with music.

We live in a society that is very aural in its perceptions, but these perceptions usually do not require any kind of active listening. We are attuned throughout life to a passive approach to what we hear. An excellent example is the Muzak that we hear in many stores, restaurants, and office buildings, which is intended solely as a soothing background designed *not* to attract attention. We hear music constantly on the radio, the television, and in the movies, but nearly always in a peripheral role. Since we are not expected to pay attention to it, we do not. Therefore, we simply do not undertake the kind of practice we need in order to be attentive to music and to perceive it in detail. However, like any skill, the ability to hear perceptively is enhanced through repetition and training. Individuals who have had limited experience in responding to music have great difficulty hearing what there is to hear in a piece of music that passes in just a few seconds. Likewise, their ability to *remember* what they have heard is impaired if they have not practiced that skill. In order to deduce the structure of a musical work, listeners must remember at the end what they heard at the beginning. These abilities require skills that most individuals in our society have not acquired.

Another difficulty in the experience of music, one that is especially noticeable in a book such as this, is the abundance of unfamiliar terminology. Music has a language of its own, most of it Italian, and familiarity with music necessitates familiarity with its vocabulary.

WHAT IS IT?

Music is the design of time using sound and silence. Musical design also is form, and at the formal level of response musical form is that shape we find in the finished work. So, at this level of response music is a symphony, concerto, suite, sonata, concert overture, opera, oratorio, cantata, mass, or requiem, to name only a few of the most familiar forms. Since we usually note these forms in our concert program—before we hear their performance—knowing what they are will guide us as to what we may expect to hear, and what to listen for.

Symphony. A symphony is a musical composition whose parameters have been shaped by, and to a large extent cannot be separated from, the development of the instruments for and the theories and styles of the historical period in which it was composed. Therefore, it is difficult to make a concise definition in a sentence or two. However, symphonies have some general characteristics. First, they are played by an orchestra. (However, "symphony" as a musical form may also apply to works composed for string quartet and chamber orchestra, for example.) Some symphonies, such as Beethoven's Symphony No. 9, utilize chorus as well as orchestra. Perhaps most important, the word *symphony* connotes a three- or four-part structure. Each of these parts is called a *movement*. Some specific designs and relationships for the movements of a symphony have evolved, and we will discuss some of these later.

Concerto. This term usually refers to a composition for solo instrument with accompaniment. During the baroque era it also encompassed the *concerto grosso,* which uses a solo group called the *concertina* and a full ensemble called the *ripieno*. The solo concerto usually has three movements, which alternate in a fast-slow-fast relationship.

Suite. If we think of the term *suite* as it frequently is used outside of music, we have an insight into its musical implications. A grouping of items of furniture in the design of a living room is called a living-room *suite*. The ensemble of trousers, vest, and jacket designed in the same fabric and style and worn together is called a *suit*. The musical suite is a grouping of dance melodies (normally six) usually unrelated except by key and contrast. It might be more correct to say that these movements are *based on* particular dance rhythms, but were composed and performed for their own sake, and not to be danced to. Suites were written primarily for keyboard instruments, specifically the harpsichord, but also for solo instrument accompanied by harpsichord, or a group of stringed or wind instruments.

Sonata. In discussing sonatas we must be careful not to confuse *sonata* with *sonata form,* a particular structure that we will discuss later. A sonata is a group of pieces loosely related and played in succession. Unlike the movements of a suite, these pieces are not all in the same key, but are in related tonalities. The first movement of a sonata generally has a special form, which has taken on particular importance in musical composition—hence its name, *sonata form.*

Concert Overture.   An overture customarily is a single-movement introduction to, for example, an opera. However, in concert it has been popular to perform many of these introductions apart from the work they introduce. As this practice became more popular composers began to write *concert overtures*—overtures with no larger work intended to follow.

Opera.   Because of its special combination of music, theatre, and architecture, we will discuss opera in detail at the end of this chapter.

Oratorio.   An oratorio is a choral work that differs from opera essentially in two ways. First, its themes are religious. Second, it is presented in concert form; that is, there is no physical action, staging, setting, costumes, or properties. The soloists in the oratorio may take the role of characters, and the work may have a plot, although perhaps the most familiar example, Handel's *Messiah,* does neither.

Cantata.   The cantata is a choral form with soloists and chorus. It is shorter and uses fewer performers than the opera or oratorio. It usually emphasizes the solo voice, and its themes may be either secular or sacred.

Mass.   The mass as a choral form concerns itself directly with the Roman Catholic service, the *Mass.* As such it includes six musical parts: the *Kyrie, Gloria, Credo, Sanctus, Benedictus,* and *Agnus Dei.* Masses may or may not be written for inclusion in the church service. The concert mass has been an important part of musical composition since the Middle Ages. Many masses have taken a special form, the *requiem mass,* or mass for

the dead—for example, Brahms's *Ein Deutsches Requiem.*

Motet.   A motet is a choral composition of *polyphonic* texture set to a sacred text. It differs from a *madrigal* only in that the madrigal uses a secular text.

HOW IS IT PUT TOGETHER?

Music is composed through the designing of sound and silence. The latter is reasonably understandable, but what of the former? What is sound? Sound is vibration that stimulates the auditory nerves. It includes sirens, speech, crying babies, jet engines, falling trees, and so forth. We might call such sources noise. However, even noise may have a part in a musical composition. Cannons and even floor polishers have found their way into serious musical works. So we must be careful in what we include or exclude from sound in music. On the other hand, musical design does depend primarily upon sound of a specific character—sound that can be controlled and shaped, sound that can be consistent in its qualities. One aspect of sound that is not limited to musical instruments but is fundamental to the designing of sound in music is tone.

Tone

Tone has four characteristics: pitch, duration, timbre, and intensity.

Pitch.   Pitch is a physical phenomenon measurable in vibrations per second. So, when we describe differences in pitch we are describing recognizable and measurable differences in sound waves. A pitch has a steady, constant frequency. A faster frequency produces a higher pitch, a slower frequency, a lower pitch. If a sounding body—a vibrating string, for example—is shortened, it vibrates more rapidly. Musical instruments designed to produce high pitches such as the piccolo, therefore tend to be small. Instruments designed to produce low pitches tend to be large—for instance, bass viols and tubas.

In Chapter 3 we noted that color comprises a range of light waves within a visible spectrum. Sound also comprises a spectrum, one whose audible pitches range from 16 to 38,000 vibrations per second. We can perceive 11,000 different pitches! Obviously that is more than is practical for musical composition. Therefore, *by convention* the sound spectrum is divided into roughly 90 equally spaced frequencies comprising seven and a half *octaves*. The piano keyboard, consisting of 88 keys (seven octaves plus two additional notes) representing the same number of equally spaced pitches, serves as an illustration (Fig. 5.1). The thirteen pitches represented by the adjacent keys of the piano from C to C in Fig. 5.1 constitute an octave. The distance in frequency from C to C# is the same as that from C# to D, and so forth. The higher C vibrates at exactly twice the frequency of the lower C. Such is the case with every note and the note one octave below it. The A one octave above the lower

one shown would vibrate at twice that rate. Again by convention, each musical note is usually tuned to a specific pitch, in vibrations per second. Normally, A is tuned to 440 vibrations per second, for example, and its octaves to 110, 220, 880, 1760, and so forth.

The thirteen equally spaced pitches in an octave are called a *chromatic scale*. However, the scales that sound most familiar to us are the major and minor scales, which consist of an octave of eight pitches. The distance between any two pitches is an *interval*. Intervals between two adjacent pitches are *half steps*. Intervals of two half steps are *whole steps*. The major scale, *do re mi fa sol la ti do* (recall the song "Doe, a deer..." from *The Sound of Music*), has a specific arrangement of whole and half steps (Fig. 5.2). Lowering the third and sixth notes of the major scale gives us the diatonic (the most common) minor scale (Fig. 5.2).

To reiterate, a scale, which is an arrangement of pitches played in ascending or descending order, is a conventional organization of the frequencies of the sound spectrum. Not all music conforms to this convention. Music of Western civilization prior to approximately 1600 A.D. does not, nor does Eastern music, which makes great use of quarter tones. In addition, some contemporary Western

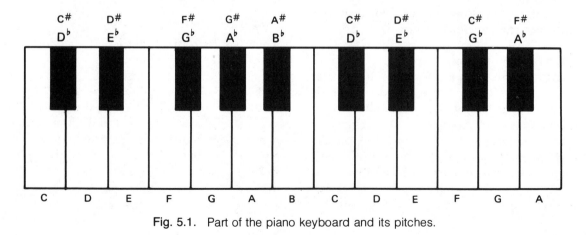

Fig. 5.1. Part of the piano keyboard and its pitches.

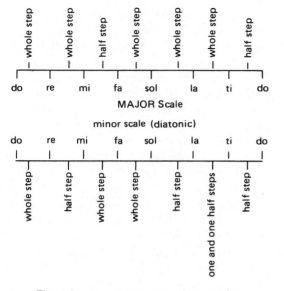

Fig. 5.2. The major and minor scales.

music departs from the conventions of tonality of the major or minor scale.

Duration. A second characteristic of tone is duration, the length of time in which vibration is maintained without interruption. Duration in musical composition is relative, and is designed within a set of conventions called musical notation. Since we are not interested here in playing or reading music, illustration of the musical-notation system is unnecessary at this point. This system consists of a series of symbols (notes) by which the composer indicates the relative duration of each pitch. The system is progressive; that is, each note is either double or half the duration of an adjacent note. Musical notation also includes a series of symbols that denote the duration of *silences* in a composition. These symbols are called *rests,* and have the same durational values as the symbols for duration of tone.

Timbre. Timbre (pronounced tam·ber) is the characteristic of tone that allows us to

distinguish a pitch played on a violin, for example, from the same pitch played on a piano. Timbre also is referred to as tone "quality" or tone "color." In addition to identifying characteristic differences among sound-producing sources, timbre characterizes differences in quality of tones produced by the same source. Here the analogy of tone "color" is particularly appropriate. A tone that is produced with an excess of air—for example, by the human voice—is described as "white." Characteristically, such tonal production results from inefficient control of breath, and creates a thin or breathy quality. Efficient control of breath produces a full, rich, "pure" tone. (Recall the term *saturation* from the discussion of color in Chapter 3.)

At this point it is helpful to note some of the various sources that produce musical tone and account for its variety of timbres.

Voice		Electronic
Soprano	⎫	Synthesizer
Mezzo-soprano	⎬ Women's	
Contralto	⎭	
Tenor	⎫	
Baritone	⎬ Men's	
Bass	⎭	

Strings	Woodwinds	Brasses
Violin	Flute	Trumpet
Viola	Piccolo	Horn
Cello	Oboe	Trombone
(Violoncello)	English horn	Tuba
Bass	Clarinet	
Harp	Bassoon	

Percussion		
Snare drum	Piano	Harpsichord
Bass drum		
Timpani		
Triangle		
Cymbal		

The piano could be considered either a stringed or a percussion instrument since it produces its sounds by vibrating strings *struck* by hammers. The harpsichord's strings are set in motion by plucking.

Intensity.   A final characteristic of tone is intensity. Any tone of any pitch, duration, or timbre can be loud, soft, or anywhere in between. Intensity is the *decibel* level of the tone, and depends upon the physical phenomenon of *amplitude* of vibration. When greater force is employed in the production of a tone the resulting sound waves are wider and cause greater stimulation of the auditory nerves. The *size* of the sound wave, not its number of vibrations per second, is changed.

Composers indicate intensity, or *dynamic level,* with a series of specific notations—like most musical terms, in Italian:

pp	pianissimo	very soft
p	piano	soft
mp	mezzo piano	moderately soft
mf	mezzo forte	moderately loud
f	forte	loud
ff	fortissimo	very loud

Melody

Melody is a succession of sounds with rhythmic and tonal organization. We can visualize melody as linear and essentially horizontal. Thus, any organization of musical tones occuring *one after another* constitutes a melody. Two other terms, *tune* and *theme,* relate to melody as parts to a whole. For example, the *tune* in Fig. 5.3 is a melody—that is, a succession of tones. However, a melody is not always a tune. For most

people the term *tune* implies singability, and there are many melodies that cannot be sung—for example, because they reach beyond the range of the human voice. A *theme* is also a melody. However, in musical composition it specifically means a central musical idea, which may be restated and varied throughout a piece. Thus, a melody is not necessarily a theme.

Related to theme and melody is the *motif,* or *motive,* a short melodic or rhythmic idea around which a composer may design a composition. For example, in Mozart's Symphony No. 40 the allegro movement (a movement lasting approximately nine minutes when all repeats are left in) is developed around a rhythmic motif of three notes:

In listening for how a composer develops melody, theme, and/or motive we can use two terms to describe what we hear: *conjunct* and *disjunct.* Conjunct melodies comprise notes close together on the musical scale. For example, the interval between the opening notes of the soprano line of J. S. Bach's chorale "Jesu Joy of Man's Desiring" from his Cantata 147 (Fig. 5.4) is never more than a whole step. Such melodic development is highly *conjunct. Disjunct* melodies contain intervals of considerable distance. However, there is no formula for determining disjunct or conjunct characteristics; there is no line at which a melody ceases to be disjunct and becomes conjunct. These are relative and comparative terms that assist us in description. For example, we would say that the opening melody of "The Star Spangled Banner" (Fig. 5.3) is more disjunct than the

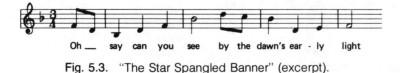

Oh — say can you see   by the dawn's ear - ly   light

Fig. 5.3. "The Star Spangled Banner" (excerpt).

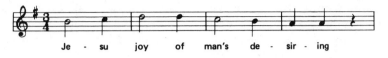

Fig. 5.4. "Jesu Joy of Man's Desiring" (excerpt).

opening melody of "Jesu Joy of Man's Desiring"—or that the latter is more conjunct than the former.

Harmony

When two or more tones are sounded at the same time we have *harmony*. Harmony is essentially a vertical arrangement, in contrast with the horizontal arrangement of melody. However, as we shall see, harmony also has a horizontal property—movement forward in time. In listening for harmony we are interested in how simultaneous tones *sound together*.

Two tones played simultaneously are an interval; three or more form a *chord*. When we hear an interval or a chord our first response is to its *consonance* or *dissonance*. Consonant harmonies sound comfortable and stable in their arrangement. Dissonant harmonies are jarring to the ear; they are tense and uncomfortable. Consonance and dissonance, however, are not absolute properties. Essentially they are conventional and, to a large extent, cultural. What is dissonant to our ears may not be so to someone else's. What is important in musical response is determining *how* the composer utilizes these two properties. Most of our music is primarily consonant. However, dissonance can be used for shock effect, for contrast, to draw attention to itself, or as a normal part of *harmonic progression*.

As its name implies, harmonic progression involves the movement forward in time of harmonies. In discussing pitch we noted the convention of the major and minor scales—that is, the arrangement of the chromatic scale into a system of *tonality*.

When we play or sing a major or minor scale we note a particular phenomenon: Our movement from *do* to *re* to *mi* to *fa* to *sol* to *la* is smooth and seems natural. But when we reach the seventh note of the scale, *ti*, something strange happens. It seems as though we *must* continue back to *do,* the *tonic* of the scale. Try it! Sing a major scale and stop at *ti.* You feel uncomfortable. Your mind tells you that you must *resolve* that discomfort by returning to *do.* That same sense of tonality—that sense of the tonic—applies to harmony. Within any scale a series of chords may be developed on the basis of the individual tones of the scale. Each of the chords has a subtle relationship to each of the other chords and to the tonic—that is, the *do* of the scale. That relationship creates a sense of progression that leads back to the chord based on the tonic.

As I indicated, scales and harmonies are conventions. However, not all conventions are arbitrary. Harmonic progression, which is based on tonality, has a physical root. Physicists call it *sympathetic vibration*. If we take two tightly stretched strings, each of the same length, on a sounding board, we easily can set the second string in motion by plucking the first. Because both strings are the same length, their sound waves are identical and the waves from the plucked string will stir the second, setting it in motion. A little experimentation shows that by dividing the second string into various lengths we can develop a systematic chart of sympathetic vibration. Length A vibrates more easily than B, which vibrates more easily than C, and so on. The relationships we would establish in such an experiment basically govern harmonic progression. Chords based on the notes (that is, the lengths of string) most easily vibrated sympathetically are closer to, and lead to, the tonic. For example, other than the same length of string or its double (the octave), the length of string, or note, most easily vibrated sympathetically is the fifth note (*sol*) of the scale; next is the fourth note, and then the second. If we played chords based on these tones in an order from difficult to easy sympathetic vibration, our progression would move us comfortably to a resolution on the tonic chord. So, harmonic progression is both conventional and physical.

The harmonic movement toward, and either resolving or not resolving to, the tonic is called *cadence*. Three different cadences are shown in Fig. 5.5. The use of cadence is one way of articulating sections of a composition or of surprising us by upsetting our expectations. A composer using a full cadence uses a harmonic progression that resolves just as our ear tells us it should. We have a sense of ending, of completeness. However, when a half cadence or a deceptive cadence is used, the expected progression is upset and the musical development moves in an unexpected direction.

As we listen to music of various historical periods we may note that in some compositions tonal centers are blurred because composers frequently *modulate* (that is, change from one *key* to another). In the twentieth century many composers, some of them using purely mathematical formulas to utilize equally all tones of the chromatic scale, have removed tonality as an arranging factor and have developed *atonal* music, or music without tonality. A convention of harmonic progression is disturbed when tonality is removed. However, we still have harmonic progression, *and* we still have harmony—dissonant or consonant.

Texture

The aspect of musical relationships known as texture is treated differently by different sources. The term itself has various spatial connotations, and using a spatial term to describe a nonspatial phenomenon creates part of the divergence of treatment. Texture in painting and sculpture denotes surface quality—that is, roughness or smoothness. Texture in weaving denotes the interrelationship of the warp and the woof—that is, the horizontal and vertical threads or fibers. The organization in Fig. 5.6 would be described as open or loose texture; that in Fig. 5.7, closed or tight. However, there is really no single musical arrangement that corresponds to either of these spatial concepts. The characteristic called *sonority* by some comes the closest. Sonority describes the relationship of tones played at the same time. A chord with large intervals between its members would have a more open, or thinner, sonority (or texture) than a chord with small intervals between its tones; that chord would have a tight, thick, or close sonority or texture. Sonority is a term that does not have universal application; some sources do

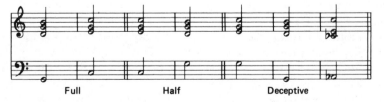

Fig. 5.5. Full, half, and deceptive cadences.

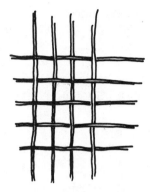

Fig. 5.6.   Open (loose) texture.

not mention it at all, and by implication, I suppose, assume it does not exist. Occasionally, the term *texture* is applied to characteristics of timbre; that is incorrect.

In a musical context *texture* (again, some sources do not use this term, and treat the following characteristics as part of harmony) usually has two, and sometimes three, characteristics: *homophony* and *polyphony* (or *counterpoint*), and sometimes *monophony*. Monophony means "one sound" and consists solely of one melodic line. There may be five hundred voices singing a melody, but if it is the same melody it is monophonic. In homophonic music one melodic line dominates and the other voices play a subordinate or supporting role. Polyphony is the development of two or more independent melodic lines. Most music is not exclusively monophonic, homophonic, or polyphonic.

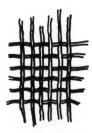

Fig. 5.7.   Closed (tight) texture.

Much music alternates, especially between homophonic and polyphonic textures.

Rhythm

Rhythm is the accented relationship of sounds and silences in time. Without rhythm we have only an aimless rising and falling of tones. Earlier we noted that each tone and silence has duration. Composing music means placing each tone into a time or rhythmical relationship with each other tone. As with the dots and dashes of the Morse code we can "play" the rhythm of a musical composition without reference to its pitches. Each symbol (or note) of the musical-notation system denotes a duration relative to each other symbol in the system.

For example, the note ♪ is half the time value of ♩ , which is half the value of ♩ , and so forth. A composer will choose one of these symbols as the basic measuring stick for his or her composition, and that symbol becomes the *beat.* So, if ♩ is assigned the beat of a piece, time might be measured ♩ ♩ ♩ ♩ ♫ , and counted

♩ ♩ ♩ ♩ ♫ . The elapsed time be-
1, 2, 3, 4, 5, 6 6½

tween 1 and 2, 2 and 3, 3 and 4, and so on, is equal.

Of course, time in music is not counted cumulatively from beginning to end. If it were, one might be counting 3,566, 3,567, 3,568, and so forth, at the end of a lengthy piece. Instead, a piece is divided into *measures,* each of which contains the same arbitrarily assigned number of beats, and time is counted cumulatively within each measure. The number of beats in a measure is normally a multiple of three or two, and constitutes triple or duple *meter,* respectively. We

can distinguish between duple and triple because of their different *accent* patterns. In triple meter we hear an accent every third
beat—ONE two three, ONE two three—
and in duple meter the accent is every other
beat—ONE two, ONE two. If there are
four beats in a measure (sometimes called
quadruple meter), the second accent is
weaker than the first—ONE two THREE
four, ONE two THREE four.

Not all rhythm in music is regular, and
not all meter is simple or consistent. Often it
is difficult to hear precisely what is happening because the composer changes metrical
patterns (in some cases almost every measure) throughout the piece. Such changes
create variety in the rhythmical structure and
add interest, and sometimes *chaos,* to it. Often, even when the meter is consistent, a
composer will disturb our expectations by
accenting normally unaccented beats. In such
cases the rhythm is said to be *syncopated.*

The development of rhythm and meter
has an *internal* order of relationships. As we
indicated, each beat is assigned a duration
relative to other durations, and beats are
clustered to form measures and thereby metrical arrangements. However, none of these
conventions indicate the amount of *actual*
time assigned to each beat. Determining the
length of a beat determines the rate of speed,
or the *tempo,* of the composition. A composer may notate tempo in two ways. The
first is by a *metronome marking,* such as ♩
= 60. This means that the piece is to be
played at the rate of sixty quarter notes
(♩) per minute. Such notation is precise.
The other method is less so, and involves
more descriptive terminology in Italian:

Largo (broad)
Grave (grave, solemn) } Very Slow

Lento
Adagio (leisurely) } Slow

Andante (at a walking pace)
Andantino (somewhat faster than
  andante)
Moderato } Moderate

Allegretto
Allegro (cheerful; faster than
  allegretto) } Fast

Vivace (vivaceous)
Presto (very quick)
Prestissimo (as fast as possible) } Very fast

The tempo may be quickened or slowed, and
the composer indicates this by the words *accelerando* (accelerate) and *ritardando* (retard,
slow down). A performer who takes liberties
with the tempo is said to use *rubato.*

Dynamics

The notations of intensity that apply to an
individual tone, such as *p*, *mp*, and *f*, also
may apply to a section of music. *Dynamics* is
the term used to refer to changes in intensity
level throughout a composition. Changes in
dynamics may be abrupt, gradual, wide, or
small. A series of symbols also governs this
aspect of music:

	Crescendo	becoming louder
	Decrescendo	becoming softer
> ∧ *sfz*	Sforzando	"with force"; a strong accent immediately followed by *p*

As we listen to and compare musical compositions we can consider the use and breadth
of dynamics in the same sense that we consider the use and breadth of palette in painting.

Structure

Musical structure, the organization of musical elements and relationships into successive
events or sections, is concerned principally

with two characteristics, variety and unity. *Variety* creates interest by avoiding monotony, and composers can use variety in every musical characteristic we have discussed in order to hold our attention or peak our interest. However, since music has design, composers must also concern themselves with *coherence*. Notes and rhythms that proceed without purpose and/or stop arbitrarily make little sense to the listener. Therefore, just as the painter, sculptor, or any other artist must try to develop design that has focus and meaning, the musician must attempt to create a coherent composition of sounds and silences—that is, a composition that has *unity*. The principal means by which an artist creates unity is repetition. As we noted in Chapter 1, the 1953 Volkswagen achieved unity through strong geometric repetition, which varied only in size. Music achieves unity through repetition in a similar fashion. However, since in music we are dealing with time, as opposed to space, repetition in music usually involves recognizable themes.

Structure can thus be seen as organization through repetition to create unity. Structure may be divided into two categories, *closed form* and *open form*. These two terms are somewhat similar to the same terms in sculpture. Closed form directs the "musical eye" back into the composition by restating at the end the thematic section that formed the beginning of the piece. Open form allows the "eye" to escape the composition by utilizing repetition of thematic material only as a departure point for further development, and by ending without repetition of the opening section. A few of the more common examples of closed and open form follow.

Closed Forms

BINARY FORM, as the name implies, consists of two parts: the opening section of the composition and its restatement. An example of binary form is the second movement of Vivaldi's *La Primavera*. We could illustrate this repetition with the letters AA.

TERNARY FORM is three-part development in which the opening section is repeated after the development of a different second section—ABA.

ALTERNATION, of which ternary form is the simplest example, utilizes a return to the A section or theme after each development—ABACADA and so forth. The first and third movements of Vivaldi's *La Primavera* illustrate this form of development. In the first movement (an example of *program music*—see also *absolute music* in the glossary) each section (B, C, D, and so on) has a textual connotation: "Song of the Birds," "The Springs Flow," "Thunder," and so forth. These different developments are woven among a recurring theme that opens the movement, alternates with the other sections, and closes the movement. This form of development also is called *rondo form*. Another example is Couperin's *Soeur Monique*, written for harpsichord.

SONATA FORM, OR SONATA-ALLEGRO FORM, takes its name from the conventional treatment of the first movement of the sonata. It is also the form of development of the first movement of many symphonies. The pattern of development is ABA or AABA. The first A section is a development of two or three main and subordinate themes known as the *exposition*. To cement the perception of section A, the composer may repeat it: AA. The B section, the *development*, takes the original themes and develops them with several *variations*. The movement then returns to the A section; this final section is called the *recapitulation*. Usually, the recapitulation section is not an exact repetition of the opening section; in fact, it may be difficult to hear in some pieces. In Mozart's Symphony No. 40 the opening movement (allegro) is in sonata-allegro form. However, the recapitulation section is identified only by a very brief restatement of the first theme, as it was heard in the exposition, not a repetition of the opening section. Then, after a lengthy *bridge,* the second theme from the exposition appears. Mozart closes the movement with a brief *coda,* in the original key, based on the first phrase of the first theme.

Open Forms

THE FUGUE is a polyphonic development of one, two, or sometimes three short themes. Fugal form, which takes its name from the Latin *fuga* ("flight"), has a traditional, though not necessary, scheme of development consisting of seven elements, only some of which may be found in any given fugue. However, two characteristics are common to all fugues: (1) counterpoint; (2) a clear dominant-tonic relationship—that is, imitation of the theme at the fifth above or below the tonic. Each voice in a fugue (as many as five or more) develops the basic subject independent from the other voices, and passes through as many of the seven elements as the composer deems necessary. Unification is achieved not by return to an opening section, as in closed form, but by the varying reoccurrences of the subject throughout.

BINARY FORM can be open if the second section is not a repeat of the first—that is, if the form is AB.

THE CANON is a contrapuntal form based on note-for-note imitation of one line by another. The lines are separated by a brief time interval—for example (the use of letters here does *not* indicate sectional development):

Voice 1: a b c d e f g
Voice 2:   a b c d e f g
Voice 3:   a b c d e f g

The interval of separation is not always the same among the voices. The canon is different from the *round,* an example of which, "Row, row, row your boat," we all sang as children. A round is also an exact melodic repeat; however, the canon develops new material indefinitely, while the round repeats the same phrases over and over. The interval of separation in the round stays constant—a phrase apart.

VARIATION FORM is a compositional structure in which an initial theme is modified through melodic, rhythmic, and harmonic treatments, each more elaborate than the last. Each section usually ends with a strong cadence, and the piece ends, literally, when the composer decides he has done enough.

HOW DOES IT STIMULATE THE SENSES?

It should be obvious by now that when we respond to any work of art we can examine it in a cause-and-effect manner to see how the artist has utilized any or all of the elements of technical and formal development to stimulate a particular sensation or expressive response in us. In music one might think that all of our sense responses must stem from what we hear. If our only exposure to music were the record or tape recording, that would be true. However, there is more to music than sitting in our easy chairs and listening to the record player. Much of the excitement of music comes from its live performance. So much of our response can be triggered by what we see as well as by what we hear. We can observe the emotional performance of the musician. What we see does have an effect on our response. If we see no involvement by the performer, we may hear very little as well. Many critics have noted this very phenomenon. We miss much of the response to a work of music if we deprive ourselves of the opportunity of seeing the performance and experiencing the *event* by limiting our exposure to music to the radio, the tape deck, or the record player.

How do the composer and the performer work on our senses through their music? The most obvious device for effecting response is the combination of rhythm and meter. We all at one time or another have heard music that caused us to involuntarily tap our toes, drum our fingers, or bounce in our seats in a purely physical response to the strongly accented beat of the music. This involuntary motor response to a "beat" is perhaps the most primitive of our sensual involvements. If the rhythm is regular and the beat strong, our body may respond as a unit. However, if the rhythm is irregular and/or the beat divided or syncopated, we may find one part of our body doing one thing and another part something else. Dynamics also have much to do with our sense response to music: the way that a composer manipulates volume and intensity in a piece can lull us to sleep or cause us to sit bolt upright in fright. A familiar example of manipulated dynamics is the second movement of Haydn's Symphony No. 94, in which the composer relaxes his audience with very soft passages and then inserts a sudden fortissimo. The result (and the name of the symphony ever since) was unabashed *surprise!*

From time to time throughout this chapter we have referred to certain historical conventions that permeate the world of music. Some of these have a potential effect on our sense response. Certain notational patterns, such as *appoggiaturas,* are a kind of musical shorthand, or perhaps mime, that conveys certain kinds of emotion to the listener. They, of course, have little meaning for us

unless we take the time and effort to study music history. Some of Mozart's string quartets indulge in exactly this kind of communication. This is another illustration of how expanded knowledge can increase the depth and value of the aesthetic experience.

The timbre of a musical composition also works on our senses. A composer's use of timbre is analogous to a painter's use of palette. Only a study of an individual work will tell us how broad or narrow the composer's use of timbre is. However, the size of the musical ensemble has a nearly automatic control of our response. A symphony orchestra can overwhelm us with diverse timbres and volumes; a string quartet cannot. Our expectations and our focus may change as we perceive the performance of one or the other. Because, for example, we know our perceptual experience with a string quartet will not involve the broad possibilities of an orchestra, we tune ourselves to seek the qualities that challenge the composer and performer within the particular medium. The difference between viewing an orchestra and viewing a quartet is similar to the difference between viewing a museum painting of huge dimension and viewing the exquisite technique of a miniature.

Texture, rhythm, meter, and timbre, in combination, have much to do with sensual response to a musical work. The combinations of these elements that a composer uses to stimulate us in many different ways are infinite. The isolation of the woodwinds, the irregular rhythms, and the melodic development of Debussy's *Prélude à l'après-midi d'un faune* combine to call up in us images of our friend Pan frolicking through the woodlands and cavorting with the nymphs on a sunny afternoon. Of course, much of what we see has been stimulated by the title of the composition. Our perception is heightened further if we are familiar with the poem by Mallarmé on which the piece is based. Titles and especially text in musical compositions may be the strongest devices a composer has for communicating directly with us. Images are triggered by words, and a text or title can stimulate our imaginations and senses to wander freely and fully through the musical development. Johannes Brahms called a movement in his *Ein Deutsches Requiem* "All Mortal Flesh is as the Grass"; we certainly receive a philosophical and religious communication from that title. Moreover, when the chorus ceases to sing and the orchestra plays alone, the instrumental melodies stimulate images of fields of grass blowing in the wind. Our senses are stimulated quite significantly.

Harmony and tonality are both of considerable importance in stimulating our senses. Just as paintings and sculpture stimulate sensations of rest and comfort or action and discomfort, so harmonies create a feeling of repose and stability if they are consonant and a sensation of restlessness and instability if they are dissonant. Harmonic progression that leads to a full cadential resolution leaves us feeling fulfilled; unresolved cadences are puzzling and perhaps irritating. Major or minor tonalities have significantly differing effects: major sounds happy; minor, sad, or mysterious. The former seems close to home, and the latter, exotic. Atonal music sets us adrift to find the unifying thread of the composition. Or we may find a new sense of comfort among harmonies that are equal—for example, in Schoenberg's Suite for Piano, Op. 25.

Melody, rhythm, and tempo are very similar to the use of line in painting, and the term *melodic contour* could be seen as a musical analogue to this element of painting. When the tones of a melody are conjunct and undulate slowly and smoothly they trace a pattern having exactly the same sensual effect as their linear visual counterpart,

〜〜 —that is, soft, comfortable,

and placid. When melodic contours are disjunct and tempos rapid, the pattern and response change: /\/\/\ .

In conclusion, it remains for us as we respond to music to analyze how each of the elements available to the composer have in fact become parts of the channel of communication, and how the composer, consciously or unconsciously, has put together a work that elicits sensory responses from us.

OPERA

We have identified opera as one of the formal divisions of music. One might ask, Why devote the time to study this particular kind of music when we do not spend an equal amount of time studying the symphony and the other forms of music we have identified? Part of the answer to this question stems from the history of the opera and from its position as a major artwork. However, one could say the same of the oratorio. Another part of the answer is that opera is more than just one of the formal divisions of music. Some would argue that opera is *drama* set to music, or even a separate discipline that is not drama or music but a third and equal art form. However, a traditional description of opera is that it is not drama set to music but rather a combination of music and drama in which music is not an equal or incidental partner but is the predominant element. It also is clear that the supportive elements of opera production such as scenery, costumes, and staging make opera (while still a form of music) a pace apart from its musical brethren.

Traditions of opera are strong, deep, and also, as some would argue, part of the problem that opera has had in gaining popular support in the twentieth century. There have been recent attempts to make opera more like contemporary drama, with greater focus on plot, character development, and so on. Even plays such as *Of Mice and Men* have been made into operas, in order to make opera less exaggerated and implausible. In addition, some individuals find great distress in the traditional inability of opera singers to act and the frequent portrayal of supposedly sexually appealing heroines by obese singers. How much of this is tradition, how much is irrelevant, and how we as audience members ought to regard it is often a source of irritation for the neophyte and the opera buff alike. However, despite opera's "problems" and the debate as to its essential characteristics, it certainly merits attention.

Many devotees of opera regard it as the purest integration of all the arts. It contains music, drama, poetry, and, in the *mise en scène,* visual art. Certainly one even could include architecture, because an opera house is a particular architectural entity. Because of opera's integration of art forms, much of

what we respond to in opera at the formal, technical, and sensual levels is discussed in other chapters of this text. But since opera tends to be the art form most removed from popular awareness, let us examine some of its basic properties.

Opera is a live art form. Recordings and television presentations make it available to a mass audience but are not substitutes for sitting in the cavernous auditorium that is an opera house and witnessing a musical and dramatic spectacle unfold on a stage perhaps 50 feet wide and 70 feet deep, filled with scenery rising 20 or 30 feet in the air, and peopled by a chorus of 100 or more people, all fully costumed and singing over a full orchestra (Figs. 5.8 and 5.9). The scope and the spectacle of such an event *is opera*. Listening to the music of opera on the radio or from a record, or watching the minuscule productions brought to us through the medium of television, *is not*.

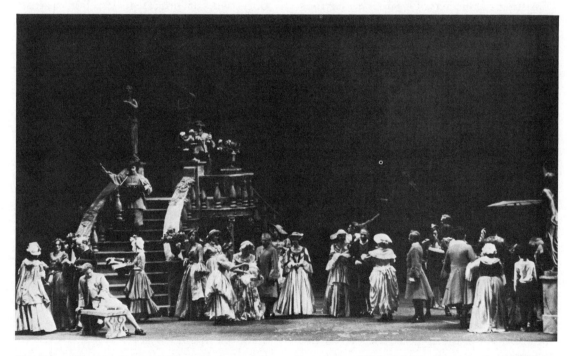

Fig. 5.8. Giacomo Puccini, *Manon Lescaux*. Opera Company of Philadelphia. Photo by Trudy Cohen.

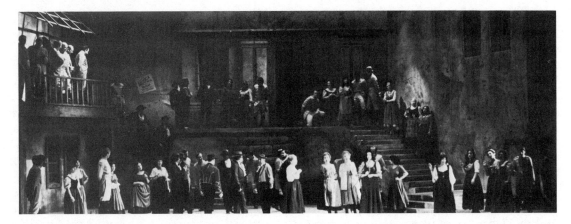

Fig. 5.9.   Georges Bizet, *Carmen*. Opera Company of Philadelphia. Composite photo by Trudy Cohen.

Opera can be divided more or less accurately into four varieties. *Opera* (without a qualifying adjective) is the serious or *tragic opera* that we perhaps think of immediately. This type also has been called *grand opera,* which implies to some an early operatic form consisting of five acts. *Opera seria* ("serious opera") is another name for tragic or grand opera.

Opéra comique, the second variety of opera, is any opera, *regardless of subject matter,* that has *spoken dialogue.* The third type, *opera buffa,* is *comic* opera (do not confuse it with opéra comique) that usually does *not* have spoken dialogue. Opera buffa usually makes great use of farce, and in the opinion of some its music is usually less profound than that of serious opera.

The fourth variety, which we will mention again in the next chapter, is *operetta.* Operetta also has spoken dialogue, but it has come to refer to a light style of opera characterized by popular themes, a romantic mood, and often a humorous tone. It is frequently considered more theatrical than musical, and its story line is usually frivolous and sentimental. Although opéra comique is the prototype of the operetta, the two are not synonomous.

As we will discover in discussing theatre, categories such as these four are helpful to a certain extent, especially in tracing the traditions of a given work. However, one must treat categories with some caution, because an individual artwork may appear to fall into one, two, or no categories. Some artists, perhaps most, feel little compulsion to limit themselves in such an arbitrary way.

Opera does have some unique characteristics. The text of an opera, which is called the *libretto,* is probably the single most important barrier to the appreciation of opera by American audiences. Since the large majority of operas in the contemporary repertoire are not of American origin, the American respondent must overcome the language barrier in order to understand the dialogue and thereby the plot. It is not a desire for snobbery or exclusivity that causes the lack of English-translation performances; rather, opera loses much of its musical character in translation. We spoke of tone color, or timbre, earlier in this chapter. There are timbre characteristics implicit in the Russian, German, and Italian languages that are lost when they are translated into English. In addition, inasmuch as opera is in a sense the Olympic Games of the vocal-music world (that is, the demands made on the human voice by the composers of opera require the highest degree of skill and training of any vocal medium), tone placement, and the vowels and consonants requisite to that placement, becomes very important to the singer. It is one thing for a tenor to sing the vowel "eh" on high B flat in the original Italian. If the translated word to be sung on the same note employs an "oo" vowel, the technical difficulty is changed considerably. So, the translation of opera from its original tongue into English is a far more difficult and complex problem than simply providing an accurate translation for a portion of the audience that does not know the text—as important as that may seem. Translation must concern itself with tone quality, color, and the execution of tones in the *tessitura* of the human voice.

Experienced opera goers may study the score before attending a performance. However, every concert program contains a plot synopsis (even when the production is in English), so that even the neophyte can know what is happening. Opera plots, unlike mysteries, have few surprise endings, and knowing the plot ahead of time does not diminish the experience of responding to the opera.

The first element in opera itself is the overture, which we discussed earlier. There are two characteristics that this orchestral introduction may have. First, it may set the mood or tone of the opera. Here the composer works directly with our sense responses, putting us in the proper frame of mind for what is to follow. In his overture to *I Pagliacci,* for example, Ruggiero Leoncavallo creates a tonal story that tells us what we are about to experience. Using only the orchestra he tells us we will see comedy, tragedy, action, and romance. If we listen to this overture, we will easily identify these elements, and in doing so understand how

relatively unimportant the work's being in English is to comprehension. Add to the "musical language" the language of body and mime, and we can understand even complex ideas and character relationships—*without* words. In addition to this type of introduction, an overture may provide melodic introductions—passages introducing the *arias* and *recitatives* that will follow.

The plot is unfolded musically through *recitative,* or sung dialogue. The composer uses recitative to move the plot along from one section to another; recitative has little emotional content, to speak of and the words are more important than the music. There are two kinds of recitative. The first is *recitativo secco,* for which the singer has very little musical accompaniment, or none at all. If there is accompaniment it is usually in the form of light chording under the voice. The second type is *recitativo stromento,* in which the singer is given full musical accompaniment.

The real emotion and poetry of an opera lies in its *arias.* Musically and poetically, an aria is the reflection of high dramatic feeling. The great opera songs with which we are likely to be familiar are arias.

In every opera there are duets, trios, quartets, and other small ensemble pieces. There also are chorus sections where everyone gets into the act. In addition, ballet or dance interludes are not uncommon in opera. These have nothing to do with the development of the plot, but are put in to add more life and interest to the dramatic production, and in some cases to provide a *seque* from one scene into another.

Although the scope of this text does not include history per se, our enjoyment of opera can be enhanced if we see it in part of its historical context. Opera traces its roots to the composition of *Euridice* by Jacopo Peri in 1600, and found expression in the baroque and classical periods. However, from the romantic period of the nineteenth century have come the major traditions of opera, which still provide the bulk of the operatic repertoire.

Bel canto, as its name implies, is a style of singing emphasizing the beauty of sound. Its most successful composer, Gioacchino Rossini, had a great sense of melody and sought to develop the *art song* to its highest level. In bel-canto singing the melody is the focus. Two other opera composers in this tradition were Gaetano Donizetti and Vincenzo Bellini.

Richard Wagner gave opera and theatre a prototype that continues to influence theatrical production—*organic unity*. Every element of his productions was integral, and was shaped so as to help create a work of total unity. Wagner was also famous for the use of *leitmotif*, a common element in contemporary film. A leitmotif is a musical theme associated with a particular person or idea. Each time that person appears or is thought of, or each time the idea surfaces, the leitmotif is played. "Lara's Theme" from the movie *Doctor Zhivago* and even the recurring theme in *Jaws* could both be thought of as leitmotifs.

Late in the nineteenth century the *verismo* movement flourished. From the same root as the word verisimilitude, with which we have dealt previously, verismo opera treated themes, characters, and events from life in a down-to-earth fashion. The composer Pietro Mascagni is reported to have said, "In my operas do not look for melody or beauty . . . look only for blood!" Certainly in the works of Mascagni, Leoncavallo, and Puccini there is plenty of blood—as well as fine drama.

No discussion of opera composers, however brief, would be complete without mention of Giuseppe Verdi. Although writing in the nineteenth century, Verdi was most closely tied stylistically to the classicism of

the previous century. His *Rigoletto, Il Trovatore,* and *La Traviata* illustrate logical musical development that uses recurring themes to provide unity. *Aida* is perhaps the most famous of the spectacular grand operas.

CHRONOLOGY OF SELECTED MAJOR PERIODS, STYLES, AND EXAMPLES FOR STUDY IN WESTERN MUSIC

c. 1100–c. 1400
Music of the Middle Ages
  Gregorian chant
  organum
  troubador music
  Machaut: *Messe de Nostre Dame*

c. 1400–c. 1600
Renaissance Music
  Dufay: *Salve Regina*
  Josquin des Prés: *Ave Maria*
  Palestrina: *Missa Salve Regina*
  Jannequin: *Chant des Oiseaux*
  Gibbons: *The Silver Swan*

c. 1600–c. 1750
Baroque Music
  J. S. Bach: Magnificat in D; Mass in B Minor; Toccata in D Minor
  Handel: *Israel in Egypt; Water Music; Messiah*
  Schütz: *The Christmas Story*
  Vivaldi: *La Primavera;* Concerto for Flute, Op. 10, No. 3

c. 1750–c. 1825
Classical Music
  Mozart: Symphony No. 40; Symphony No. 41
  Haydn: Symphony No. 45; Symphony No. 94
Transitional Music
  Beethoven: Symphony No. 3; Symphony No. 9

c. 1825–c. 1900
Romantic Music
  Berlioz: *Harold in Italy*
  Brahms: *Ein Deutsches Requiem*
  Chopin: Etudes, Op. 25

Liszt: *Les Préludes*
Mahler: Symphony No. 9
Moussorgsky: *Pictures at an Exhibition*
Schubert: Symphony No. 8 (*Unfinished*)
R. Strauss: *Don Quixote*
Tchaikovsky: Symphony No. 6 (*Pathétique*)
Romantic Opera (see the previous section)

c. 1900–
Impressionism
  Debussy: *Prélude à l'après-midi d'un faune*
Serialism, Twelve-tone Technique, Dodecaphony
  Schoenberg: Variations for Orchestra, Op. 31
Aleatory Music
  Cage: *Fontana Mix*

Chapter 6

THEATRE

Like the other performing arts, theatre is an interpretative discipline. Between the playwright and the audience stand the director and the designers, all artists in their own right, but each functioning to communicate the playwright's artwork to the audience. At the same time, each of these artists, and the actors as well, seeks to add his or her own artistic communications to the process. Sometimes the play becomes subordinate to what is expressed by the interpreters.

WHAT IS IT?

Theatre is the design of time, sound, and two- and three-dimensional space, utilizing the live performer. Our formal response to a theatrical production depends upon the basic nature, or *genre* (see the glossary), of the play from which the production evolves. Genres in theatre are tragedy, drama, melodrama, comedy, farce, and others. Some are products of specific periods of history and illustrate trends in dramatic literature or theory that no longer exist. Others are still developing, and as yet lack definite form. The genres we will examine are relatively fixed in their definition and development; they are the major genres of theatre history, including the twentieth century. Our response to genre is a bit different from our formal response or identification in music, for example, because we seldom find generic identification in the theatre program. Some plays are well-known examples of a specific genre, and in these cases, as with a symphony, we can see how the production develops the conventions of that form. Other plays, however, are not well known or may be open to interpretation (or may be arbitrarily interpreted by the director). As a result, we can draw our conclusions only *after* the performance has finished.

Tragedy. By convention, tragedy requires an unhappy ending and an ennobling of the victim. It also requires events of significance and dignity that transcend everyday life. In the past these criteria have been met through the use of poetry and the portrayal of personages of high stature, such as kings. Tragedies are as old as recorded history. Our experience with this genre dates to the classical Greek theatre of the fifth century B.C. Aristotle, in his *Poetics,* describes in great detail the characteristics of tragedy, and much of his categorization shapes the basis for our discussion even today. There is some debate, however, surrounding the definition of tragedy and the claim that its heroes must be larger than life. Can a play with an unhappy or tragic ending have a hero who is a common person and still be a tragedy? Another characteristic that seems to be standard for a tragic hero is what many have called the "tragic flaw." Very simply, the tragic flaw is that attribute of the hero, usually excessive pride, by which he creates his own downfall.

It should be obvious from this brief discussion that tragedy, like so many other genres, is a complex *theoretical* entity. If we were to go on with our examination, we would subdivide tragedy into Greek, Elizabethan, modern, and perhaps a few other varieties. For our purposes, however, we will stop here with the exhortation that a fuller understanding of the genre will bring greater satisfaction in experiencing it in the theater.

Drama. The term *drama* often is used as a synonym for theatre. Such usage is not entirely accurate. As a genre, drama refers to plays that have serious intent but do not fall within the definition of tragedy. In a drama we do not necessarily have an unhappy ending, but the subject matter is treated in a serious fashion. The events tend to be of lesser *magnitude* than in tragedy. The heroes are of everyday stuff.

Melodrama. Melodrama is a genre characterized by sensationalism and sentimentality. The personages and their characters tend to be stereotyped; problems and solutions tend to be all good or all evil. Black is black and white is white; there are no grays either in people or in issues. Plots tend to be overly romantic, and the action exaggerated. In a typical melodrama such as *Uncle Tom's Cabin* we see scenes such as Little Eva carrying her baby across the ice on a raging river in the middle of a snowstorm. Much of what we see in modern movies and on television is melodrama.

Comedy. We tend to think of plays that make us laugh as comedies. This description is not always accurate. Many dramas, and even tragedies, have comic moments or scenes. However, comedy *is* typified by humorous treatment of subject matter, whether or not the subject matter is frivolous. Comedies can have serious themes, and by skillful writing a playwright can cause us to laugh at what is essentially not a funny matter. Sometimes a playwright wishes us to believe we are seeing a comedy. We may laugh throughout the play. Only after leaving the theater might we have cause to question the nature of what we experienced.

Comedies, like tragedies, come in various types and from various historical periods. They also date from ancient Greece and find reference in Aristotle's *Poetics.* Aristotle wrote that tragedy shows people as better than they are; comedy shows them as worse.

Farce. The principal difference between comedy and farce lies in the latter's exaggeration in the actions of the actors and in the situations. Some writers suggest that farce is to comedy what melodrama is to tragedy. Typically a farce relies for its effect on broad, slapstick humor filled with "sight gags" and action. A comedy rests mainly on its dialogue. If we look to the medium of film, we find in The Three Stooges examples of farce familiar to all of us.

Musical Comedy. We are all familiar with musical comedy, sometimes called operetta, and I made some allusions to it in the section on opera in the last chapter. Musical comedy has been called the United States' unique contribution to the world of theatre. Whether or not this is true, the musical comedy is a popular theatrical genre in the United States. It is characterized by the interspersing of dialogue and vocal solos, choruses, and dances; the ratio of dialogue to music varies greatly from one musical comedy to another. The genre apparently has changed over a period of years, beginning in the 1950s. It may be more accurate to refer to more recent musical comedies as *musicals,* because the themes and subjects of many of them are serious, and even tragic, as in *West Side Story, A Little Night Music,* and *No Strings.*

Since in the theatre we witness a quickly passing parade of complex messages, we need to respond to many things in many ways. Asking ourselves questions about how a play may meet the criteria of the genres we have just discussed will help us discern some of the basic intent of the artists who are communicating with us.

HOW IS IT PUT TOGETHER?

Obviously we can read plays and analyze them. This, however, is not adequate for understanding a theatrical production. Theatre is not literature; it is an art of time and space that transpires with live actors in the confines of some form of theatrical environment. Studying a script is even less a means of responding to theatre than merely studying a score is in responding to music. So, we must examine the entire scope of a theatrical production if we are to understand our response to it.

Character, Message, and Spectacle Plays

To one degree or another every play has elements of character, message, and spectacle. I think it can be helpful to us in responding to a play to try to determine which of these three is the principal focus of the play. Obviously, some plays will appear to fall into more than one category and some into none.

Character Plays. Character plays focus on the development of the characters of the personages. For the sake of accuracy, the *dramatis personae,* or "cast of characters," are called *personages.* The term *character* is used in its psychological sense to mean the composite of mental factors that motivate the actions of the personages. In a character play we focus upon why individuals do what they do, how they change, and how they interact with the other individuals as the play unfolds. Tennessee Williams's *The Glass Menagerie* is an illustration of a character play.

Message Plays. A message play focuses on a theme, a specific idea communicated by the playwright to the audience. Its intent is basically instructive. The most obvious form of message play is the propaganda play, of which Clifford Odets's *Waiting for Lefty* is an excellent American example.

Spectacle Plays. Spectacle plays, of which melodramas are an example, focus neither on character nor on message. There may be elements of both in a spectacle play, but characters are superficially drawn and stereotyped and the themes are trite or shallow. Instead, the spectacle play focuses on "action." Most contemporary Americans are surprised to learn that the novel *Ben Hur* was also produced as a stage play, and that the great chariot race for which the movie version is famous actually was done on the stage with two chariots, eight horses, and a complex arrangement of treadmills and revolving background scenery. It is difficult to imagine any character development or message that could compete with this spectacle for the audience's attention.

Language

An important response to what is in a production is to the language. It is the author's most direct communicative link with us, and it immediately tells us part of what we can expect from the play. A continuum extending from verisimilitude to theatricality is helpful to consider. Dialogue that sounds to us like everyday speech is high in verisimilitude. Poetry, on the other hand, is high in theatricality. We also must listen for the relationship of the language to the overall presentation of the play. Some might call this characteristic *symbolism*. In any case, *how* does the play's language reveal character, theme, or magnitude? In other words, does the author wish us to read between the lines of dialogue? Do the words imply more than what first meets the ear?

Structure

Dissecting the structure of a play is a difficult operation. Even "theatre people" do not agree on the terminology and procedures involved in putting a play together and making it work. Our task is complicated by the failure of most playwrights to adhere to neat formulas when they write. They do whatever they believe is necessary to accomplish their aims. Nevertheless, we can and should understand some basic concepts about play structure. The rudiments of play structure are *exposition, complication,* and *denouement.*

Exposition. In the exposition of a play the playwright gives us essential background information. He or she is setting the stage for what we will see as the play progresses. How much time or space (if any) is allotted to the

exposition depends entirely on the playwright and the play. Some playwrights lay the exposition as quickly and succinctly as possible; others continue nearly to the final curtain to "fill us in" about what happened prior to the point at which the play began.

Complication. If we regard the situation of a play when the curtain opens as the status quo, then usually something—an event or decision—happens to upset that status quo and thereby to cause the play to move forward. If and when that happens, we have moved into the complication section of the play. In this section we might say "the plot thickens." The outlaws ride into town, and all is thrown into turmoil. Here the playwright twists the events of the plot and subplots.

Denouement. If an author wishes to resolve all these complications (some do not), then at some *point* we will reach a *climax,* after which the complications will be resolved. That resolution is called the *denouement.* In many plays the denouement is achieved through a logical sequence of events emanating from the characters of the personages. In early Greek tragedies, however, the complications were so complex that the only means by which the author could undo them was divine intervention. Whenever some device other than logical character development is used to bring about the denouement, we call that device a *deus ex machina,* or "god in a machine"—referring to the method of entrance used by the gods in the theatre of ancient Greece. Whether the denouement is logical or contrived, a structural pattern that builds to a peak and then resolves to a conclusion is called *pyramidal.*

The Protagonist. Inside the structural pattern of a play some kind of action must take place. We must ask ourselves, How does this play work? How do we get from the beginning to the end? Most of the time we take that journey via the actions and decisions of the *protagonist,* or central personage. Deciding the protagonist of a play is not always easy, even for directors. However, it is important to understand whom the play is about if we are to understand the play. In Terence Rattigan's *Cause Célèbre* we could have three different responses depending upon whom the director decided was the protagonist. The problem is this: There are two central feminine roles. A good case could be made for either as the central personage of the play. Or they both could be equal. What we understand the play to be about depends on whom the director chooses to focus.

Dynamics

Every production has its own dynamic patterns, which we can chart (for example, as in Fig. 6.1). The structural pattern of a play, about which we just spoke, is made clear to us by the dynamic patterns the director establishes. These patterns also help to hold the interest of the audience. Scientific studies indicate that attention or interest is not a constant factor; human beings are able to concentrate on specific items only for very brief periods. Therefore, in order to hold audience attention over the two-hour span of a production it is essential to employ devices

whereby from time to time interest or attention is allowed to peak and then relax. However, the peaks must be carefully controlled. A production should build to a high point of dramatic interest. Usually this point is the climax and occurs late in the play. However, each scene or act has its own peak of development—again, to maintain interest. So, the rise from the beginning of the play to the high point of dramatic interest is not a steady rise, but a series of peaks and valleys. Each successive peak is closer to the ultimate one. The director controls where and how high these peaks occur by controlling the dynamics of the actors—volume and intensity (both bodily and vocal). (These are the same two qualities that make up dynamics in music.)

The importance of dynamics is best illustrated by situations in which dynamics are uncontrolled. I once saw a college production of Arthur Miller's *All My Sons,* a very dramatic play centering upon morality. The climax of the play occurs near the end when the central personage discovers that his decision to allow defective aircraft engines to be sold to the air force caused the death of his own son. The difficulty for the director and actors is that there are scenes of conflict and emotion preceding the climax. In this production the dynamic level went too high too soon. Not only did this cause the climax to

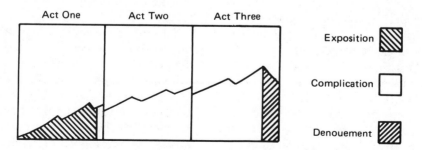

Fig. 6.1. Hypothetical dynamic and structural development of a three-act play.

be anticlimactic, but (since the dynamic level stayed at that peak) it also caused the production to be monotonous.

The Actor

Although it is not always easy to tell which functions in a production are the playwright's, which the director's, and which the actor's, the responsibility for one function is perfectly clear: the main channel of communication between the playwright and the audience is the actors. It is through their movements and speech that the audience perceives the play.

Our purpose in this discussion is not to study acting. However, we can look for two elements in an actor's portrayal of a role that will enhance our response. The first is *speech*. Language, as we noted a moment ago, is the playwright's words. Speech is the manner in which the actor delivers those words. Speech, like language, can range from high verisimilitude to high theatricality, and it is possible to utter language that is highly verisimilar in speech that is highly theatrical. If speech adheres to normal conversational rhythms, durations, and inflections, we respond in one way. If it utilizes extended vowel emphasis, long, sliding inflections, and dramatic pauses, we respond quite differently—even though the playwright's words are identical in both cases.

The second element of an actor's portrayal that aids our understanding is the physical reinforcement he or she gives to the character's basic motivation. Most actors try to identify a single basic motivation for their character. That motivation is called a *spine*. Everything that pertains to the decisions the personage makes is kept consistent for the audience because those decisions (and actions) stem from this basic drive. Actors will translate that drive into something physical that they can *do* throughout the play. For example, Blanche, a central personage in

Tennessee Williams's *A Streetcar Named Desire,* is driven by the desire to arrange or rearrange whatever she comes in contact with. More specifically, she must *clean* what she encounters, because of the way she regards herself and the world around her. Ideally, the actress playing Blanche will discover that element of Blanche's personality as she reads the play and develops the role. In order to make that spine clear to us in the audience, the actress will translate it into physical action. Therefore, we will *see* Blanche constantly smoothing her hair, rearranging and straightening her dress, cleaning the furniture, brushing imaginary dust from other personages' shoulders, and so forth. Nearly every physical move she makes will relate somehow to the act of cleaning. Of course, these movements will all be subtle and played down. Nevertheless, if we are attentive we can find them, and thereby understand the nature of the character we are perceiving.

Mise en Scène

There is another channel of communication between the playwright and the audience—the environment within which the actors work. We may call the elements of this environment the *technical* elements of a production, or we may use the French term, *mise en scène*. This term implies not just scenery, lighting, properties, and costumes but also the interrelationship of audience and stage space.

Part of our response to a production is shaped by the design of the space in which the play is produced. The earliest and most natural arrangement is the theatre-in-the-round, or *arena* theater (Fig. 6.2), in which the audience surrounds the playing area on all sides. Whether the playing area is circular, square, or rectangular is irrelevant. Some argue that the closeness of the audience to the stage space in an arena theater provides the

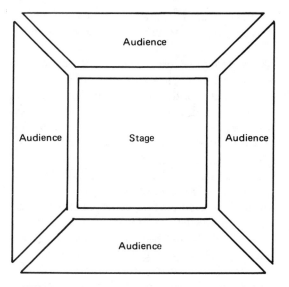

Fig. 6.2.   Ground plan of an arena theater.

most intimate kind of theatrical experience. A second possibility is the *thrust,* or three-quarter, theater (Fig. 6.3), in which the audience surrounds the playing area on three sides. The most familiar illustration of this theater is what we understand to be the theater of the Elizabethan or Shakespearean period. The third actor-audience relationship, and the one most widely utilized in the twentieth century, is the *proscenium* theater, in which the audience views the action through a "picture-frame" opening (Fig. 6.4). In this type of theater the audience sits on only one side.

There also are experimental arrangements of audience and stage space. On some occasions acting areas are placed in the middle of the audience, creating little "island stages." In certain circumstances these small stages create quite an interesting set of responses and relationships between actors and audience.

Common experience indicates that the physical relationship of the acting area to the audience has nearly a causal effect on the depth of audience involvement. Experience has also indicated that a certain amount of separation is necessary for certain kinds of emotional responses. We call this mental and physical separation *aesthetic distance.* The proper aesthetic distance allows us to become involved in what we know is fictitious or even unbelievable.

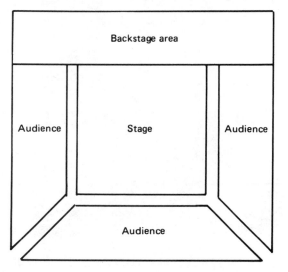

Fig. 6.3.   Ground plan of a thrust theater.

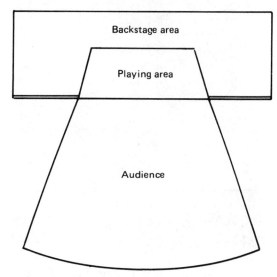

Fig. 6.4.   Ground plan of a proscenium theater.

Mise en scène also implies visual reinforcement involving scenery, lighting, costumes, and properties, each of which has specific goals in the production. The *mise en scène* may or may not have independent communication with the audience; this is one of the options of the director and designers. It is interesting to note that before the nineteenth century there was no coordination of the various elements of a theatre production. This, of course, had all kinds of interesting, and in some cases catastrophic, consequences. However, for the last century most theatre productions have adhered to what is called the organic theory of play production. That is, everything, visual and oral, is designed with a single purpose. Each production has a specific goal in terms of audience response, and all of the elements in the production attempt to achieve this end.

Scene Design.   Simply stated, the purpose of scene design in the theater is to create an environment conducive to the production's ends. The scene designer uses the same tools of composition—line, form, mass, color, repetition, and unity—as the painter. In addition, since a stage design occupies three-dimensional space and must allow for the movement of the actors in, on, through, and around the elements of scenery, the scene designer becomes a sculptor as well. Figures 6.5–6.8 illustrate how emphasis on given elements of design highlight different characteristics in the production. C. Ricketts's design for *The Eumenides* (Fig. 6.5) stresses

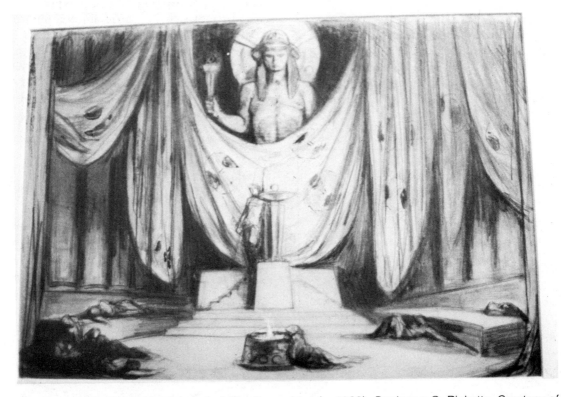

Fig. 6.5.   Scene design for Aeschylus' *The Eumenides* (c. 1922). *Designer:* C. Ricketts. Courtesy of The Victoria and Albert Museum, London.

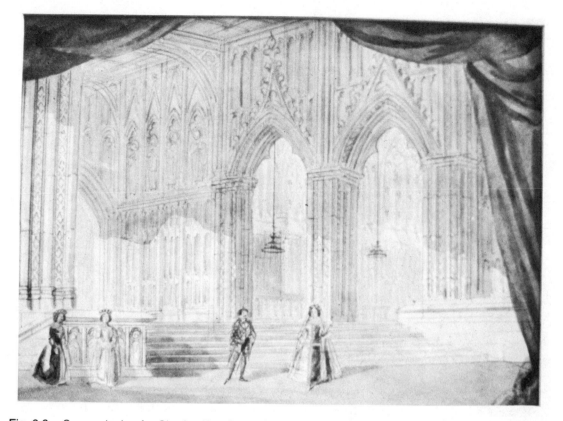

Fig. 6.6.   Scene design for Charles Kean's production of Shakespeare's *Richard II,* Princess Theatre, London (1857). *Designer:* Thomas Grieve. Courtesy of The Victoria and Albert Museum, London.

formality, assymetricality, and symbolism. Thomas Grieve's *Richard II* (Fig. 6.6) is formal, but light and spacious. His regular rhythms and repetition of arches create a completely different feeling from the one elicited by Ricketts's design. William Telbin's *Hamlet* (Fig. 6.7) with its strong central triangle and monumental scale, creates an overwhelming weight that, while utilizing diagonal activity in the sides of the triangles, cannot match the action of Robert Burroughs's zigzagging diagonals juxtaposed among verticals in his design for *Peer Gynt* (Fig. 6.8). Unlike the painter or sculptor, however, the scene designer is limited by the stage space, the concepts of the director (as

opposed to his own), the amount of time and budget available for the execution of his design, and elements of practicality: can the design withstand the wear and tear of the actors over the period of time for which the production will run? These are the constraints, and also the challenges, of scene design.

Lighting Design.   Lighting designers are perhaps the most crucial of all the theater artists in modern productions, because without their art nothing done by the actors, the costume designer, the property master, the director, or the scene designer would be seen by the audience. On the other hand, lighting designers work in an ephemeral medium.

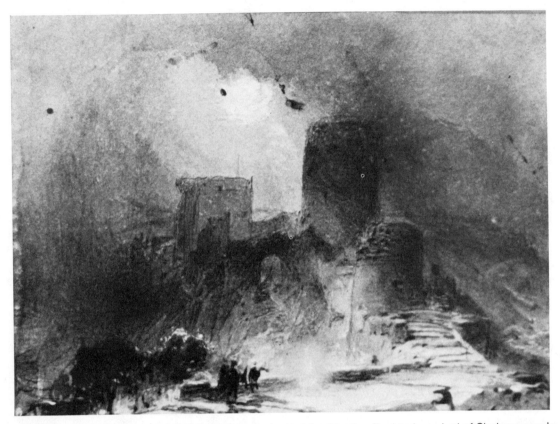

Fig. 6.7. Scene design (probably an alternate design) for Charles Fechter's revival of Shakespeare's *Hamlet,* Lyceum Theatre, London (1864). *Designer:* William Telbin. Courtesy of The Victoria and Albert Museum, London.

They must sculpt with light and create shadows that fall where they desire them to fall; they must "paint" over the colors provided by the other designers. In doing so they use lighting instruments with imperfect optical qualities. Lighting designers do their work in their mind, unlike scene designers, who can paint a design and then calculate it in feet and inches. Lighting designers must imagine what their light will do to an actor, to a costume, to a set. They must enhance the color of a costume, accent the physique of an actor, and reinforce the plasticity of a setting. They also try to reinforce the dramatic structure and dynamics of the play. They

work within the framework of light and shade. Without shadows and highlights the human face and body become imperceptible. A human face without shadows cannot be seen clearly more than a few feet away. However, in a theater such small movements as the raising of an eyebrow must be seen clearly as much as one hundred feet away. It is the lighting designer who, through proper use of light and shade, makes this possible.

Costume Design. One is tempted to think of the costumes of the theatre merely as clothing that has to be researched to reflect a particular historical period and constructed to fit a particular actor. But costuming goes beyond that. Costume designers work with the entire body of the actor. They design hair styles and clothing (and sometimes make-up) to suit a specific purpose or occasion, a character, a locale, and so forth (Figs. 6.9 and 6.10). A costume outlines the actor's figure for the audience to see.

The function of stage costuming is threefold. First, it *accents*. That is, it shows the audience which personages are the most important in a scene, and it shows the relationships between personages. Second, it *reflects*—a particular era, time of day, climate, season, location, or occasion. The de-

signs in Fig. 6.9 reflect a historical period. We recognize different historical periods primarily through silhouette, or outline. Costume designers may merely suggest full detail or may actually provide it, as has been done in Fig. 6.9. We see here the designer's concern not only for period but also for character in her choice of details, color, texture, jewelry, and also hair style. Notice the length to which the designer goes to indicate detail, providing not only front but also back views of the costume, and also a head study showing the hair without a covering. Third, stage costuming *reveals*—the style of the performance, the characters of the personages,

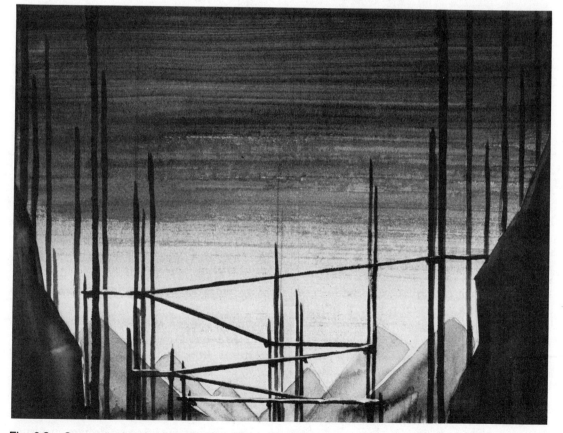

Fig. 6.8. Scene design for Ibsen's *Peer Gynt,* The University of Arizona Theatre. *Director:* Peter R. Marroney. *Scene designer:* Robert C. Burroughs.

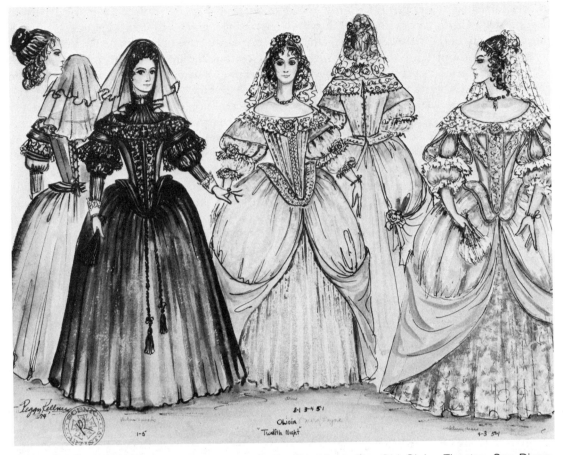

Fig. 6.9. Costume designs for Shakespeare's *Twelfth Night,* The Old Globe Theatre, San Diego, California. *Director:* Craig Noel. *Costume designer:* Peggy J. Kellner.

and the personages' social position, profession, cleanliness, age, physique, and health. In Fig. 6.10 the concern of the designer is clearly less with historical period than with production style and character. This costume design reveals the high emotional content of the particular scene, and we see at first glance the deteriorated health and condition of King Lear. The contrast provided by the king in such a state heightens the effect of the scene, and details such as the bare feet, the winter furs, and the storm-ravaged cape are precise indicators of the pathos we are expected to

find and respond to in it. Costume designers work, as do scene and lighting designers, with the same general elements as painters and sculptors: the elements of composition. A stage costume is an actor's skin: it allows him to move as he must, and occasionally it restricts him from moving as he should not.

Properties. Properties fall into two general groups: *set props* and *hand props*. Set properties are part of the scene design: furniture, pictures, rugs, fireplace accessories, and so on. Along with the larger elements of the set, they identify the mood of the play and the character of those who inhabit the world they portray. Hand properties are used by the actors to portray characters of the personages: cigarettes, cigars, ashtrays, papers, pencils, glasses, and so forth. The use of properties can be significant to our understanding of a play. For example, if at the opening curtain all properties appear to be neat and in order, we receive a particular message. If as the play develops the actors disrupt the properties so that at the end of the play the entire scene is in disarray, that simple transition can help illustrate what may have happened in the play.

Style

In describing the relationship of the *mise en scène* to the play, we have noted the designers' use of compositional elements. The use of these elements relative to "life" is part of that amorphous quality we call *style*. All of the elements of a production can be placed

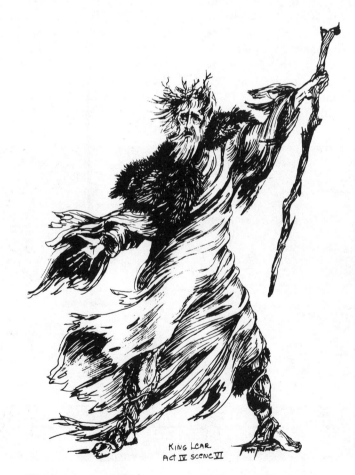

Fig. 6.10. Costume design for Shakespeare's *King Lear,* The Old Globe Theatre, San Diego, California. *Director:* Edward Payson Call. *Costume designer:* Peggy J. Kellner.

on a continuum, one end of which is theatricality and the other, verisimilitude. Items high in verisimilitude we recognize as being like those items with which we deal in everyday life: language, movements, furniture, trees, rocks, and so forth. As we progress on our continuum from verisimilitude to theatricality the elements of the production express less and less relationship to everyday life. They become distorted, exaggerated, and perhaps even nonobjective. Items far removed from verisimilitude, then, are high in theatricality. Poetry, as we noted, is high in theatricality; everyday speech is high in verisimilitude. The position of the various elements of a production on this continuum suggests the style of the play, in the same sense that brush stroke, line, and palette indicate style in painting.

Figures 6.11–6.17 illustrate the range of visual styles between verisimilitude and theatricality. Figure 6.11 is a proscenium setting high in verisimilitude—including a full ceiling over the setting. Figure 6.12 is an arena setting high in verisimilitude; it reflects the basically lifelike overall style of the presentation. However, the requirement of the arena configuration that there be *no walls* can cause problems in some productions. Note that some theatricality—specifically, the empty picture frame—is present in the decoration of this set. This is not an inconsistency since the play develops as a "flashback" in the mind of its main personage. In Fig. 6.13 the designer has attempted to heighten the theatrical nature of the production by using set props high in verisimilitude and a setting that is representational but pushed toward theatricality by the use of open space where one might expect solid walls in this pros-

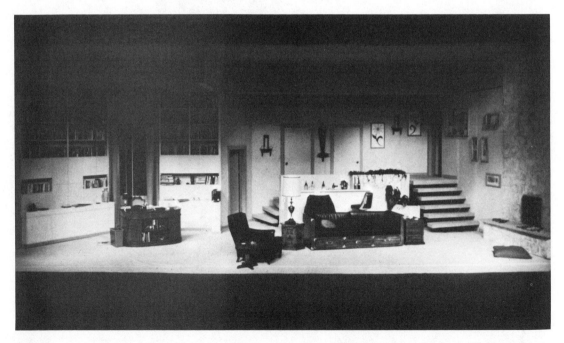

Fig. 6.11. A proscenium setting for Jean Kerr's *Mary, Mary,* The University of Arizona Theatre. *Director:* H. Wynn Pearce. *Scene and lighting designer:* Dennis J. Sporre.

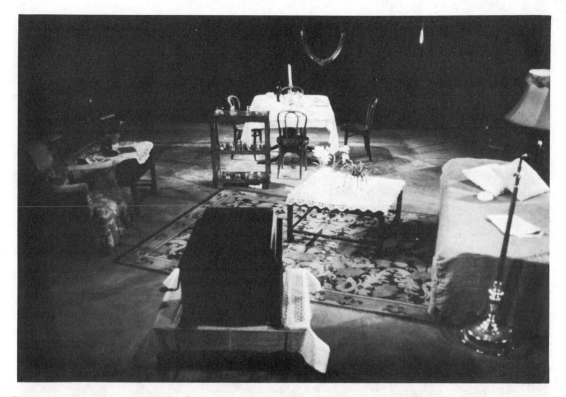

Fig. 6.12. An arena setting for Tennessee Williams's *The Glass Menagerie,* State University of New York at Plattsburgh. *Director:* H. Charles Kline. *Scene and lighting designer:* Dennis J. Sporre.

cenium production. The setting in Fig. 6.14 moves further toward theatricality and indicates clearly through exaggerated detail and two-dimensionality the whimsical and "fun" nature of the production. The designs in Figs. 6.15 and 6.16 create a purely formal and theatrical environment. No locale is specifically depicted, but the use of representational detail (in Fig. 6.16 various areas of the set served as "locations" and had realistic furniture) keeps the setting tied to the overall style of the actors. Finally, in Fig. 6.17 neither time nor place is indicated or remotely suggested. Here the emphasis is on reinforcement of the high action of the production. The steep ramps throughout the set make it impossible for the actors to walk

from one level to the next; the setting *forces* them to *run.*

In this series of illustrations I have used my own designs, not out of vanity but to make a further point regarding style. In most arts the artist's *style* is unique—a recognizable mark on his or her artwork. Some artists change their style, but they do so by their own choice. Interpretive artists such as costume, scene, and lighting designers, and to a degree conductors as well, must submerge their personal style to that of the work with which they are involved. The playwright or the director sets the style, and the scene designer adapts to it and makes *his or her design* reflect it.

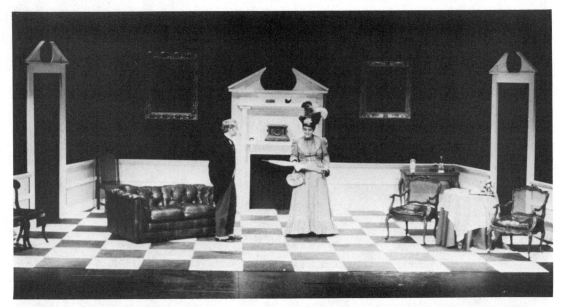

Fig. 6.13. A proscenium setting for Oscar Wilde's *The Importance of Being Earnest,* The University of Arizona Theatre. *Director:* William Lang. *Costume designer:* Helen Workman Currie. *Scene and lighting designer:* Dennis J. Sporre.

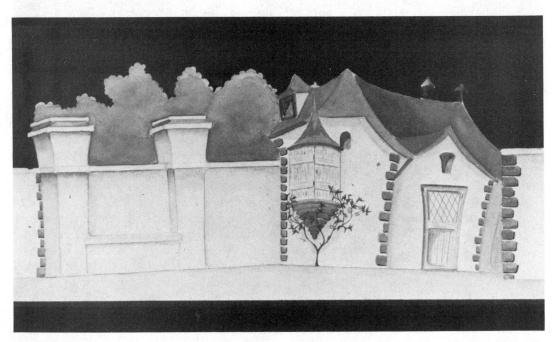

Fig. 6.14. Scene design for Jerry Devine and Bruce Montgomery's *The Amorous Flea* (musical), The University of Iowa Theatre. *Director:* David Knauf. *Scene and lighting designer:* Dennis J. Sporre.

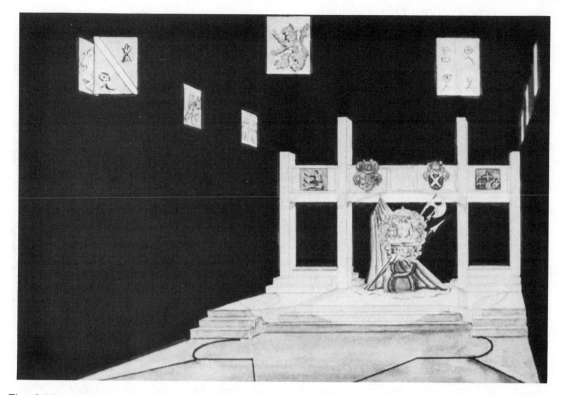

Fig. 6.15. A thrust setting for Shakespeare's *King John,* University of Illinois at Chicago Circle. *Director:* Donald Dickenson. *Scene and lighting designer:* Dennis J. Sporre.

HOW DOES IT STIMULATE THE SENSES?

The specific treatment given to each of the elements we have just discussed stimulates our senses in a particular manner. We respond to the play's structure and how it works; we respond to dynamics. We are stimulated by the theatricality or verisimilitude of the language of the playwright and the movements and speech of the actors. We find our response shaped by the relationship of the stage space to the audience, and by the sets, lights, properties, and costumes. All of these elements bombard us simultaneously with complex visual and aural stimuli. How we respond, and how much we are able to respond, determines our ultimate reaction to a production.

Perhaps the theatre is unique in its ability to stimulate our senses, because only in the theatre is there a direct appeal to our emotions through the live portrayal of other individuals involved directly in the human condition. Being in the presence of live actors gives us much more of life in the two hours in which we share their company than we could experience outside the confines of the theater in that same time span. That phenomenon is an experience difficult to equal. The term we use to describe our reaction to and involvement with what we experience in a theatrical production is *empathy.* Empathy causes us to cry when individuals whom we

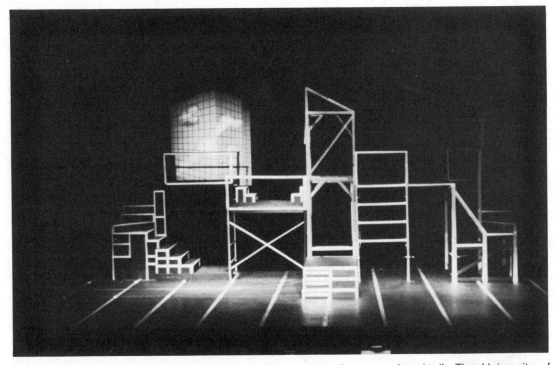

Fig. 6.16. A proscenium setting for Stephen Sondheim's *Company* (musical), The University of Arizona Theatre. *Director:* Peter R. Marroney. *Scene and lighting designer:* Dennis J. Sporre.

know are only actors become involved in tragic or emotional situations. Empathy makes us wince when an actor slaps the face of another actor, or when two football players collide at full speed. Empathy is our mental and physical involvement in situations in which we are not direct participants.

Now let us examine a few of the more obvious ways a production can appeal to our senses. In plays that deal in *conventions* the language may act as virtually the entire stimulant of our senses. Through the language the playwright sets the time, the place, the atmosphere, and even the small details of decoration. We become our own scene, lighting, and even costume designer, imagining what the playwright tells us ought to be there. In the opening scene of Shakespeare's *Hamlet* we find Bernardo and Francisco, two

guards. The hour is midnight; it is bitter cold; they are on guard; we are in Denmark; a ghost appears, in "warlike form." How do we know all of this? In a modern production we might *see* it all through the work of the costume and set designers. But this need not be the case, because the playwright gives us all of this information *in the dialogue*. Shakespeare wrote for a theater that had no lighting instruments save for the sun. His theatre (such as we know of it) probably used no scenery. The costumes were the street clothes of the day. The theatrical environment was the same whether the company was playing *Hamlet, Richard III,* or *The Tempest.* So what needed to be seen needed to be imagined. The language provided the stimuli for the audience.

We also respond to what we see. We examined dynamics earlier. A sword fight performed with flashing action, swift movements, and great intensity sets us on the edge of our chair. We are helpless to respond otherwise. Although we know the action is staged and the incident fictitious, we are caught in the excitement of the moment. We also can be gripped and manipulated by events of a quite different dynamic quality. In many plays we witness "character assassination" as one life after another is laid bare before us. The intense but subtle movements of the actors—both bodily and vocal—can pull us here and push us there, emotionally, and perhaps cause us to leave the theater feeling as if a rock were resting in our stomach. Part of our response is caused by subject matter, part by language, but much of it is the result of careful manipulation of dynamics.

Mood is an important factor in the communication that occurs in the theater. Before the curtain is up our senses are tickled by stimuli designed to put us in the mood for what follows. The houselights in the theater may be very low, or we may see a *cool* or *warm* light on the front curtain. *Music* fills the theater. We may recognize the raucous tones of a 1930s jazz piece or the melancholy of a ballad. Whatever the stimuli, they are all carefully designed to *cause* us to begin to react the way the director wishes us to react. Once the curtain is up the assault on our senses continues. The palette utilized by the scene, lighting, and costume designers helps communicate the mood of the play and other messages about it. The rhythm and variation in the *mise en scène* capture our interest and reinforce the rhythmic structure of the play. In Fig. 6.8 the use of line and form as well as color provides a formal and infinite atmosphere reflecting the epic grandeur of Ibsen's *Peer Gynt*.

The degree of plasticity or three-

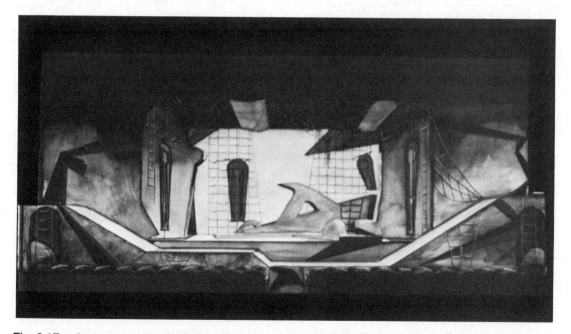

Fig. 6.17.   Scene design for Euripides' *The Bacchae*, University of Illinois at Chicago Circle. *Director:* William Raffeld. *Scene and lighting designer:* Dennis J. Sporre.

dimensionality created by the lighting designer's illumination of the actors and the set
causes us to respond in many ways. If the
lighting designer has placed the primary
lighting instruments directly in front of the
stage, plasticity will be diminished and the
actors will appear washed-out or two-
dimensional. We respond quite differently to
that visual stimulant than to the maximum
plasticity and shadow resulting from lighting
coming nearly from the side.

We also react to the *mass* of a setting.
Scenery that towers over the actors and appears massive in weight is different in effect
from scenery that seems minuscule in comparison with the human form. The settings
in Figs. 6.5, 6.6, 6.7, and 6.13 are different
from one another in scale, and each places
the actors in a different relationship with
their surroundings. In Fig. 6.13 the personages are at the center of their environment; in
Fig. 6.7 they are clearly subservient to it.

Finally, focus and line act on our senses.
Careful composition can create movement,
outlines, and shadows that are crisp and
sharp. Or it can create images that are soft,
fuzzy, or blurred. Each of these two devices
is a stimulant; each has the potential to elicit a
relatively predictable response. Perhaps in no
other art is such an arsenal of communicative
weapons so available and full of potential for
the artist. We, as respondents, benefit
through nearly total involvement in the life
situation that comes to us over the foot-
lights.

CHRONOLOGY OF SELECTED MAJOR PERIODS AND EXAMPLES FOR STUDY IN THEATRE

c. 500 B.C.–100 A.D.
Greek Theatre
  Aeschylus: *The Oresteia*
  Sophocles: *Oedipus the King; Antigone; Electra*

Euripides: *Cyclops; Medea*
Aristophanes: *The Birds; The Frogs*
Roman Theatre
  Plautus: *The Pot of Gold; Miles Gloriosus*

c. 1200–c. 1500
Medieval Theatre
  mystery and miracle plays: *Everyman; Adam*
  farce: *Maître Pierre Pathelin*

c. 1500–c. 1700
Italian-Renaissance Theatre
  commedia dell'arte
  Machiavelli: *Mandragola*
Elizabethan Theatre
  Shakespeare: *Romeo and Juliet; Richard II; The Tempest*
  Beaumont and Fletcher: *The Knight of the Burning Pestle*
Neoclassic French and Spanish Theatre
  Lope de Vega: *Fuenteovejuna*
  Corneille: *Le Cid*
  Racine: *Phèdre*
  Moliere: *Tartuffe; The School for Wives*

c. 1660–c. 1800
English Restoration and Jacobean Theatre
  Congreve: *The Way of the World; Love for Love*
  Cibber: *Love's Last Shift*
  Sheridan: *The School for Scandal*
French Comedy
  Beaumarchais: *The Marriage of Figaro*
Early American Theatre
  Tyler: *The Contrast*

c. 1800–c. 1875
Alexandre Dumas *fils*: *La Dame aux Camélias*
Boucicault: *The Octoroon*

c. 1875–c. 1920
Ibsen: *Ghosts; Peer Gynt*
Shaw: *Pygmalion; St. Joan*
Chekhov: *The Sea Gull*
Gorki: *The Lower Depths*

c. 1920–
O'Neill: *Ah Wilderness!; Desire Under the Elms*

Miller: *After the Fall*
Williams: *The Glass Menagerie; A Streetcar Named Desire*
Giraudoux: *Amphitryon '38*
Brecht: *The Threepenny Opera; The Good Woman of Setzuan*

Pinter: *The Homecoming*
Shaffer: *The Royal Hunt of the Sun*
Ionesco: *The Chairs*
Beckett: *Waiting for Godot*
Albee: *Who's Afraid of Virginia Woolf?*
Innaurato: *Gemini*

Chapter 7

FILM*

It is only within the last decade that the film has become accepted as a legitimate form of art and that serious and responsible critics and scholars have begun to examine the component parts of film and how they interact with the general form of the film to create both form and style. Of the forms of art considered in this volume, the film is the most familiar and the most easily accessible; it is usually accepted almost without conscious thought, at least in terms of the story line or the star image presented or the basic entertainment value of the product. Yet all these elements are carefully crafted out of editing techniques, camera usage, juxtaposition of image, and structural rhythms—among others. It is these details of cinematic construction that can enhance the viewing of a film

---

*The text for this chapter was prepared by M. Ellis Grove. I have edited and expanded where necessary to conform to the rest of the text.

and can raise the film from mere entertainment into the realm of serious art. Bernard Shaw once observed that "details are important; they make comments." The perception of the details of the film is not as easy as it might seem, since at the same time serious students are searching them out the entertainment elements of the film are drawing their attention away from the search. Because of these entertainment elements and the inundation of our society with film, the serious perception of the art of the film is not an easy one, but time and a conscious effort can reward the student with insights that are not those of the casual film viewer.

WHAT IS IT?

Film is the design of time and of three-dimensional space compressed into a two-dimensional image. Of all the arts discussed in this volume, film is the only one that also is an invention. Once the principles of photography had evolved and the mechanics of recording and projecting cinematic images were understood, society was ready for the production of pictures that could move, be presented in color, and eventually talk.

If you examine a strip of film, you will notice that it is only a series of pictures arranged in order the length of the strip. Each of these pictures, or *frames,* is about four fifths of an inch wide and three fifths of an inch high. If you study the frames in relation to one another, you will see that even though each frame may seem to show exactly the same scene the position of the objects in the separate frames are slightly different. When this film, which contains sixteen frames per foot of film, is run on a projecting device and passed before a light source at the rate of twenty-four frames per second (sixteen to eighteen frames per second for silent films), the frames printed on it are enlarged through the use of a magnifying lens, are projected on a screen, and appear to show movement. However, the motion picture, as film is popularly called, does not really move but only seems to. This is due to an optical phenomenon called *persistence of vision,* which according to legend was discovered by the astronomer Ptolemy sometime around the second century. The theory behind persistence of vision is that it takes the eye a fraction of a second to record an impression of an image and send it to the brain. Once the impression is received, the eye retains it on the retina for about one tenth of a second after the actual image has disappeared. The film projector has built into it a device that pulls the film between the light source and a lens in a stop-and-go fashion, the film pausing long enough at each frame to let the eye take in the picture. Then a shutter on the projector closes, the retina retains the image, and the projection mechanism pulls the film ahead to the next frame. Holes, or *perfora-*

tions, along the right-hand side of the filmstrip enable the teeth on the gear of the driving mechanism to grasp the film and not only move it along frame by frame but also hold it steady in the gate or slot between the light source and the magnifying lens. It is this stop-and-go motion that gives the impression of continuous movement; if the film did not pause at each frame, the eye would receive only a blurred image.

The motion picture was originally invented as a device for recording and depicting motion. But once this goal was realized, it was quickly discovered that this machine could also record and present stories—in particular, stories that made use of the unique qualities of the medium of film.

Our formal response to film recognizes three basic techniques of presentation. These are narrative film, documentary film, and absolute film.

Narrative Film.   The narrative film is one that tells a story; in many ways it uses the techniques of theatre. The narrative film follows the rules of literary construction in that it begins with expository material, adds levels of complications, builds to a climax, and ends with a resolution of all the plot elements. As in theatre, the personages in the story are portrayed by professional actors under the guidance of a director; the action of the plot takes place within a *mise en scène* that is designed and constructed primarily for the action of the story but that also allows the camera to move freely in photographing the action. Many narrative films are genre films, constructed out of familiar literary styles—the western, the detective story, and the horror story, among others. In these films the story elements are so familiar to the audience that it usually knows the outcome of the plot before it begins. The final showdown between the "good guy" and the "bad guy," the destruction of a city by an unstoppable monster, and the identification of the murderer by the detective are all familiar plot elements that have become clichés or stereotypes within the genre; their use fulfills audience expectations. Film versions of popular novels, and stories written especially for the medium of the screen, are also part of the narrative-film form, but since film is a major part of the mass-entertainment industry the narrative presented is usually material that will attract a large audience and thus assure a profit.

Documentary Film.   Documentary film is an attempt to record actuality using primarily either a sociological or journalistic approach. It is normally not reenacted by professional actors, and often is shot as the event is occurring, at the time and place of its occurrence. The film may use a narrative structure, and some of the events may be ordered or compressed for dramatic reasons, but its presentation gives the illusion of reality. The footage shown on the evening television news, television programing concerned with current events or problems, and full coverage either by television or film companies of a worldwide event, such as the Olympics, are all kinds of documentary film. All convey a sense of reality as well as a recording of time and place.

Absolute Film.   Absolute film is to narrative film as absolute music is to program music. It is simply film that exists for its own sake, for its record of movement or form. It does not use narrative techniques—although documentary techniques can be used in some instances. Created neither in the camera nor on location, absolute film is built carefully, piece by piece, on the editing table or through special effects and multiple-printing techniques. It tells no story but exists solely as movement or form. Absolute film is rarely longer than twelve minutes (one reel) in length, and it usually is not created for commercial intent but is meant only as an artistic experience. Narrative or documentary films may contain sections that can be labeled absolute, and these sections can be studied either in or out of the context of the whole film.

HOW IS IT PUT TOGETHER?

Magnitude and Convention

In addition to considering whether a film is narrative, documentary, or absolute, the student of film must also realize both the magnitude of the film and the film's use of certain conventions. In considering the magnitude of a film one must be aware of the means by which the film is to be communicated. In other words, was the film made for a television showing or for projection in a large film theater? Due to the size of the television receiver, large panoramas or full-scale action sequences are not entirely effective on the TV—they become too condensed. TV films, to be truly effective, should be built around the close-up and around concentrated action and movement, since the TV audience is closer to the image than the viewers in a large theater. Scenes of multiple images with complex patterns of movement or scenes of great violence will become confusing because of the intimacy of television, and will seem more explicit than they really are. On the other hand, when close shots of intimate details are enlarged through projection in a theatre they may appear ridiculous. The nuance of a slightly raised eyebrow that is so effective in the living room will appear either silly or overly dramatic when magnified on a sixty-foot screen. Today's moviemakers, when creating a film, must be aware of how it will appear if translated to the home screen or enlarged in a theater; their work ought to be designed to accommodate the size of either medium.

The film, as with theatre, has certain conventions or customs that the viewer accepts without hesitation. When an exciting chase scene takes place no one asks where the orchestra is that is playing the music that enhances the sequence; they merely accept the background music as part of the totality of the film. A film photographed in black and white is accepted as a recording of reality, even though the viewers know that the real world has color while this particular reel world does not. When a performer sings and dances in the rain in the middle of a city street no member of the audience worries if the orchestra is getting wet or wonders if the performer will be arrested for creating a public spectacle. The conventions of the musical film are equally acceptable to an audience conditioned to accept them.

This consideration of conventions is especially important to the acceptance of the silent film as a form of art. The silent film should not be thought of as a sound film without sound but as a separate entity with its own special conventions. These conventions revolve around the methods used to indicate sound and dialogue without actually using them. The exaggerated pantomime and acting styles, the use of titles, character stereotyping, and visual metaphors are all conventions that were accepted during the silent era but appear ludicrous today, due to changes in style and taste and improvements in the devices used for recording and projecting film. The action in the silent film was recorded and presented at a speed of sixteen to eighteen frames per second; when that action is presented today on a projector that operates at twenty-four frames per second the movement becomes too fast and appears to be jerky and disconnected. However, once you learn to accept these antiquated conventions, you may find that the silent film is an equally effective form of cinematic art.

Editing

Film is rarely recorded in the order of its final presentation; it is filmed in bits and pieces and put together, after all the photography is finished, as one makes a jigsaw puzzle or builds a house. The force or strength of the final product depends upon the editing process used, the manner in which the camera and the lighting are handled, and the movement of the actors before the camera. Naturally, the success of a film depends equally on the strength of the story presented and the ability of the writers, actors, directors, and technicians who have worked on the film. However, this level of success is based on the personal taste of the audience and the depth of perception of the individual, and therefore does not lie within the boundaries of this discussion.

Perhaps the greatest difference between film and the other arts discussed within this volume is the use of *plasticity,* the quality of film that enables it to be cut, spliced, and ordered according to the needs of the film and the desires of the filmmaker. If twenty people were presented with all the footage shot of a presidential inauguration and asked to make a film commemorating the event, you would probably see twenty completely different films; each filmmaker would order the event according to his or her own views and artistic ideas. The filmmaker must be able to synthesize a product out of many diverse elements. This concept of plasticity is, then, one of the major advantages of the use of the machine in consort with an art form.

It is the editing process, then, that creates or builds the film, and within that process are many ways of meaningfully joining shots and scenes to make a whole. Let's examine some of these basic techniques. The *cut* is simply the joining together of shots during the editing process. A *jump cut* is a cut that breaks the continuity of time by jumping forward from one part of the action to another part that obviously is separated from the first by an interval of time, location, or camera position. It is often used for shock effect or to call attention to a detail, as in commercial advertising on television. The *form cut* cuts from an image in a shot to a different object that has a similar shape or contour; it is used primarily to make a smoother transition from one shot to another. For example, in D. W. Griffith's silent film *Intolerance,* attackers are using a battering ram to smash in the gates of Babylon. The camera shows the circular frontal area of the ram as it is advanced towards the gate. The scene cuts to a view of a circular shield, which in the framing of the shot is placed in exactly the same position as the front view of the ram.

Montage can be considered the most aesthetic use of the cut in film. It is handled in two basic ways: first, as an indication of compression or elongation of time, and, second, as a rapid succession of images to illustrate an association of ideas. A series of stills from Leger's *Ballet Mechanique* (Fig. 7.1) illustrates how images are juxtaposed to create comparisons. For example, a couple goes out to spend an evening on the town, dining and dancing. The film then presents a rapid series of cuts of the pair—in a restaurant, then dancing, then driving to another spot, then drinking, and then more dancing. In this way the audience sees the couple's activities in an abridged manner. Elongation of time can be achieved in the same way. The second use of montage allows the filmmaker to depict complex ideas or draw a metaphor visually. Sergei Eisenstein, the Russian film director, presented a shot in one of his early films of a Russian army officer walking out of the room, his back to the camera and his hands crossed behind him. Eisenstein cuts immediately to a peacock strutting away from the camera and spreading its tail. These

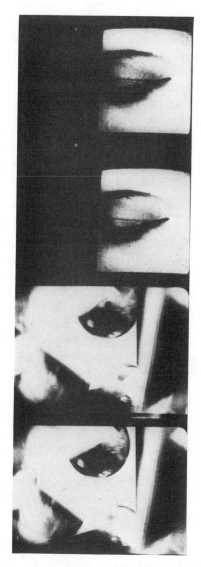

Fig. 7.1. *Ballet Mechanique* (1924). A film by Fernand Leger.

two images are juxtaposed, and the audience is allowed to make the association that the officer is as proud as a peacock.

Camera Viewpoint

Camera position and viewpoint are as important to the structure of film as is the editing process. How the camera is placed and moved can be of great value to filmmakers as an aid in explaining and elaborating upon their cinematic ideas. In the earliest days of the silent film the camera was merely set up in one basic position; the actors moved before it as if they were performing before an audience on a stage in a theater. However, watching an action from one position became dull, and the early filmmakers were forced to move the camera in order to add variety to the film.

The Shot.   The *shot* is what is recorded by the camera over a particular period of time, and is the basic unit of filmmaking. Several varieties are used. The *master shot* is a single shot of an entire piece of action, taken in order to facilitate the assembly of the component shots of which the scene will finally be composed. The *establishing shot* is a long shot introduced at the beginning of a scene to establish the interrelationship of details, a time, or a place, which will be elaborated upon in subsequent shots. The *long shot* is a shot taken with the camera a considerable distance from the subject. The *medium shot* is taken nearer to the subject. The *close-up* is a shot taken with the camera quite near the subject. A *two-shot* is a close-up of two persons with the camera as near as possible while keeping both subjects within the frame. A *bridging shot* is a shot inserted in the editing of a scene to cover a brief break in the continuity of the scene.

Objectivity.   An equally important variable of camera viewpoint is whether the scene is shot from an objective or subjective viewpoint. The *objective viewpoint* is that of an omnipotent viewer, roughly analogous to the technique of third-person narrative in literature. In this way filmmakers allow their audience to watch the action through the eyes of a universal spectator. However, filmmakers who wish to involve their audience more deeply in a scene may use the *subjective viewpoint:* the scene is presented as if the audience were actually participating in it, and the action is viewed from the filmmaker's perspective. This is analogous to the first-person narrative technique, and is usually found in the films of the more talented directors.

Cutting within the Frame

Cutting within the frame is a method used to avoid the editing process. It can be created by actor movement, camera movement, or a combination of the two. It allows the scene to progress more smoothly and is used most often on television. In a scene in John Ford's *Stagecoach* the coach and its passengers have just passed through hostile Indian territory without being attacked; the driver and his passengers all express relief. Ford cuts to a long shot of the coach moving across the desert and *pans,* or follows, it as it moves from right to left on the screen. This movement of the camera suddenly reveals in the foreground, and in close-up, the face of a hostile Indian watching the passage of the coach. In other words, the filmmaker has moved from a long shot to a close-up without the need of the editing process. He has also established a spatial relationship. The movement of the camera and the film is smooth and does not need a cut to complete the sequence. In a scene from *Jaws* (Fig. 7.2) the camera moves from the distant objects to the face in the foreground, finally including them both in the frame; the pan across the scene in so doing is accomplished without editing of the film.

Dissolves

During the printing of the film negative transitional devices can be worked into a

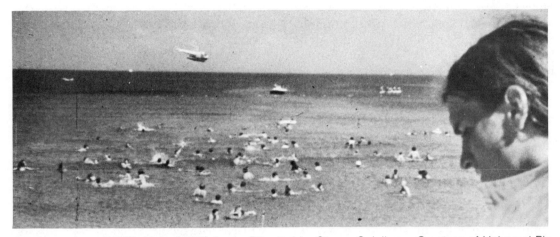

Fig. 7.2. *Jaws* (1975). Universal Pictures. Directed by Steven Spielberg. Courtesy of Universal Pictures.

scene. They are usually used to indicate the end of the scene and the beginning of another. The camera can cut or jump to the next scene, but the transition can be smoother if the scene fades out into black and the next scene fades in. This is called a *dissolve*. A *lap dissolve* occurs when the fade-out and the fade-in are done simultaneously and the scene momentarily overlaps. A *wipe* is a form of optical transition in which a line moves across the screen, eliminating one shot and revealing the next, much in the way a windshield wiper moves across the windshield of a car. In silent film the transition could also be created by closing or opening the aperture of the lens; this process is called an *iris-out* or an *iris-in*.

Movement

Camera movement also plays a part in film construction. The movement of the camera as well as its position can add variety or impact to a shot or a scene. Even the manner in which the lens is focused can add to the meaning of the scene. If the lens clearly shows both near and distant objects at the same time, the camera is using *depth of focus*. In Fig. 7.2 foreground and background are equally in focus. In this way actors can move in the scene without necessitating a change of camera position. Many TV shows photographed before an audience usually use this kind of focus. If the main object of interest is photographed clearly while the remainder of the scene is blurred or out of focus, the camera is using *rack* or *differential focus*. With this technique the filmmaker can focus the audience's attention on one element within a shot.

There are many kinds of physical (as opposed to apparent) camera movement that can have a bearing upon a scene. The *track* is a shot taken as the camera is moving in the same direction, at the same speed, and in the same place as the object being photographed. A *pan* is taken by rotating the camera horizontally while keeping it fixed vertically. The pan is usually used in enclosed areas, particularly TV studios. The *tilt* is a shot taken while moving the camera vertically or diagonally; it is used to add variety to a sequence. A *dolly shot* is taken by moving the camera towards or away from the subject. Modern sophisticated lenses can accomplish the same movement by changing the focal length. This negates the need for camera movement, and is known as a *zoom shot.*

Of course, the camera cannot photograph a scene without light, either natural or artificial. Most television productions photographed before a live audience require a flat, general illumination pattern. For close-ups stronger and more definitely focused lights are required in order to highlight the features, eliminate shadows, and add a feeling of depth to the shot. Cast shadows or atmospheric lighting (in art, *chiaroscuro*) is often used to create a mood, particularly in films made without the use of color. Lighting at a particular angle can heighten the feeling of texture, just as an extremely close shot can. These techniques add more visual variety to a sequence.

If natural or outdoor lighting is used and the camera is hand-held, an unsteadiness in movement is found in the resulting film; this technique and effect is called *cinema verité.* This kind of camera work, along with natural lighting, is found more often in documentary films or in sequences photographed for newsreels or television news programing. It is one of the conventions of current-events reporting, and adds to the sense of reality necessary for this kind of film recording.

These techniques and many others are all used by filmmakers to ease some of the technical problems in making a film. They can be used to make the film smoother or more static, depending upon the needs of the story line, or to add an element of commentary to the film. One school of cinematic thought believes that camera technique is best when it is not noticeable; another, more recent way of thinking believes that the obviousness of all the technical aspects of film adds meaning to the concept of cinema. In any case, camera technique is present in every kind of film made, and is used to add variety and commentary, meaning and method, to the shot, the scene, and the film.

HOW DOES IT STIMULATE THE SENSES?

The basic aim of film, as with any art, is to involve its audience in its product, either emotionally or intellectually. Of course, there is nothing like a good plot with well-written dialogue delivered by trained actors to create audience interest. But there are other ways in which filmmakers may enhance their final product, techniques that manipulate the audience toward a deeper involvement or a heightened intellectual response. Figure 7.3 illustrates how angles and shadows within a frame help create a feeling of excitement and variety. An in-depth study of the films of Fellini, Hitchcock, or Bergman may indicate how directors can use some of the technical aspects of film to underline emotions or strengthen a mood or an idea in their films.

It is in the area of technical detail that perception is most important for students of the film. They should begin to cultivate the habit of noticing even the tiniest details in a scene, for often these details may add a commentary that an average member of the audience may miss. For example, in Hitchcock's *Psycho,* when the caretaker of the motel (Tony Perkins) wishes to spy upon the guests in cabin 1 he pushes aside a picture that hides a peephole. The picture is a reproduction of *The Rape of the Sabine Women.* Hitchcock's irony is obvious. Thus, perception becomes the method through which viewers of film may find its deeper meanings as well as its basic styles.

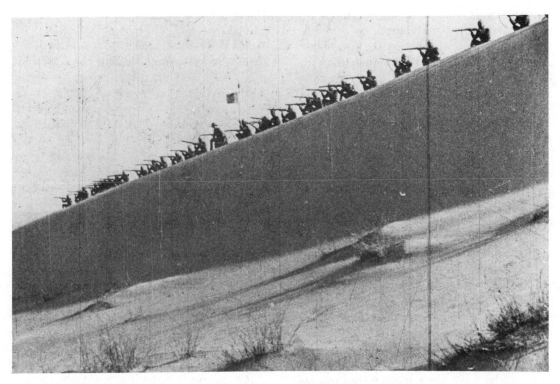

Fig. 7.3.   Still from an unidentified silent film.

Crosscutting

There are many techniques that filmmakers can use to heighten the feeling they desire for their film to convey. The most familiar and most easily identified is that of *crosscutting*. Crosscutting is an alternation between two separate actions that are related by theme, mood, or plot but are usually occurring within the same period of time. Its most common function is to create suspense. Consider this familiar cliché. Pioneers going west in a wagon train are beseiged by Indians. The settlers have been able to hold them off, but ammunition is running low. The hero has been able to find a cavalry troop, and they are riding to the rescue. The film alternates between views of the pioneers fighting for

their lives and shots of the soldiers galloping to the rescue. The film continues to cut back and forth, the pace of cutting increasing until the sequence builds to a climax—the cavalry arriving in time to save the wagon train. The famous chase scene in *The French Connection,* the final sequences in *Wait Until Dark,* and the sequences of the girl entering the fruit cellar in *Psycho* are built for suspense through techniques of crosscutting.

A more subtle use of crosscutting, *parallel development,* occurs in *The Godfather, Part I.* At the close of that film Michael Corleone is acting as godfather for his sister's son; at the same time his men are destroying all his enemies. The film alternates between views of Michael at the religious service and sequences showing violent death. This parallel construction is used to draw an ironic comparison; actions are juxtaposed. By developing the two separate actions the filmmaker allowed the audience to draw their own inferences and thereby added a deeper meaning to the film.

Tension Build-up and Release

If the plot of a film is believable, the actors competent, and the director and film editor talented and knowledgeable, a feeling of tension will be built up. If this tension becomes too great, the audience will seek some sort of release, and an odd-sounding laugh, a sudden noise, or a loud comment from a member of the audience may cause the rest of the viewers to laugh, thus breaking the tension and in a sense destroying the atmosphere so carefully created. Wise filmmakers therefore build into their film a *tension release* that deliberately draws laughter from the audience, but at a place in the film where they wish them to laugh. This tension release can be a comical way of moving, a gurgle as a car sinks into a swamp, or merely a comic line. It does not have to be too obvious, but it should be present in some manner. After a suspenseful sequence the audience needs to be relaxed; once the tension release does its job, the audience can be drawn into another suspenseful or exciting situation.

Sometimes, in order to shock the audience or maintain their attention, a filmmaker may break a deliberately created pattern or a convention of film. In *Jaws,* for example, each time the shark is about to appear a four-note musical *motif* is played. The audience thereby grow to believe that they will hear this warning before each appearance, and so they relax. However, toward the end of the film the shark suddenly appears without benefit of the motif, shocking the audience. From that point until the end of the film they can no longer relax, and their full attention is directed to it.

Direct Address

Another method used to draw attention is that of *direct address*. It is a convention in most films that the actors rarely look at or talk directly to the audience. However, in *Tom Jones,* while Tom and his landlady are arguing over money Tom suddenly turns directly to the audience and says, "You saw her take the money." The audience's attention is focused on the screen more strongly than ever after that. This technique has been effectively adapted by television for use in commercial messages. For example, a congenial person looks at the camera (and you) with evident interest and asks if you are feeling tired, run-down, and sluggish. He assumes you are and proceeds to suggest a remedy. In a sense, the aside of nineteenth-century melodrama and the soliloquy of Shakespeare were also ways of directly addressing an audience and drawing them into the performance.

Of course, silent films could not use this type of direct address to the audience; they had only the device of titles. However, some of the silent comedians felt that they should have direct contact with their audience, and so they developed *a camera look* as a form of direct address. After an especially destructive moment in his films Buster Keaton would look directly at the camera, his face immobile, and stare at the audience. When Charlie Chaplin achieved an adroit escape from catastrophe he might turn toward the camera and wink. Stan Laurel would look at the camera and gesture helplessly (Fig. 7.4), as if to say "How did all this happen?" Oliver Hardy, after falling into an open manhole, would register disgust directly to the camera and the audience. These were all ways of commenting to the audience and letting them know that the comedians knew they were there. Some sound comedies adapted this technique. In the "road" pic-

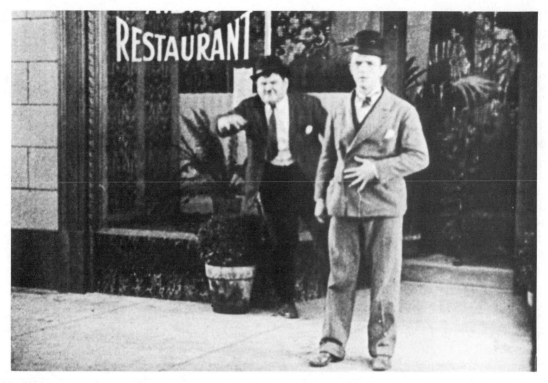

Fig. 7.4. *Your Darn Tootin'* (1928). A Hal Roach Production for Pathe Films. Directed by Edgar Kennedy.

tures of Bob Hope and Bing Crosby both stars, as well as camels, bears, fish, and anyone else who happened to be around, would comment on the film or the action directly to the audience. However, this style may have been equally based on the audience's familiarity with radio programs, in which the performer usually spoke directly to the home audience.

Structural Rhythm

Much of the effectiveness of a film relies on its success as a form as well as a style. By that I mean that filmmakers create rhythms and patterns that are based on the way they choose to tell their stories or that indicate deeper meanings and relationships. The *structural rhythm* of a film is the manner in which the various shots are joined together and juxtaposed with other cinematic images, both visual and aural.

Symbolic images in film range from the very obvious to the extremely subtle, but they are all useful to filmmakers in directing the attention of the audience to the ideas inherent in the philosophical approach underlying the film. This use of symbolic elements can be found in such clichés as the hero dressed in white and the villain dressed in black, in the more subtle use of water images in Fellini's *La Dolce Vita,* or even in the presence of an X whenever someone is about to be killed in *Scarface.*

Sometimes, symbolic references can be enhanced by form cutting—for example, cutting directly from the hero's gun to the villain's gun. Or the filmmaker may choose to repeat a familiar image in varying forms, using it as a composer would use a motif in music. Hitchcock's shower sequence in *Psycho* is built around circular images: the shower head, the circular drain in the tub, the mouth open and screaming, and the iris of the unseeing eye. In *Fort Apache* John Ford uses clouds of dust as a curtain to cover major events; the dust is also used to indicate the ultimate fate of the cavalry troop. Grass, cloud shapes, windblown trees, and patches of color have all been used symbolically and as motifs. Once they perceive such elements, serious students of film will find the deeper meanings of a film more evident and their appreciation of the film heightened.

Another part of structural rhythm is the repetition of certain visual patterns throughout a film. A circular image positioned against a rectangular one, a movement from right to left, an action repeated regularly throughout a sequence—all can become observable patterns or even thematic statements. The silent film made extreme use of thematic repetition. In *Intolerance* D. W. Griffith develops four similar stories simultaneously and continually crosscuts between them. This particular use of form enabled him to develop the idea of the similarity of intolerance throughout the ages. In their silent films Laurel and Hardy often built up a pattern of "you do this to me and I'll do that to you"; they called it "tit for tat." Their audience would be lulled into expecting this pattern, but at that point the film would present a variation on the familiar theme (a process quite similar to the use of *theme and variation* in musical composition). The unexpected breaking of the pattern would surprise the audience into laughter.

Parallel development, discussed earlier, can also be used to create form and pattern throughout a film. For example, Edwin S. Porter's *The Kleptomaniac* alternates between two stories: a wealthy woman caught shoplifting a piece of jewelry, and a poor woman who steals a loaf of bread. Each sequence alternately shows crime, arrest, and punishment; the wealthy woman's husband bribes the judge to let her off, while the poor woman is sent to jail. Porter's final shot shows the statue of justice holding her scales, one weighted down with a bag of gold. Her blindfold is raised over one eye, which is looking at the money. In this case, as in others, the form is the film.

When sound films became practicable filmmakers found many ways of using the audio track, in addition to just recording dialogue. The track could be used as symbolism, as a motif that reinforced the emotional quality of a scene, or for stronger emphasis or structural rhythm.

Some filmmakers believe that a more realistic feeling can be created if the film is cut rather than dissolved. They feel that cutting abruptly from scene to scene gives the film a staccato rhythm that in turn augments the reality they hope to achieve. A dissolve, they think, creates a slower pace and tends to make the film *legato* and thus more romantic. If the abrupt cutting style is done to the beat of the sound track, a pulsating rhythm is created for the film sequence; this in turn is communicated to the audience and adds a sense of urgency to the scene. In Fred Zinneman's *High Noon* the sheriff is waiting for the noon train to arrive. The sequence is presented in *montage,* showing the townspeople, as well as the sheriff, waiting. The shot is changed every eight beats of the musical track. As the time approaches noon the shot is changed every four beats. Tension mounts. The feeling of rhythm is enhanced by shots of a clock's pendulum swinging to the beat of the sound track. Tension continues to build. The train's whistle sounds. There is a series of rapid cuts of faces turning and looking, but there is only silence on the sound track, which serves as a tension release. This last moment of the sequence is also used as transition between the music and silence. In other films the track may shift from music to natural sounds and back to the music again. Or a pattern may be created of natural sound, silence, and a musical track. All depends on the mood and attitude the filmmaker is trying to create. In Hitchcock's films music often is used as a tension release or an afterthought, as Hitchcock usually relies on the force of his visual elements to create structural rhythm.

Earlier in this chapter I mentioned the use of motif in *Jaws*. Many films make use of an audio motif to introduce visual elements or convey meaning symbolically. Walt Disney, particularly in his pre-1940 cartoons, often uses his sound track in this manner. For example, Donald Duck is trying to catch a pesky fly, but the fly always manages to elude him. In desperation Donald sprays the fly with an insecticide. The fly coughs and falls to the ground. But on the sound track we hear an airplane motor coughing and sputtering and finally diving to the ground and crashing. In juxtaposing these different visual and audio elements, Disney is using his track symbolically.

John Ford often underlines sentimental moments in his films by accompanying the dialogue of a sequence with traditional melodies; As the sequence comes to a close the music swells and then fades away to match the fading out of the scene. In *The Grapes of Wrath,* when Tom Joad says good-bye to his mother "Red River Valley" is played on a concertina; as Tom walks over the hill the music becomes louder, and when he disappears from view it fades out. Throughout this film, this familiar folk song serves as a thematic reference to the Joad's home in Oklahoma and also boosts the audience's feelings of nostalgia. In *She Wore a Yellow Ribbon* the title of the film is underlined by the song of the same name, but through the use of different tempos and timbres the mood of the song is changed each time it is used. As the cavalry troop rides out of the fort the song is played in a strong 4/4 meter with a heavy emphasis on the brass; the sequence is also cut to the beat of the track. In the graveyard sequences the same tune is played by strings and reeds in 2/4 time and in a much slower tempo, which makes the song melancholy and sentimental. In the climactic fight sequence in *The Quiet Man* John Ford cuts to the beat of a spritely Irish jig, which enriches the comic elements of the scene and plays down the violence.

Our discussion in these last few paragraphs only touches the surface of the techniques and uses of sound in film; of course, there are other ways of using sound and the other elements discussed thus far. But part of the challenge of the film as an art form is the discovery by the viewer of the varying uses to which film technique can be put, and this in turn enhances further perceptions.

Film is basically a visual art; the pictures tell the story. How these pictures are recorded, arranged, and enhanced can raise the mechanical, commercial movie form into a work of art. Full response to that art demands an informed and knowledgeable audience. Perception or visual literacy is the key to that audience.

CHRONOLOGY AND SELECTED EXAMPLES FOR STUDY IN CINEMATOGRAPHY

1889–1914: The Growth of the Machine; Cinematic Archaeology

1895 *Baby's Lunch.* Lumiere Brothers. France.
1902 *A Trip to the Moon.* George Malies. France.
1903 *The Great Train Robbery.* Edwin S. Porter. USA.
1905 *Rescued by Rover.* Cecil Hepworth. England.
1909 *A Corner in Wheat.* D. W. Griffith. USA.

1911 *The Lonedale Operator.* D. W. Griffith. USA.

1912 *Queen Elizabeth.* Louis Mercanton. France.
Starring Sarah Bernhardt.

1913 *Judith of Bethulia.* D. W. Griffith. USA.

1914 The Star system begins.
Tillie's Punctured Romance. Mack Sennett. USA.
Starring Charlie Chaplin.
The Birth of a Nation. D. W. Griffith. USA.

1915–1928: The Art of the Silent Film; The Growth of the Studio System

1916 *Intolerance.* D. W. Griffith. USA.

1917 *Easy Street.* Charlie Chaplin. USA.

1919 *The Cabinet of Dr. Caligari.* Robert Weine.
Germany. Expressionism.

1922 *Nanook of the North.* Robert Flaherty. USA.
Documentary.

1923 *Greed.* Eric Von Stroheim. USA. Naturalism.

1924 *The Last Laugh.* F. W. Murnau. Germany.
Impressionism.

1925 *Potemkin.* Sergei Eisenstein. USSR. Realism
and montage.
The Gold Rush. Charlie Chaplin. USA.

1927 *Ben Hur.* Fred Nible. MGM. USA.
The Jazz Singer. Alan Crosland. Warner Brothers.
USA. Starring Al Jolson.

1928 *The Lights of New York.* Bryan Foy. USA.
Steamboat Willie. Walt Disney. USA. Starring
Mickey Mouse.

1929–1953: The Sound Era; Television

1929 *Un Chien Andalou.* Luis Bunuel. France.
Surrealism.

1930 *Anna Christie.* Clarence Brown. MGM. USA.
Starring Greta Garbo.
Little Caesar. Mervyn LeRoy. Warner Brothers.
USA. Starring Edward G. Robinson.

1935 *The Thirty-Nine Steps.* Alfred Hitchcock.
England.
The Informer. John Ford. RKO. USA.

1936 *Night Mail.* John Grierson. England.
Documentary.

1937 *The River.* Pare Lorentz. USA. Documentary.

1939 *Gone with the Wind.* Victor Fleming.
MGM–Selznick. USA.

Stagecoach. John Ford. United Artists. USA.

1941 *Citizen Kane.* Orson Welles. RKO. USA.

1944 *Henry V.* Laurence Olivier. England.

1945 *House on 92nd Street.* Henry Hathaway.
Twentieth Century-Fox. USA. DocuDrama.
Open City. Roberto Rossellini. Italy. Neorealism.

1946 *Great Expectations.* David Lean. England.

1948 *The Bicycle Thief.* Vittorio De Sica. Italy.

1949 The emergence of television.

1952 3-D films; Cinerama begins.

1953 *The Robe.* Henry Koster. Twentieth
Century-Fox. USA. CinemaScope.
The Moon is Blue. Otto Preminger. United
Artists. USA. No production seal of approval.

**1956–   Foreign Influences; Independent
Studio Production**

1956 *The Seventh Seal.* Ingmar Bergman. Sweden.
Metaphysical allegory.

1957 *The Bridge on the River Kwai.* David Lean.
Columbia. USA.

1959 *The 400 Blows.* François Truffaut. France.
Auteurism.
Breathless. Jean-Luc Godard. France.
Room at the Top. Jack Clayton. England.

1960 *L'Avventura.* Michelanglo Antonioni. Italy.
Subjective realism.
Psycho. Alfred Hitchcock. Paramount. USA.

1963 *8½.* Federico Fellini. Italy. Abstraction.
Tom Jones. Tony Richardson. England.

1967 *Bonnie and Clyde.* Arthur Penn. USA. Warner
Brothers–Seven Arts.

1968 *2001.* Stanley Kubrick. MGM. USA.

1969 *M.A.S.H.* Robert Altman. Twentieth
Century-Fox. USA.

1972 *The Godfather, Part I.* Francis Ford Coppola.
USA. Paramount.

1975 *Jaws.* Steven Spielberg. USA. Universal.

1978 *Superman.* Richard Donner. Warner
Brothers. USA. The force of special effects.

1979 *All That Jazz.* Bob Fosse. Twentieth
Century-Fox–Columbia. USA. Biographical
surrealism.
Manhattan. Woody Allen. United Artists. USA.
The film is the man.

Chapter 8

DANCE

Dance is one of the most natural and universal of human activities. In virtually every culture, regardless of location or level of development, we find some form of dance. Dance appears to have sprung from humans' religious needs. For example, scholars are relatively sure that the theatre of ancient Greece developed out of that society's religious, tribal dance rituals. So, there can be no doubt that dance is part of human communication at its most fundamental level. We can see this expression even in little children, who, before they begin to paint, sing, or imitate, begin to dance.

Most of us at one time or another have participated in some form of dancing. Doubtless, we hardly believe that participation approximates art. However, we do have some understanding of what the term *dance* means. In addition, nearly every city or town, regardless of its size, seems to have a local dance studio or ballet teacher. However, if our exposure to high-quality dance

has been limited, we may feel that the art of dance is totally foreign to us. The quality of what we see has an effect on our desire to see more. So, unless we live in a city where quality dance is easily accessible, we are probably less enthusiastic about dance than about any other art form.

WHAT IS IT?

Dance is the design of time, sound, and two- and three-dimensional space. In general it takes one of three forms: ballet, modern dance, and folk dance.

Ballet. Ballet is considered classical or formal dance; it is rich in traditions and rests heavily upon a set of prescribed movements and actions, as we shall see. In general a ballet is a highly theatrical dance presentation consisting of solo dancers, duets, and choruses, or *corps de ballets.* According to

Anatole Chujoy in the *Dance Encyclopedia,* the basic principle in ballet is "the reduction of human gesture to bare essentials, heightened and developed into meaningful patterns."

Modern Dance.   Modern dance is a large and relatively indefinable category of dance. We call it modern although its roots are early in the twentieth century. It began as a revolt against the stylized and tradition-bound elements of the ballet. The basic principle of modern dance probably could be stated as an emphasis on natural and spontaneous or un-inhibited movement, in strong contrast with the conventionalized and specified movements of the ballet. Typical of modern dance are abstract ideas as well as emotions relating to the human condition. While there are narrative elements in many modern dances, there may be less emphasis on them than in traditional ballet. There also are differences in the use of the body, the use of the dance floor, and the interaction with the *mise en scène.*

Folk Dance.   Folk dance, like folk music, is that body of dances identified with, or stemming from, a particular ethnic or sociocultural group. It is similar to folk music in that we do not know the artist who developed it; there is no choreographer of record for folk dances. They began as a necessary or informative part of certain cultures, and their characteristics are stylistically identifiable with a given culture. They developed over a period of years, without benefit of authorship, passing from one generation to another. They have their prescribed movements, their prescribed rhythms, and their prescribed music and costume. At one time or another they may have become formalized—that is, committed to some form of record. But they are part of a heritage, and not the creative result of an artist or a group of interpretative artists, as is the case with the other forms of dance.

HOW IS IT PUT TOGETHER?

Dance is an art of time and space that utilizes many of the elements of the other arts. In the *mise en scène* and in the line and form of the human body it involves many of the compositional elements of pictures, sculpture, and theatre. Dance also relies heavily on the elements of music—whether or not music accompanies the dance presentation. However, the essential ingredient of dance is the human body and its varieties of expression. So, it is with the human body that we will begin our examination of how a dance work is put together.

Formalized Movement

The most obvious repository of formalized movement in dance is ballet. All movement in ballet is based upon five basic leg, foot, and arm positions. In the *first position* (Fig. 8.1) the dancer stands with weight equally

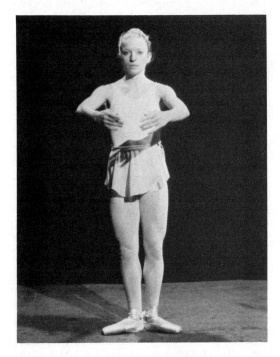

Fig. 8.1.   First position.

distributed between the feet, heels together, and toes open and out to the side. In ballet all movements evolve from this basic *open* position; the feet are never parallel to each other and both pointing straight forward. The *second position* (Fig. 8.2) is achieved by opening the first position the length of one's foot, again with the weight placed evenly on both feet. In the *third position* (Fig. 8.3) the heel of the front foot touches the instep of the back foot; the legs and feet must be well turned out. In the *fourth position* (Fig. 8.4) the heel of the front foot is opposite the toe of the back foot. The feet are parallel and separated by the length of the dancer's foot; again, the weight is placed evenly on both feet. The *fifth position* (Fig. 8.5) is the most frequently used of the basic ballet positions. The feet are close together with the front heel touching the toe of the back foot. The legs and the feet must be well turned out in order to achieve this position correctly, and the weight is

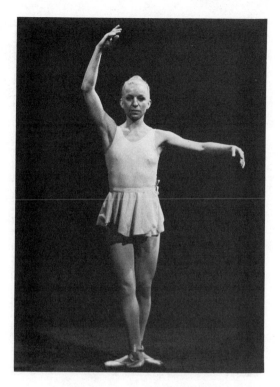

Fig. 8.3.   Third position.

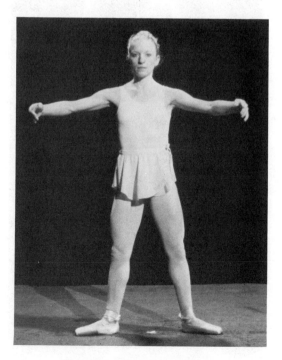

Fig. 8.2.   Second position.

placed evenly on both feet. As is clear from Figs. 8.1–8.5, each position changes the attitude of the arms as well as that of the legs and feet. From these five basic positions a series of fundamental movements and poses is developed; these are the core of every movement of the human body in formal ballet.

Some of the fundamental ballet poses and movements can be recognized throughout a dance work, including modern dance; a few lend themselves to photographic illustration. Figure 8.6 shows a *demi-plié* in first position. This half-bend of the knees can be executed in any position. The *grand plié* shown in Fig. 8.7, also in first position, carries the bend to its maximum degree. The *arabesque* is a pose executed on one foot with arms and foot extended. It can appear in a variety of positions; it is seen in Fig. 8.8 in the *penche,* or leaning position. The *port de bras* (Fig. 8.9) is

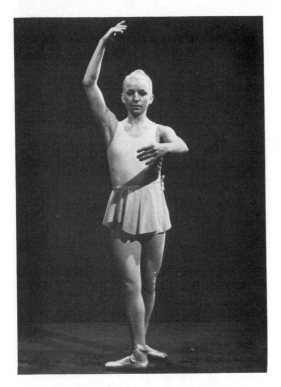

Fig. 8.4.   Fourth position.

that we see a limited number of movements and poses, turns and leaps, done over and over again. In this sense these bodily compositions form a kind of theme and variation, and they are interesting in that right alone.

In addition, it is possible for us to find a great deal of excitement in the bodily movements of formal ballet if for no other reason than the physical skills required for their execution. The standards of quality that are applied to a ballet dancer are based on the ability of the dancer to execute these movements properly. Just as in gymnastics or figure skating, the strength and grace of the individual in large part determines his or her qualitative achievement. It goes without saying, however, that ballet is far more than just a series of gymnastic exercises.

Perhaps the most familiar element of bal-

simply the technique of moving the arms correctly. As might be imagined, many variations can be made upon the five basic positions. For example, the *grande seconde* (Fig. 8.10) is a variation upon second position in which the leg is elevated to full height. The leg also is elevated in the *demi-hauteur,* or "half height" (Fig. 8.11). Full height requires extension of the leg at a 90-degree angle to the ground; half height requires a 45-degree extension. Movements carry the same potential for variety. For example, in the *ronds de jambe à têrre* (Fig. 8.12) the leg from the knee to and including the foot is rotated in a semicircle. Other basic movements (defined in the glossary) include the *assemblé, changement de pied, jeté, pirouette,* and *relevé.* As we develop expertise in perceiving dance it will become obvious to us in watching formal ballet (and to a lesser degree, modern dance)

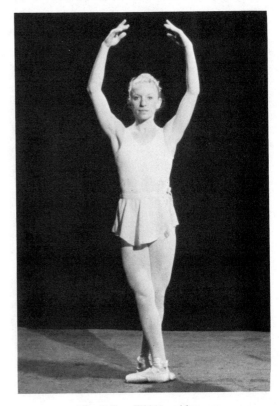

Fig. 8.5.   Fifth position.

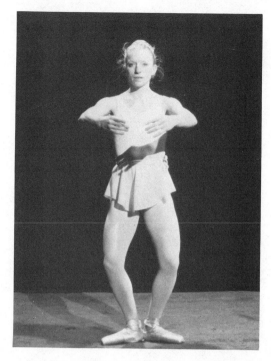

Fig. 8.6.   Demi-plié in first position.

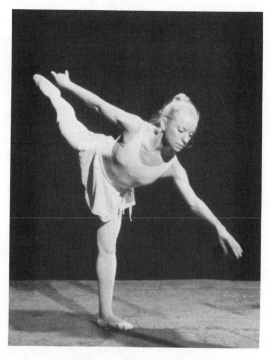

Fig. 8.8.   Arabesque (penche).

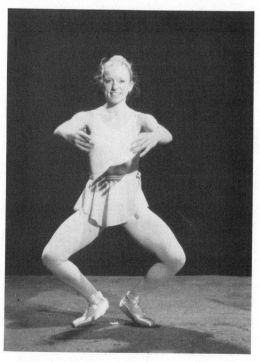

Fig. 8.7.   Grand plié in first position.

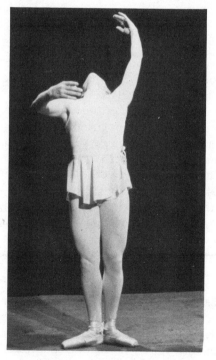

Fig. 8.9.   Port de bras.

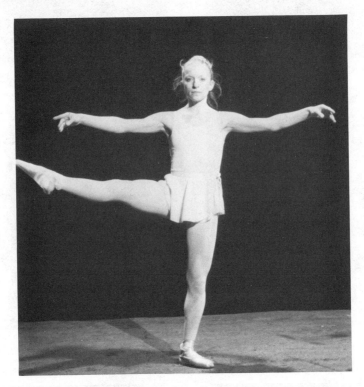

Fig. 8.10.   Grande seconde.

let is the female dancer's toe work or dancing *on point* (Fig. 8.13). A special kind of footgear is required for toe work (Fig. 8.14). Dancing on point is a fundamental part of the female dancer's development. It usually takes a minimum of two years of thorough training and development before a dancer can begin to do toe work. Certain kinds of turns are not possible without toeshoes and the technique for using them—for example, spinning on point or being spun by a partner.

We have focused on ballet in this discussion of formalized movement because it is the most familiar of the traditional, formalized dance forms. Ballet, however, is not alone in adhering to formalized patterns of movement. It is, in part, formalized movement that allows us to distinguish among folk and other dances, such as the *pavane,* the *galliard,* the *waltz,* and the *mambo.* All have formal or conventional patterns of movement. Perhaps only modern dance resists formal movement, and even then not completely.

Line, Form, and Repetition

The compositional elements of line, form, and repetition apply to the use of the human body in exactly the same sense that they apply to those elements in painting and sculpture—the latter especially. The body of the dancer can be analyzed as sculptural, three-dimensional form that reflects the use of line, even though the dancer is continually in motion. The body as a sculptural form moves from one pose to another, and if we were to take a stop-action movie of a dance

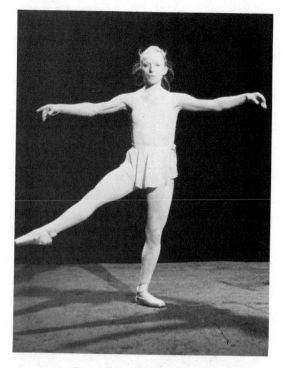

Fig. 8.11.   Demi-hauteur.

the individual dancer's body as well as combinations of dancers' bodies in duets, trios, or the entire corps de ballet (Figs. 8.15 and 8.16).

Mime

Within any dance form, modern dance included, there may be elements of bodily movement that we call *mime*. Bodily movement is *mimetic* whenever it suggests the kinds of movements we associate with people or animals. It is also mimetic if it employs any of the forms of conventional sign language, such as the Delsarte system. Of course, if there are narrative elements in the dance and the dancer actually portrays a character in the theatrical sense, there also may be mimetic action. Only when the movement of the dance is purely an emo-

we could analyze, frame by frame or second by second, the compositional qualities of the human body. The human form in every illustration in this chapter, including those that show groupings of dancers, can be analyzed as a composition of line and shape. Dance, therefore, can be seen at two levels: first, as a type of pictoral communication employing symbols that occur only for a moment; second, as the design of transition with movement between those moments.

Because the dancer moves through time, the concept of repetition becomes an important consideration in analyzing how a dance work is put together. The relationship of the movements to each other as the dance progresses from beginning to end shows us a repetitional pattern that is very similar to theme and variation in music. So, *choreographers* concern themselves with the use of

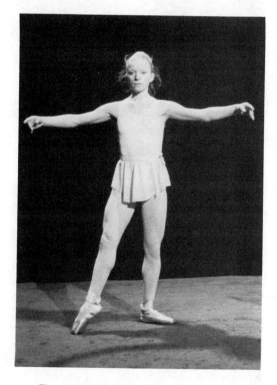

Fig. 8.12.   Ronds de jambe à têrre.

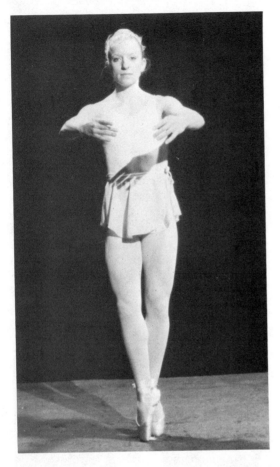

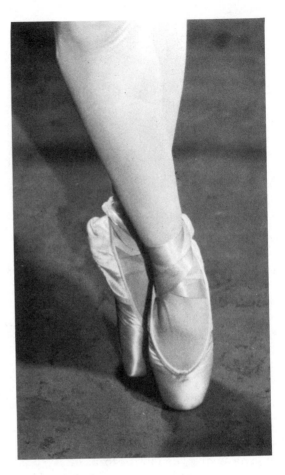

Fig. 8.13.   On point.

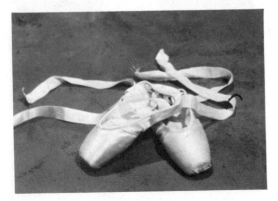

Fig. 8.14.   Toeshoes.

tional expression of the dancer can we say that it is free of mime.

Idea Content

Our consideration of the presence or absence of mime leads us to a consideration of how dance communicates its idea content. There are three general possibilities. First, the dance may contain *narrative* elements; that is, it may tell a story. Second, the dance may communicate through *abstract* ideas. There is a specific theme to be communicated in this case, but no story line. The ideas are abstract

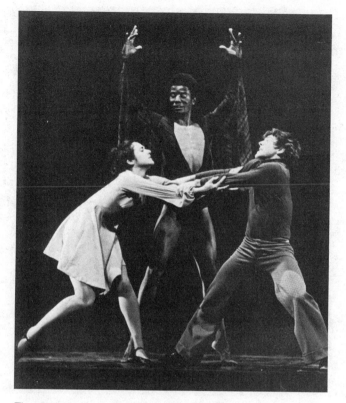

Fig. 8.15. *Nameless Hour.* Jazz Dance Theatre at Penn State. The Pennsylvania State University. *Choreographer:* Jean Sabatine. Photo by Roger Greenawalt.

and general and relate to some aspect of human emotion or the human condition. The third possibility is the absence of narrative or abstract communication. The work may be a *divertissement,* or diversion. In general, formal ballet usually has strong narrative elements. However, some ballets are divertissements. Ballet usually does not concern itself with abstract ideas. Modern dance, on the other hand, often concerns itself with abstract ideas; it may have narrative elements as well. Folk dances usually do not reflect abstract ideas, but may show characteristics of narrative or divertissement.

A final variable of idea content in dance is the presence or absence of *ethnic influence.* It is interesting to note how elements of dance reflect sociocultural background. Jazz dance, for example, may stimulate us to consider the black heritage in America. Other dances, though modern, may be based on dance forms that have roots in ancient cultures. The presence of narrative, abstract idea, divertissement, and/or ethnic influence and how they relate to the overall structure of dance are important considerations for us in analyzing and responding to dance.

Music

We associate music with dance as a matter of course. Most of the time music serves as a basis for the bodily movement of the work

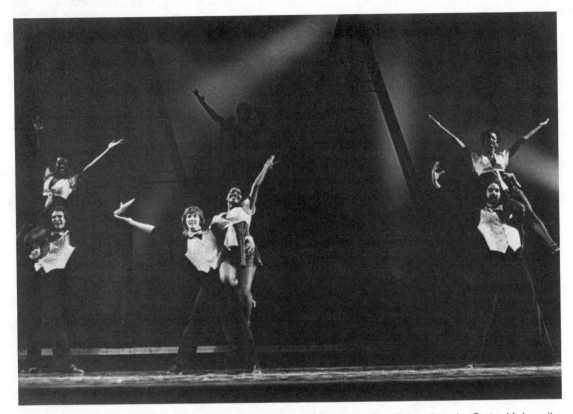

Fig. 8.16. *Family Tree.* Jazz Dance Theatre at Penn State. The Pennsylvania State University. *Choreographer:* Jean Sabatine. Photo by Roger Greenawalt.

we are perceiving, although it is not necessary for dance to be accompanied by music. However, it is impossible to have dance without one element of music—rhythm. Every action of the dancer's body has some relationship in time to every other movement, and those relationships establish rhythmical patterns that are musical regardless of the presence or absence of auditory stimuli.

When we hear music accompanying a dance we can respond to the relationship of the dance to the musical score. The most obvious relationship we will see and hear is the one between the gestures and footfalls of the dancer and the beat of the music. In some cases the two are in strict accord; the *beat-*

for-beat relationship is one to one. In other cases there may be virtually no perceivable beat-for-beat relationship between the dancer's movements and the accent or rhythmic patterns of the musical score.

Another relationship is that of the *dynamics* of the dance to those of the music. Of prime importance in this relationship is the intensity, or *force,* of the dance movement. Moments of great intensity in a dance can manifest themselves in rapid movement and forceful leaps. Or they may be reflected in other qualities. We must discern how the actual performance employs dynamics.

We can use the same kind of analysis in dance as we did in theatre in plotting dynamic levels and overall structure. For maximum interest there must be variety of intensity. So, if we chart the relationship of the peaks and valleys of dynamic levels, we are likely to conclude that the dynamic structure of a dance is quite similar to the dynamic structure of a play in that it tends to be pyramidal: it builds to a high point and then relaxes to a conclusion. This kind of analysis applies whether or not narrative elements are present.

Mise en Scène

Because dance is essentially a visual and theatrical experience, part of our analysis and response must be to those theatrical elements of dance that are manifested in the environment of the presentation. In other words, we can respond to the *mise en scène* of the dance (Fig. 8.16). We can note the elements of verisimilitude in the *mise en scène* and how those elements reflect or otherwise relate to the aural and visual elements of the dance. A principal consideration here is the interrelationship of the dance with properties, settings, and the floor of the theatrical environment. The dance may utilize *properties* in significant or insignificant ways. As for *settings,* some dances employ massive stage designs. Others have no setting at all; they are performed in a neutral environment. Again, part of our response is to the relationship of the elements of the setting to the rest of the dance.

The principal difference between formal ballet and modern dance lies in the use of the *dance floor.* In formal ballet the floor acts merely as an agent from which the dancer springs and to which the dancer returns. But in modern dance the floor assumes an integral role in the dance, and we are likely to see the dancers sitting on the floor, rolling on it—in short, *interacting with* the floor. So, consideration of the use of the floor in dance concerns not only whether or not it is employed as an integral part of a dance, but also

how that use of the floor relates to the idea content of the dance.

In discussing the relationship of *costume* to dance, we would do well to return to the section on costume design in Chapter 6 to note the purposes of costume, because those purposes apply to the dance in the same manner that they apply to a theatre production. In formal dance the costume is likely to be traditional, conventional, and neutral. There is little representation of the story line of a romantic ballet in the traditional tights and *tutu* of the female dancer (Fig. 8.17). However, in folk dance and modern dance (as well as in many compositions in formal ballet) we are likely to see costumes high in verisimilitude. Costumes may help portray character, locality, and other aspects of the dance (Figs. 8.15 and 8.16).

In addition, it is especially important that the costume allow the dancer to do whatever

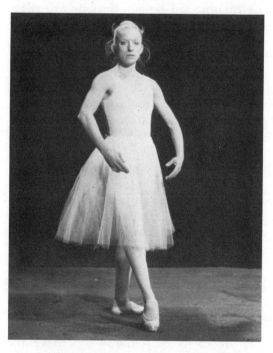

Fig. 8.17. Traditional tights and tutu.

it is that the choreographer expects him or her to do. In fact, costume may become an integral part of the dance itself. An extreme example of this is Martha Graham's *Lamentation,* in which a single dancer is costumed in what could best be described as a tube of fabric—no arms, no legs, just a large envelope of cloth. Every movement of the dancer stretches that cloth so that the line and form of the dancer is not the line and form of a human body but rather the line and form of a human body enveloped in a moving fabric.

The final element of the dance costume to be considered, and one of great significance, is footgear. Dancers' footgear ranges from the simple, soft, and supple ballet slipper to the very specialized toeshoe of formal ballet, with street shoes, character oxfords, and a variety of representational or symbolic footwear in between. In addition, modern dance often is done in bare feet. Of course, the fundamental requirements of footgear are comfort and enough flexibility to allow the dancer to do whatever he or she must do. Footgear, whether it be toeshoe, ballet slipper, character oxford, or bare feet, must be appropriate to the surface of the stage floor. Great care must be taken to insure that the dance floor is not too hard, too soft, too rough, too slippery, or too sticky. The floor is so important that many touring companies take their own floor with them to insure that they will be able to execute their movements properly. There have been cases in which professional dance companies refused to perform in local auditoriums because the floor was dangerous for the dancers.

Lighting

Inasmuch as the entire perception of a dance relies on perception of the human body as a three-dimensional form, the work of the lighting designer is of critical importance in the art of dance. How we perceive the human form in space depends on how that body is lit. Certainly our emotional and sense response is highly shaped by the nature of the lighting that plays on the dancer and the dance floor.

HOW DOES IT STIMULATE THE SENSES?

The complex properties of the dance make possible perhaps the most diverse and intense communicative stimuli of any of the arts. We noted earlier that opera is a synthesis of all of the arts. The dance, as well, integrates elements of all of the arts, and it does so in such a way as to communicate in a highly effective manner.

We noted previously that it is possible to respond at different levels to an artwork. To some extent we can respond even at a level of total ignorance. In many ways artworks are like onions. If they lack quality we can call them rotten. But more important, and more seriously, an artwork, like an onion, has a series of skins. As we peel away one that is obvious to us, we reveal another and another and another, until we have gotten to the core of the thing. There will be levels of understanding, levels of meaning, levels of potential response for the uninitiated as well as the thoroughly sophisticated viewer. The more sophisticated a *balletomane* one becomes, the fuller one's understanding and response becomes.

Line and Form

Like every other artwork that exists in space, the dance appeals to our senses through the compositional qualities of line and form. These qualities exist not only in the human body but in the visual elements of the *mise en scène.* Essentially, horizontal line stimulates a sense of calm and repose. Vertical lines suggest grandure and elegance. Diagonal lines stimulate a feeling of action and movement (Fig. 8.16), and curved lines, grace. As we respond to a dance work we can note how the human body expresses line and form, not only when it is standing still but also when it moves through space. If we are alert and perceptive we will note not only how lines and forms are created, but also how they are repeated from dancer to dancer and from dancer to *mise en scène*.

Often, the kind of line created by the body or body characteristics of the dancer is a key to understanding the work of the choreographer. George Balanchine, for example, insists that his dancers be almost skin and bone; you will not see a corpulent or overly developed physique in his company. So, bodies themselves appeal to our senses, and choreographers capitalize on that appeal in their dance conceptions.

Dynamics

We noted in Chapter 5 that the beat of music is a fundamental appeal to our senses. Beat is the aspect of music that sets our toes tapping and our fingers drumming. Probably our basic response to a dance is to the dynamics expressed by the dancers and in the music. A dancer's use of vigorous and forceful action, high leaps, graceful turns, or extended pirouettes appeals directly to us, as does the tempo of the dance. Variety in dynamics— the louds and softs and the highs and lows of bodily intensity as well as musical sound—is the dancer's and choreographer's means of providing interest, just as it is the actor's, the director's, and the painter's.

Sign Language

The dancer, like the actor, can stimulate us directly because he or she is another human being and can employ many symbols of communication (Fig. 8.15). Most human communication requires us to learn a set of symbols, and, therefore, we can respond to the dance at this level only when we have mastered this language. There are systems of sign language, such as the Delsarte, in which the positions of the arms, the hands, and the head have meanings. Likewise, in our response to the hula dance, experts tell us, we ought not concentrate on the vigorous hip movements of the dancer but rather on the hand movements, each of which communicates an idea. But until we learn what each of these movements means, we cannot respond in any significant way. However, there is a set of universal body symbols to which all of us respond (so psychologists tell us), regardless of our level of familiarity or understanding. For example, a smile has the same meaning regardless of culture or language. The gesture of acceptance in which the arms are held outward with the palms up also has the same universal meaning. The universal symbol of rejection is the hands held in front of the body with the palms out as if to push away. When dancers employ universal symbols we respond to their appeal to our senses just as we would in normal conversation.

Color

Although the dancer uses facial and bodily expressions to communicate some aspect of the human condition, we do not receive as direct a message from them as we do from the words of the actor. So, to enhance the dancer's communication the costume, lighting, and set designers must strongly reinforce the mood of the dance through the *mise en scène* they create. The principal means of expression of mood is color. In dance lighting designers are free to work in much more obvious ways with color because they do not have to create patterns of light and shadow as high in verisimilitude as those of their counterparts in the theatre. As a result, they do not have to worry if the face of a dancer is red or blue or green, an attribute that would be disastrous in a play. So, we are apt to see much stronger, colorful, and more suggestive lighting in the dance than in theatre.

Colors will be more saturated, intensity will be much higher, and the qualities of the human body, as form, will be explored much more strongly by light from various directions. The same is true of costumes and settings. Because dancers obviously do not portray a role in a highly verisimilar way, their costume can be very communicative in an abstract way. On the other hand, scene designers must be careful to utilize color in such a way that the dancer receives the focus in the stage environment. In any but the smallest of stage spaces it is very easy for the human body to be overpowered by the elements of the *mise en scène* since it occupies much more space. So, scene designers, in contrast with lighting designers, must be careful to provide a background against which the dancer will stand out in contrast. Nevertheless, scene designers use color as forcefully as they can to help reinforce the overall mood of the dance.

The examples of how dance affects our senses that we have just noted are rudimentary ones. Perhaps more than any other art, dance causes us to ascend beyond our three cognitive questions—what is it? how is it put together? how does it affect the senses?—and dwell in that fourth level of meaningful response—what does it mean to me? Our emotional response to dance is the level of response to which dance appeals most significantly. Modern dance, with its emphasis on the human condition, directs its appeal especially to that fourth level of affective response. Nevertheless, our understanding of our cognitive responses helps us respond emotionally to what the choreographer and the dancers have set forth for us.

SELECTED EXAMPLES FOR STUDY IN DANCE

Dance Music
Stravinsky: *The Firebird; The Rite of Spring*
Copland: *Appalachian Spring*

Films
Ballet with Edward Villella (LCOA). Contains excerpts—*Pas de Deux, Giselle, Apollo,* and *Rubies*—choreographed by George Balanchine.
Dance: Anna Sokolow's "Rooms" (IU).
Dance: Echoes of Jazz (IU).
Dance: Four Pioneers (IU).
Dance: New York City Ballet (IU).
Dance: Robert Joffrey Ballet (IU).
Seraphic Dialogue (Martha Graham) (IU).
Martha Graham Dance Company (Parts 1, 2, and 3) (IU).

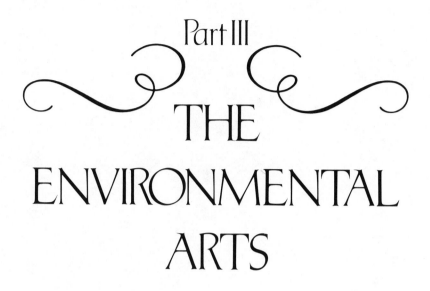

Part III

THE ENVIRONMENTAL ARTS

Landscape Architecture

Architecture

Chapter 9

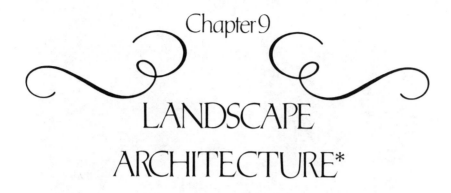

LANDSCAPE ARCHITECTURE*

WHAT IS IT?

Landscape architecture as an art and science is the design of three-dimensional outdoor space. Its purposes are to accommodate people's functions, improve their relationship with their man-made and natural environments, and enhance their pursuit of their activities. Typical landscape designs include streetscapes, malls, urban plazas, shopping centers, parks and playscapes, and residential, commercial, and industrial areas. The discipline, then, includes large and small spaces, rural, suburban, and urban spaces, and public as well as private areas. As a science and an art the design and planning process that takes place in landscape architecture manifests reasoned judgments as well as intuitive and creative interpretation.

---

*The text for this chapter was prepared by Donald Girouard. I have edited and arranged it to conform to the rest of the book.

The purpose and design structure of contemporary landscape design trace their roots to early history. The concept of private gardens arranged in formal geometric patterns appeared in early Egyptian times and found its way into classical Greek and Roman civilization. Eventually the Moorish influences in Spain resulted in a transition from rigid, confined spaces to designs that included views beyond the garden walls (Fig. 9.1). The Renaissance gardens of France and Italy continued the formal geometric and symmetrical arrangements.

The antithesis of formal landscape design can be traced to the early Chinese and Japanese gardens. The veneration of nature in these two cultures promoted the development of a very informal, natural landscape with emphasis on the use of the natural elements of ground form, stone, sand, plants, and water. The influence of this informal, natural setting was evident in a style of landscape design that evolved in England

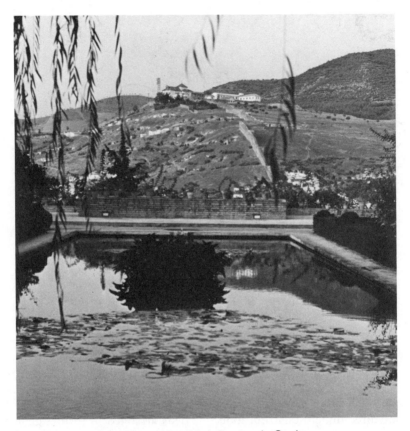

Fig. 9.1.   Moorish influence in Spain.

during the eighteenth century (Fig. 9.2). The style was one that exemplified asymmetrical arrangements and informality. The English parks designed in this style formed the basis for the concept of Central Park in New York City, designed in the 1850s by the father of landscape architecture in America, Frederick Law Olmsted, and his partner Calvert Vaux.

The twentieth century revolted against the *eclecticism* of preconceived symmetrical forms and patterns of design. The concept of functionalism—signified by the maxim "form follows function"—left its mark on present-day landscape design. In fact, contemporary landscape architecture reflects to some degree all of these influences.

What has evolved from this history is an art form that embraces the organization and arrangement of land and the spaces above it, including the natural and man-made physical elements that give form and character to the spaces on the land. The result is a three-dimensional pattern of elements and spaces that have functional and visual *harmony* and create meaningful experiences for the people using them.

HOW IS IT PUT TOGETHER?

Several factors link the landscape architecture of the past and present. These include *the function of the design, the people for whom the spaces are created,* and *the influences of the particular site and its surroundings.* In addition, the compositional elements of *unity, scale, time, space and mass, light and shade, and texture and color* persist in landscape architecture.

Space

The landscape designer assumes an intermediary role between an expressed need by a client and the eventual users of the space or spaces he or she creates. *Space,* then, is a basic medium of landscape design. It can take its form from the arrangement of living walls of plants, from concave or convex land forms, from structural walls of brick or concrete, or from buildings. The floor of the space and the overhead plane of sky or tree canopy form the other units of spatial definition.

Intent. An important aspect of space is its character, or quality. *Character* refers to the *intent* of the designer to create a landscape whose elements are harmonious and unified and support intended functions and experiences. For example, the spatial character of an area designed to support quiet park activities might use natural colors and textures, flowing land forms, indigenous plants, curving forms, lines and spaces, and soothing sounds. In addition, the *scale,* or size, of the elements and spaces, if appropriate to humans, may create a feeling of intimacy rather than of grandeur or monumentality.

Sequence. Another basic consideration in landscape design is *time and space,* or *sequence.* Sequence involves movement through space and from space to space. Designers can con-

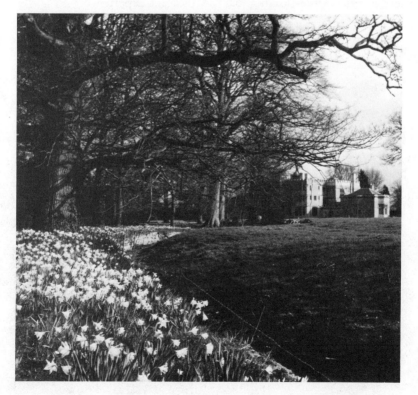

Fig. 9.2.   Informal design in eighteenth-century England.

trol a desired response by the way they organize this movement. Spaces can be connected in sequential movement up or down, from narrow to wide, from closed to open, from large to small, or in controlled random movement, depending upon the function and experiences desired.

Within a given space landscape designers can create light or dark spaces depending on the *density,* mass, texture, and color of the enclosing elements. In addition, they can induce sequential movement through space by contrasting dark with light, shade with sun, and so forth, in their design of spaces.

The Floor. In most landscape design the *floor* of the space becomes a basic organizational element. The floor contains the walks or roads that define movement, and the linear qualities of these arteries—free-flowing or rigid and straight—form the backbone of spatial function and our experience of the designed spaces.

The Design Process

The Client. The process of designing outdoor spaces can be thought of as including three phases. Phase one is the analysis of the client's program of functions to determine their interrelatedness and how they should be organized in a logical sequence. The design of a shopping area, for example, would consider the main entry drive leading to the parking area near the stores, an area close to the stores for pickup of passengers, a walk from the parking area to the stores, and so forth. The designer must consider the logic of the sequence as well as ensuring that the change from driver to pedestrian is a safe yet pleasant experience.

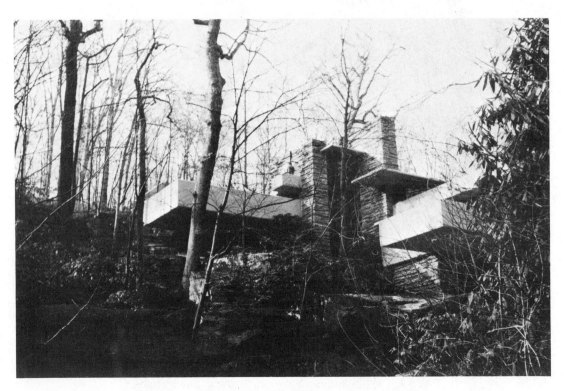

Fig. 9.3. *Falling Water. Architect:* Frank Lloyd Wright.

The Site.   Second, the site and its surroundings must be analyzed. This entails looking at the natural or man-made landscape and its existing character to determine if it is strong enough to manifest itself in the design character to be established. In the case of a rugged, mountainous area with craggy, steep slopes, angular forms, and heavy natural forests, the designer can complement these qualities with the form, materials, textures, and colors he or she uses in the design. On the other hand, the designer can use delicate curving forms, smooth textures, and vivid colors as a contrast with the natural backdrop, creating a foil that enhances both what exists and what is designed (Fig. 9.3). Other aspects of the site that the landscape designer must consider include views into and from the site; the climatic influences of sun and wind exposure to determine orienta-

tion; the topographic limitations or potentials of the site.

Synthesis.   Having analyzed these factors, the landscape architect *synthesizes* the functions with the site and produces the final three-dimensional form.

HOW DOES IT STIMULATE THE SENSES?

The analysis of how a landscape design is synthesized does not consist merely of an explanation of the factors we have mentioned. Landscape architecture is a space-time experience that includes people as participants. Therefore, readers must project themselves into space and time and become a participant in the spaces. The effects of land-

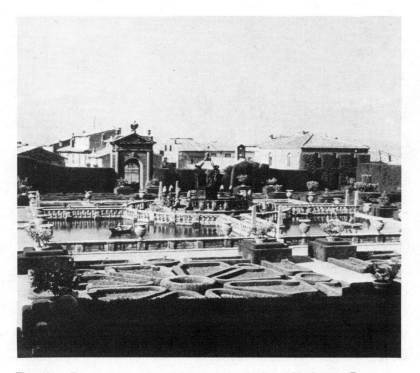

Fig. 9.4.   Formal symmetry in landscape design. Villa Lante, Rome. First level.

scape design on the senses can then become more meaningful and understandable.

Formality

Villa Lante, created in 1564 for a wealthy cardinal, is an excellent example of formal symmetrical design (Figs. 9.4–9.8). Set outside Rome, the villa served as a summering place where one could escape the heat of the city. It was sited on a hillside so that it could capture welcome breezes.

The designer's inheritance of the time was *formal composition,* an arrangement that tends to express and emphasize human will by announcing clear order and the relationship of parts in achieving unity and balance. The relationship of the design to the hillside is crisply delineated vertically and horizontally by dividing the hillside into four specific levels

that are separated twice by vertical walls and twice by clearly defined geometric shapes.

A single, dominant centerline forms the spine of the design, but almost without exception one cannot walk along it. Consequently, one views the central focal points on a diagonal, which yields far less awareness of the overall symmetry. In most cases the strongest organizational factor of landscape design is the path or road system that guides people through space.

The first level of the villa (Fig. 9.4), near a village, is monumental in scale and is well juxtaposed with the adjoining buildings in the composition. The gate and broad expanse of the floor of the space are conventions used to create the relationship of *scale* between humans and the space. The gate also creates a transition from the village to the

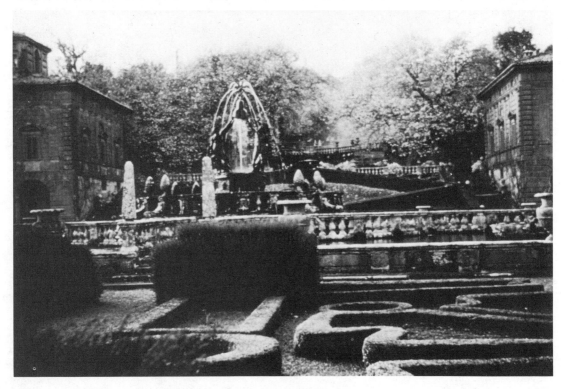

Fig. 9.5. Villa Lante.

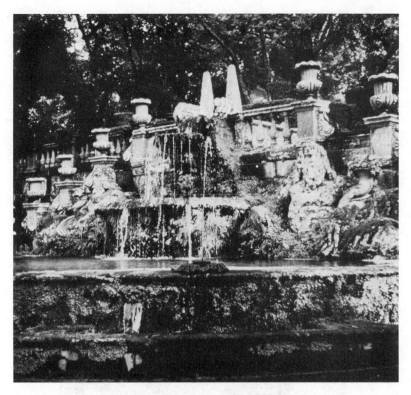

Fig. 9.6.   Villa Lante. Second level.

villa. The pool and fountain begin to set the theme of a summering place and to complement the red and green colors of the garden beds. The chromatic effects are subdued. The water becomes a definite link between the various levels of the design, and this repetition of an element also helps to create unity.

Looking in the other direction up the hill (Fig. 9.5), we find two twin structures tucked into the base of the slope. This architectural treatment creates a strong definition between the hillside and the level plane. In addition, it narrows the space to form an entry, which emphasizes movement up the hill. Sloping planes of lawn lead to the second level.

The second level (Fig. 9.6) has a fountain as a *focal point* along the centerline axis, and introduces sound as a part of the experience. In addition, the design incorporates an overhead canopy of trees to create a more intimate scale and to introduce a change from the light, open space below. Moving into and through the space, one becomes more aware of and comes in closer contact with the textural qualities of the materials of the design.

The third level (Fig. 9.7) is reached by a set of stairways, and again the convention of a focal area in the center of the space is used. The long basin gives added depth to the illusion of perspective. Space encloses more, water continues, space modulates in size and feeling between levels, and our attention is drawn upward.

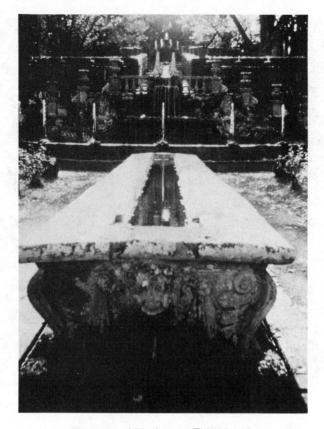

Fig. 9.7. Villa Lante. Third level.

Above this level is a sloping cascade of water that directs our attention to yet another focal point, which in turn leads to a backdrop in the wooded hillside (Fig. 9.8). This progression of space also must be viewed and experienced as one moves in the opposite direction, down to the open terrace below. The water, which begins in a natural grotto, eventually finds itself in the quiet basin below. The downward progression allows for looking down and across the town, and the spaces continually open up to reveal the countryside. This movement from beginning to end in landscape design is planned as such; it does not just happen.

Informality

Let's look now at a pleasure garden designed in the 1960s in Montreal, Canada (Figs. 9.9–9.12). The finished design was to be primarily a sensory experience. The design expresses *informality*. Focal points are introduced on an informal axis, a walkway, but not on any centerline of vision. They are casually dispersed, but controlled. Water, plants, and natural elements dominate the design. The scale is decidedly intimate: the designer puts us in close contact with the textures, sounds, and colors of nature.

The view in the illustration (Fig. 9.9) is

not seen as one enters the space of the design, but attention is drawn to this part of the garden by its sounds. The experience of this part of the garden sets the theme for what is to occur as one moves through the sequence. The plants introduce a play of shade and shadow, darks and lights, and all elements seem in harmony with one another.

Movement through the space changes gradually and at times the walls seem alive (Fig. 9.10). The axis of the design is informal and moves us at a casual pace. The walkway through the garden is designed at points to reinforce the slow pace and informality so as to encourage close union with the elements.

Plants are used as accents and masses throughout the composition. Openings focus attention or allow the eye to explore the effects that have been created (Fig. 9.11). Very little use of color is made; earth tones, grays, and greens dominate and unify the composition and our experience of it. The spatial qualities and the character of the design are easily perceived in its theme, and the cadence of movement supports the sensory experience.

The final point of focus is contained in a larger space with a major backdrop of greenery and architecture (Fig. 9.12). One could easily compare this part of the garden to a

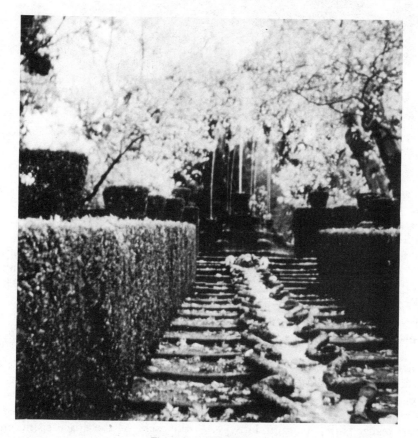

Fig. 9.8.   Villa Lante.

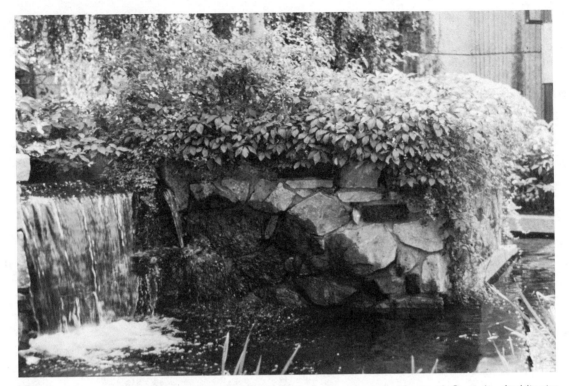

Fig. 9.9.   Informality in landscape design. Garden, Place Bonaventure, Montreal, Canada. *Architects:* Sasaki, Dawson, DeMay Associates.

painted landscape with foreground, middle ground, and background. Turning back in the sequence, one would find it hard to imagine this rooftop garden surrounded by hotel rooms and lobbies.

Composition

In both Villa Lante and the garden in Place Bonaventure, *focal points* are distributed along a sequence. Moreover, *spatial size* is varied in both designs, and there are similarities in the use of *materials*. The opening and closing of space, the use of overhead planes, shade and shadows, and darks and lights, and emphasis on contact with sound and texture are realized in each design. However, the garden exhibits no obvious order or pattern and is continuously intimate in scale,

whereas the villa contrasts monumentality with intimacy, for emphasis.

Function

The sculpture in Fig. 9.13 identifies a playground space designed in Washington, D.C. in the 1960s (Figs. 9.14–9.17). The client was a governmental body. The site was near an urban school. The goal was to provide for recreational needs of various age groups in a densely populated area where daily access to large, attractive state parks miles away is impossible. A playground at this site would provide facilities where they were needed and be accessible on a daily basis. The potential users of the space spent most of their recreational energy on sidewalks, in streets, and on vacant lots. Fulfilling a social function, therefore, was the major consideration in this design.

The urban setting, with its familiar rectangular forms and concrete, brick, wood, and steel materials, represented an existing environmental character that would give substance and form to the final design (Fig. 9.14). In order to meet the requirements of providing activities for various age groups on a small site, different levels were provided for different spaces; walks and steps serve as transitions between spaces (Fig. 9.15). The steps also function as places from which to observe the various activities. The older group can enjoy basketball, the younger group the play-apparatus area, and families or older groups picnics or seating under the shade of the roof. These uses are compatible with one another. Moreover, the spaces are close to one another so that a variety of experiences can be enjoyed, and are sequenced for easy movement from one to the next. The organization is decidedly informal: it reflects free movement and choice, in direct contrast with the walks and streets that govern most experiences in the city.

The use of *scale* in the design—that is, the use of spaces and objects appropriate to the size and age of the persons using them—creates *harmony* between the playground and its users (Fig. 9.16). Children can easily orient themselves to the spaces and objects. They are not awed by their size, but rather are invited to carry on their activities because

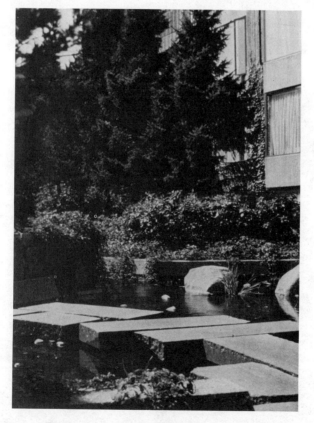

Fig. 9.10.   Garden, Place Bonaventure.

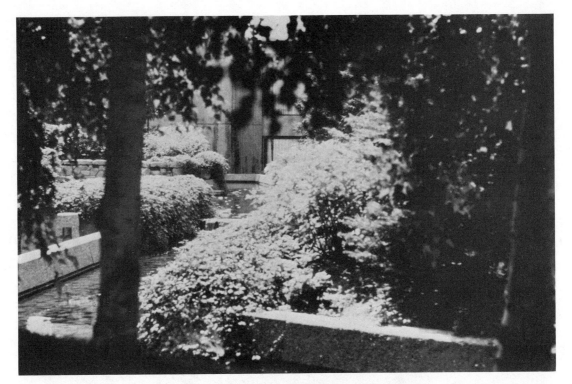

Fig. 9.11.　Garden, Place Bonaventure.

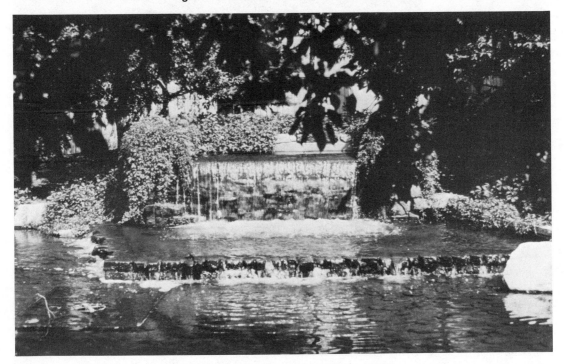

Fig. 9.12.　Garden, Place Bonaventure.

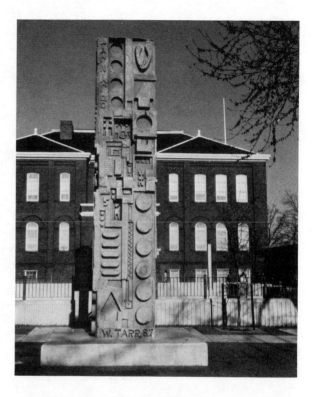

Fig. 9.13. Sculpture at site of playground illustrated in Figs. 9.14–9.17.

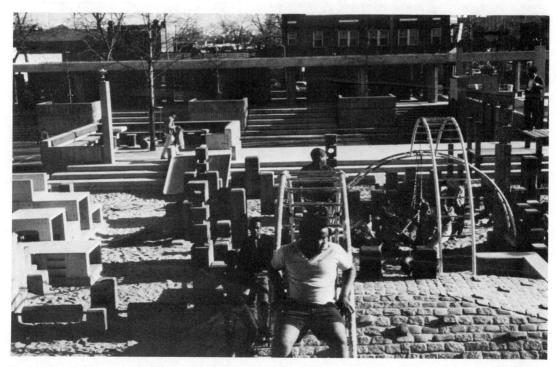

Fig. 9.14. Function in landscape design. Playground, Washington, D.C. *Designer:* M. Paul Friedberg.

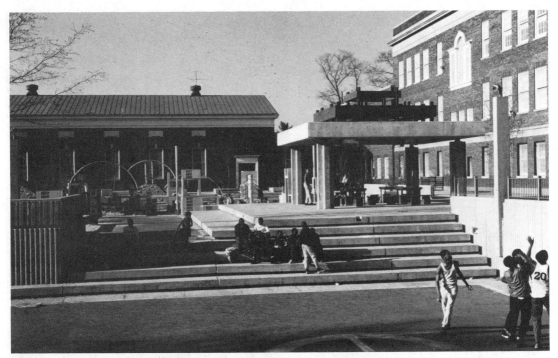

Fig. 9.15.   Playground, Washington, D.C.

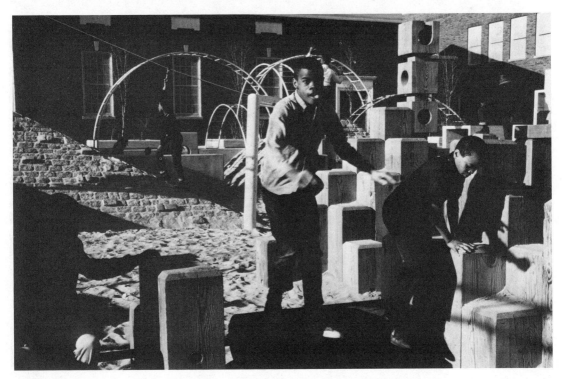

Fig. 9.16.   Playground, Washington, D.C.

the designer's use of scale adds to the experience of the space and enhances relationships among user, objects, and spaces.

One might characterize the design quality of the space in this playground as one of dynamic action (Fig. 9.17). The solid materials of stone, concrete, wood, and steel, the forms of varying height, the texture and colors, the play of horizontal, vertical, and angled lines and forms, the variety of enclosed and open space, the play of shade and shadows and of dark and light areas—all embody the designer's expression and composition, support human usage, and provide sensual pleasure.

SUMMARY

A landscape design comes from the analysis of the client's expressed needs, the users, the site, and its environment. Reason and intuition combine to create functional spaces and at the same time exhibit an artist's appreciation for the use of artistic elements to create not only unity and harmony among geometric forms but also functional and visual variety and interest. The result is a stimulation of a *predetermined response from the user*.

All the factors, then—space and time, people, functions and experiences, site and surroundings, plus the designer's sensitivity to creating appropriate design qualities—are interrelated. Landscape design is unique in that it can stimulate the senses only by the full participation of the "audience" in the use of its spaces. A person's reaction to the various stimuli in the landscape can encourage active or passive participation. The medium of space—the elements constituting its boundaries or existing within it—create the

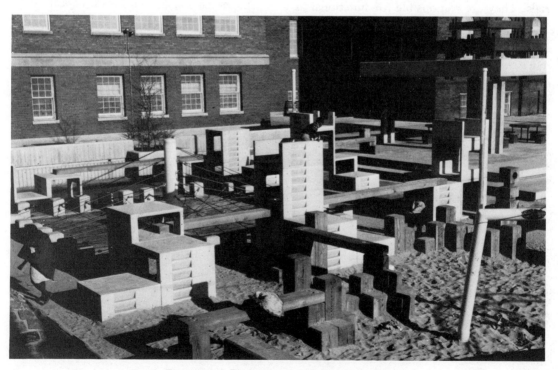

Fig. 9.17. Playground, Washington, D.C.

atmosphere for reaction. Large, open spaces can produce fright unless a scale suitable to humans is used. Dark, poorly lit, narrow spaces can cause one to hurry ahead to the relief of an area open to the sky. Active forms and bright colors can stimulate playful participation. Horizontal forms and planes, curving line and spaces, the dappled shade of a tree, the warmth of the sun, and quiet natural colors can combine to create a feeling of relaxation. Dynamic forms, bold colors, elements in motion, looping paths, the sounds of voices, music, and water, intersecting planes, and large and small spaces, apparently unorganized—all can stimulate the senses and create the setting for yet another type of experience.

Landscape designers usually try to stimulate a predetermined response by their organizational pattern, definition of form and spaces, uses of lines, textures, and scale, and choice of natural and/or man-made materials. They are responsible for functional as well as sensual qualities. However, the true test of landscape design rests with the people who use and experience the space.

SELECTED EXAMPLES FOR STUDY IN LANDSCAPE ARCHITECTURE

1000–1600
Alhambra and Generalife, Granada. c. 1240.
Villa Medici, Rome. c. 1540.
Villa D'Este, Tivoli. c. 1549.

1600–1800
Vaux-le-Vicomte, Melun, France. Le Nôtre. 1656.
Versailles, France. Le Nôtre. c. 1661–2.
Hampton Court, London. Christopher Wren. 1699.
Mount Vernon, Potomac River. 1743.
Villa Balbianello, Lake Como. c. 1785.

1800–1900
Birkenhead Park, near London. John Paxton. 1843.
Central Park, New York City. Frederick Law Olmsted and Calvert Vaux. 1868.

1900–
Mellon Square, Pittsburgh. Simonds and Simonds.
Constitution Plaza, Hartford. Sasaki, Dawson, DeMay Associates. 1960s.
Copley Square, Boston. Sasaki, Dawson, DeMay Associates. 1960s.
Ghirardelli Square, San Francisco. Lawrence Halprin and Associates. 1960s.

Chapter 10

ARCHITECTURE

In approaching architecture as an art, it is virtually impossible for us to separate aesthetic properties from practical or functional properties. In other words, architects first have a particular function to achieve in their building. That function is their principal concern. The aesthetics of the building are important, but they must be tailored to the overall practical considerations. For example, when architects set about to design a 110-story skyscraper they are locked into an aesthetic form that will be vertical rather than horizontal in emphasis. They may attempt to counter verticality with strong horizontal elements, but the physical fact that the building will be taller than it is wide is the basis from which the architects must work. If their desire is to make the building appear light and airy, they must consider, for example, the fact that a computer center with its exceptionally heavy equipment may be planned for the fifth floor of that building.

Their structural design must take into account the weight of the computer center. Then they can consider the aesthetic properties of lightness and airiness.

Architecture often is described as the art of *sheltering*. To consider it as such we must use the term sheltering very broadly. Obviously there are types of architecture within which people do not dwell and under which they cannot escape the rain. Architecture encompasses more than buildings. So, we can consider architecture as the art of sheltering people both physically and spiritually from the raw elements of the unaltered world.

WHAT IS IT?

As we noted, architecture can be considered the art of sheltering. In another large sense, it is the design of three-dimensional space to create practical enclosure. Its basic forms are residences, churches, and commercial buildings. Each of these forms can take innumerable shapes, from single-family residences to the ornate palaces of kings to high-rise condominiums and apartments. We also could expand our categorization of architectural forms to include bridges, walls, monuments, and so forth.

HOW IS IT PUT TOGETHER?

In examining how a work of architecture is put together we will limit ourselves to nine fundamental elements: structure, line, repetition, balance, scale, proportion, context, space, and climate.

Structure

There are many systems of construction or systems of structural support. We will deal with only a few of the more prominent.

Masonry. The most obvious example of masonry is the brick wall, and masonry structures are built upon that principle. Stones, bricks, or blocks are joined with mortar, one on top of the other, to provide basic, structural, weight-bearing walls of a building, a bridge, and so forth (Fig. 10.1). There is a limit to what can be accomplished with a masonry structure because of the pressures that play on the joints between blocks and mortar and the foundation on which they rest. However, when one considers that office buildings such as Chicago's

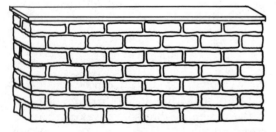

Fig. 10.1. Masonry Wall.

Monadnock Building (Fig. 10.2) are skyscrapers and that their structure is completely masonry (that is, there are no interior steel beams assisting in the support of the building), it becomes obvious that much is possible with this elemental method of construction. It must be noted here that masonry *structure* means that masonry is the exclusive supportive element in the building. A skyscraper or residence that has a steel framework or frame construction over which bricks and mortar have been placed is not a masonry structure, because the masonry elements are not the elements supporting the building. It is also important to recognize the difference between structure and *style.* As will become obvious, many buildings exhibit what appear to be structural elements —post-and-lintel, archways, and so on. However, closer analysis may prove these elements to be decorative and not supportive. A decorative element that does not support is not structural.

Post-and-Lintel. *Post-and-lintel* structure (Figs. 10.3–10.6) consists of horizontal beams (lintels) laid across the open spaces between vertical supports (posts). In this architectural system the traditional material is stone. Post-and-lintel structure is similar to *post-and-beam* structure, in which series of vertical posts are joined by horizontal members, traditionally of wood. The wooden members of post-and-beam structure are held together by nails, pegs, or lap joints.

Because of the lack of tensile strength in its fundamental materials, stone, post-and-lintel structure is limited in its ability to define space. *Tensile strength* is the ability of a material to withstand bending. If we lay a slab of stone across an open space and support it only at each end, we can span only a narrow space before it cracks in the middle and falls to the ground. On the other hand, stone has great *compressive strength*—the

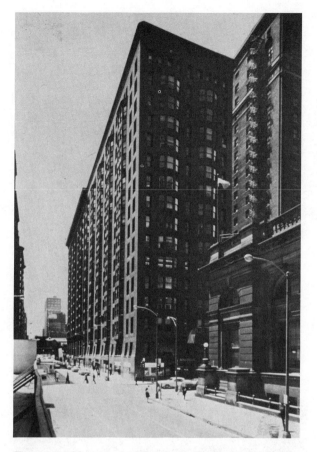

Fig. 10.2. Monadnock Building, Chicago. *Architects:* Burnam and Root.

ability to withstand compression or crushing.

A primitive example of post-and-lintel structure is Stonehenge, that ancient and mysterious religious configuration of giant stones in Great Britain (Fig. 10.3). The ancient Greeks refined this system to high elegance; the most familiar of their post-and-lintel creations is the Parthenon (Fig. 10.4). A more detailed view of this style and structure can be seen in Figs. 10.5 and 10.6.

The Greek refinement of post-and-lintel structure is a *prototype* for buildings throughout the world and across the centuries. So it makes sense to pause to examine the Greek style in more detail. One of the more interesting aspects of the style is its treatment of columns and *capitals*. Figure 10.7 shows the three basic Greek orders, or styles—Ionic, Doric, and Corinthian. These, of course, are not the only styles of post-and-lintel structure. Column capitals can be as varied as the imagination of the architect who designed them. Their primary purpose is to act as a transition for the eye as it moves from post to lintel. Figure 10.8 shows another column capital, from the entrance of Westminster Cathedral in London, which

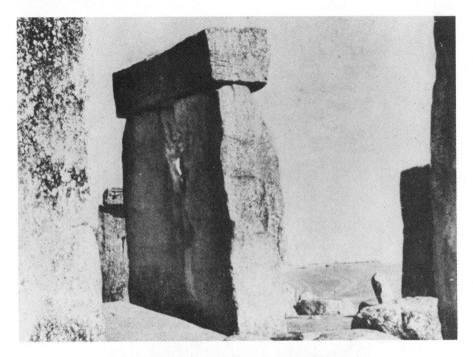

Fig. 10.3. Stonehenge, England.

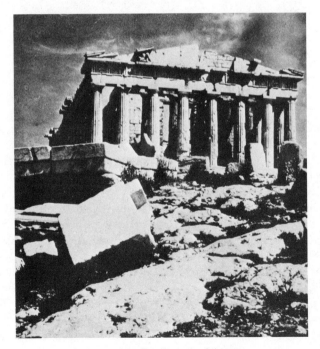

Fig. 10.4. Parthenon, Athens.

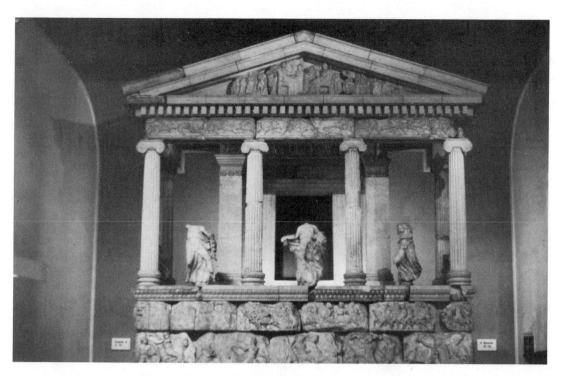

Fig. 10.5. Greek temple. British Museum, London.

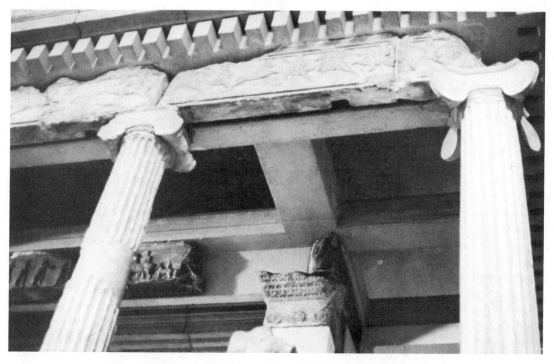

Fig. 10.6. Greek temple, roof detail. British Museum, London.

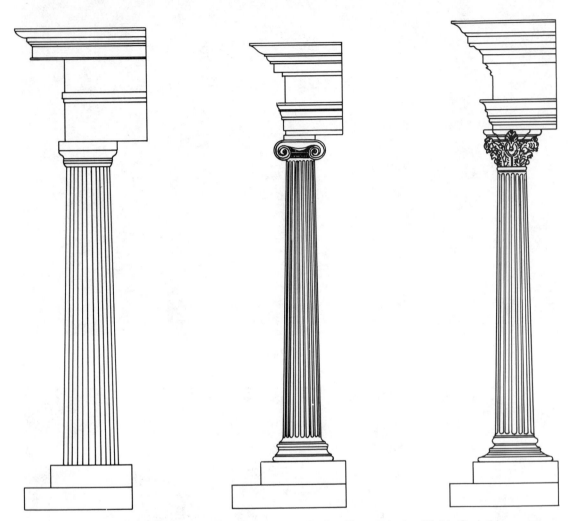

Fig.10.7. Greek columns and capitals. *Left:* Doric. *Center:* Ionic. *Right:* Corinthian.

reflects a religious theme. Figure 10.9 shows a column capital designed to look like a bunch of grapes. Columns also may express a variety of detail. A final element, present in some columns, is *fluting*—vertical ridges cut into the column (Fig. 10.6).

Arch. A third type of architectural structure is the arch. As we indicated earlier, post-and-lintel structure is limited in the amount of unencumbered space it can achieve. The

arch, on the other hand, can define large spaces, since its stresses are transferred outward from its center (the *keystone*) to its legs. So it does not depend on the tensile strength of its material.

There are many different styles of arches, some of which are illustrated in Fig. 10.10. The characteristics of different arches may have structural as well as decorative functions. For example, the pointed arch is capable of spanning greater distances than the

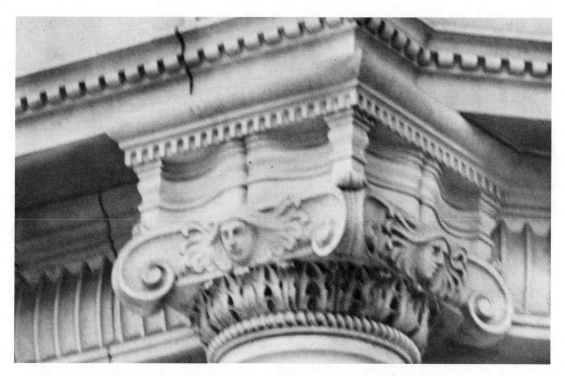

Fig. 10.8. Column capital, central portal, Westminster Cathedral, London.

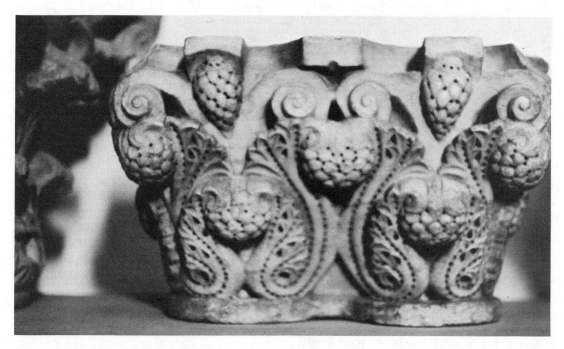

Fig. 10.9. Column capital, Egypt, eight century A.D. British Museum, London.

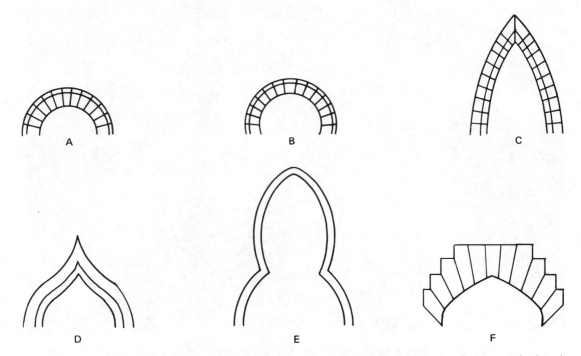

Fig. 10.10. The arch. *A.* Round (Roman) arch. *B.* Horseshoe (Moorish) arch. *C.* Lancet (pointed, Gothic) arch. *D.* Ogee arch. *E.* Trefoil arch. *F.* Tudor arch.

round arch because of the way it transfers stress from its center to its legs.

The transfer of stress from the center of an arch outward to its legs dictates the need for a strong support to keep the legs from caving outward. Such a reinforcement is called a *buttress* (Fig. 10.11). The designers of Gothic cathedrals sought to achieve a sense of lightness. Since stone was their basic building material, they recognized that some system had to be developed that would overcome the bulk of a stone buttress. Therefore, They developed a system of buttresses that accomplished structural ends but were light in appearance. These structures are called *flying buttresses* (Fig. 10.12).

Several arches placed side by side form an *arcade* (Fig. 10.13). Arches placed back to back to enclose space form a *tunnel vault*

(Fig. 10.14). When two tunnel vaults intercept at right angles, as they do in the floor plan of the traditional Christian cathedral, they form a *groin vault* (Fig. 10.15). The protruding masonry indicating diagonal juncture of arches in a tunnel vault or the juncture of a groin vault is *rib vaulting* (Fig. 10.16).

When arches are joined at the top with their legs forming a circle, the result is a *dome* (Fig. 10.17). The dome, through its intersecting arches, allows for more expansive, freer space within the structure. However, if the structures supporting the dome form a circle, the result is a circular building. To permit squared space beneath a dome, the architect can transfer weight and stress through the use of *pendentives* (Fig. 10.18).

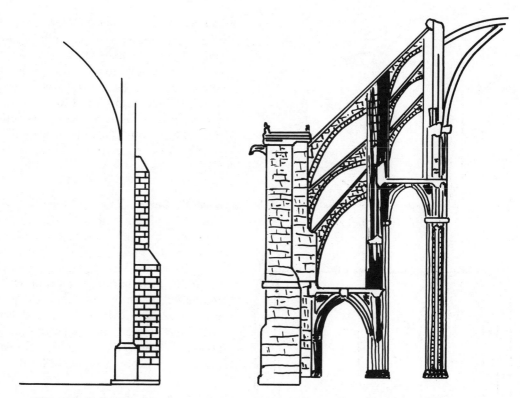

Fig. 10.11. Buttress.

Fig. 10.12. Flying buttresses.

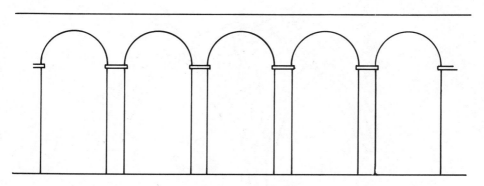

Fig. 10.13. Arcade.

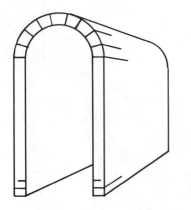

Fig. 10.14. Tunnel vault.

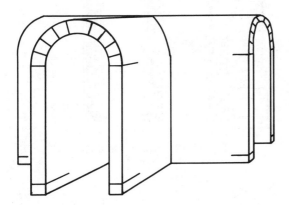

Fig. 10.15. Groin vault.

Cantilever. A *cantilever* is an overhanging beam or floor supported only at one end (Fig. 10.19). Although not a twentieth-century innovation—many nineteenth-century barns in the central and eastern parts of the United States employed it—the most dramatic uses of cantilever have emerged with the introduction of modern materials such as steel beams and prestressed concrete (Fig. 10.20).

Geodesic Dome. The geodesic dome (Fig. 10.21) is a unique, modern structural system invented by an American architect, R. Buckminster Fuller. Consisting of a network of metal rods and hexagonal plates, the dome is a light, inexpensive, yet strong and easily assembled building. Although it has no apparent size limit (Mr. Fuller claims he could roof New York City, given the funds), its potential for variation and aesthetic expressiveness seems somewhat limited.

Line, Repetition, and Balance

Line and repetition perform the same compositional functions in architecture as in painting and sculpture. In his Marin County Courthouse (Fig. 10.22) Frank Lloyd Wright

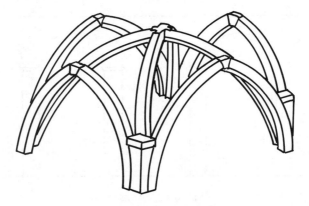

Fig. 10.16. Ribbed vault.

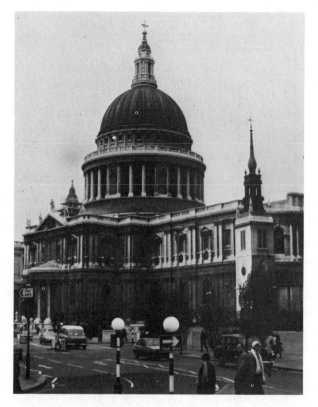

Fig. 10.17. Dome. St. Paul's Cathedral, London.

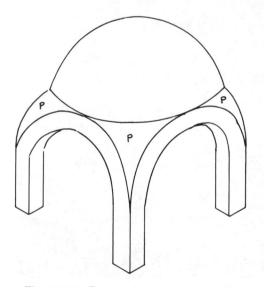

Fig. 10.18. Dome with pendentives (P).

takes a single motif, the arc, varies only its size and repeats it almost endlessly. The result, rather than being monotonous, is dynamic and fascinating.

Let's look at three other buildings. The main gate of Hampton Court Palace (Fig. 10.23), built in the English Tudor style around 1515 by Thomas Wolsey, at first appears haphazard to us because we seem to see virtually no repetition. Actually, this section of the palace is quite symmetrical, working its way left and right of the central gatehouse in mirror images. However, the myriad of chimneys, the imposition of the main palace, which is not centered on the main gate, and our own vantage point cause an apparent clutter of line and form that prompts our initial reaction. Line and its resultant form

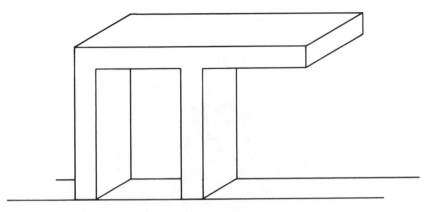

Fig. 10.19. Cantilever.

give Hamptom Court Palace the appearance of a substantial castle.

Although it seems impossible, Fig. 10.24 is the same Hamptom Court Palace. Figure 10.23 reflects the style and taste of England during the reign of Henry VIII (who appropriated the palace from its original owner, Cardinal Wolsey). Later monarchs found the cumbersome and primitive appearance unsuited to their tastes, and Christopher Wren

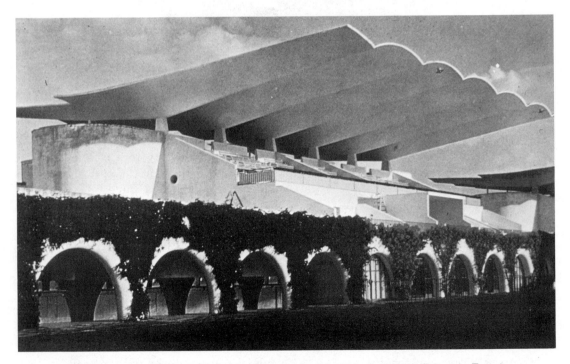

Fig. 10.20. Grandstand, Zarzuela Race Track, Madrid. *Architect:* Eduardo Torroja.

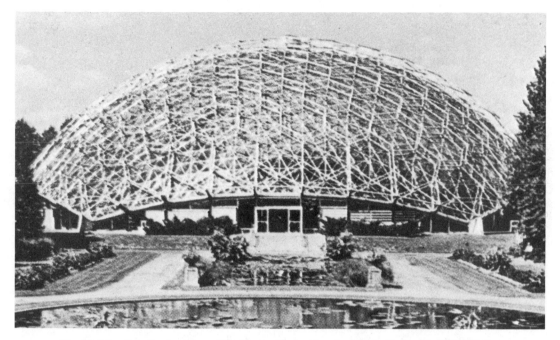

Fig. 10.21. Geodesic dome. Climatron, St. Louis. *Architect:* R. Buckminster Fuller.

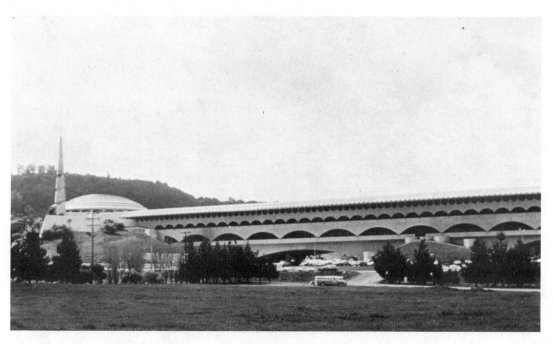

Fig. 10.22. Marin County Courthouse, California. *Architect:* Frank Lloyd Wright.

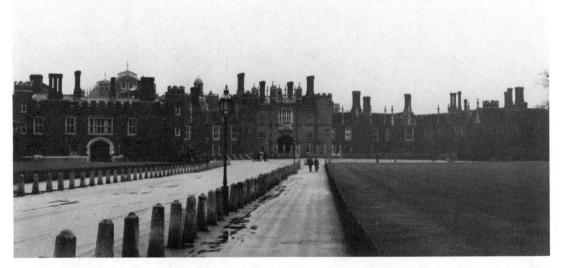

Fig. 10.23. Hampton Court Palace, England. Tudor entry.

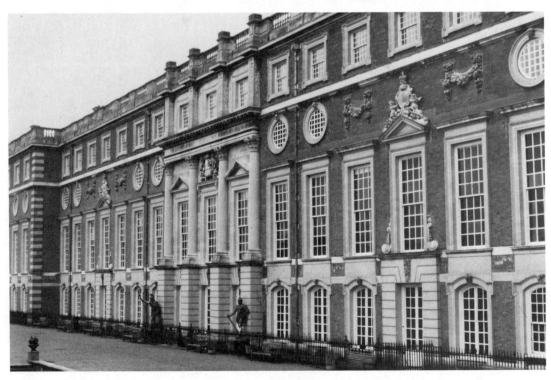

Fig. 10.24. Hampton Court Palace. Wren facade.

was commissioned to plan a "new" palace. So, in 1689, in the reign of William and Mary, renovation of the palace proper began. The result was a new and classically oriented facade.

As we can see in Fig. 10.24, Wren has designed a sophisticated and overlapping system of repetition and balance. Note first that the facade is symmetrical. The outward wing seen at the far left of the photograph is duplicated at the right (but not seen in the photo). In the center of the building are four attached columns surrounding three windows. The middle window forms the exact center of the design, with mirror-image repetition on each side. Now note that above the main windows is a series of relief sculptures, pediments (triangular casings), and circular windows. Now return to the main row of windows at the left border of the photo and count toward the center. The outer wing contains three windows; then seven windows; then the central three; then seven; and finally the three of the unseen

outer wing. Patterns of threes and sevens are very popular in architecture, and Wren has established a pattern of three in the outer wing, repeated it at the center, and then repeated it within each of the seven-window groups to create yet three additional patterns of three! How is it possible to create three patterns of three with only seven windows? First, locate the center window of the seven. It has a pediment and a relief sculpture above it. On each side of this window are three windows (a total of six) without pediments. So, we have *two* groupings of three windows each. Above each of the outside four windows is a circular window. The window on each side of the center window does not have a circular window above it. Rather, it has a relief sculpture, the presence of which joins these two windows with the center window to give us our third grouping of three. Line, repetition, and balance in this facade form a marvelous perceptual exercise and experience.

Buckingham Palace (Fig. 10.25) and the

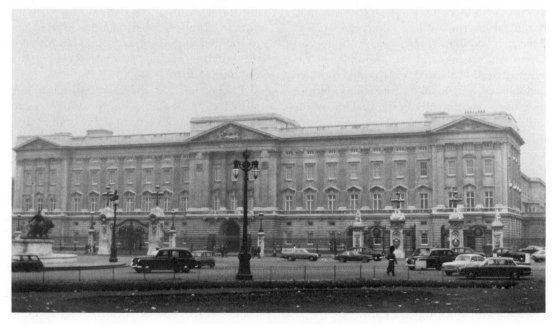

Fig. 10.25. Buckingham Palace, London.

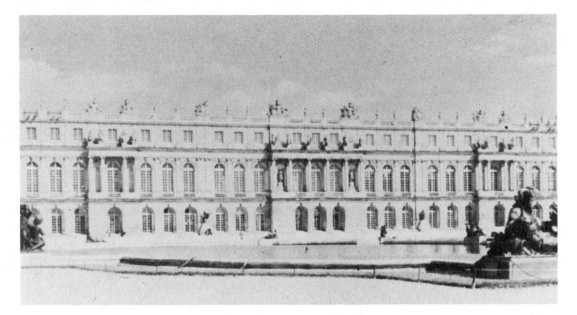

Fig. 10.26. Palace of Versailles, France.

Palace of Versailles (Fig. 10.26) illustrate different treatments of line and repetition. Buckingham Palace uses straight line exclusively, with repetition of rectilinear and triangular form. Like Hampton Court Palace, it exhibits *fenestration* groupings of threes and sevens, and the building itself is symmetrically balanced and divided by three pedimented, porticolike protrusions. Notice how the predominantly horizontal line of the building is broken by the three major pediments and given interest and contrast across its full length by the window pediments and the verticality of the attached columns.

Contrast Buckingham Palace with the Palace of Versailles, in which repetition occurs in groupings of threes and fives. Contrast is provided by juxtaposition and repetition of curvilinear line in the arched windows and baroque statuary. Notice how the horizontal line of the building, despite three porticoes, remains virtually undisturbed, in contrast with Buckingham Palace.

Scale and Proportion

The mass, or *scale,* and proportion of a building and its component elements are very important compositional qualities. Scale refers to the building's size and the relationship of the building and its decorative elements to the human form.

Proportion, or the relationship of individual elements in a composition to each other, also plays a role in the overall analysis and appearance of a design. Let's step outside architecture for a familiar example. The Concorde supersonic airliner appears to be a rather large plane when we view it on the movie screen or on television. Yet if we were to see the plane in actuality, we would be surprised to find that it is not particularly large—in comparison with a DC10, a Boeing 747, or even a Boeing 707. The proportion of the Concorde's window area to its overall size is misleading when we see the plane out of context with the human body.

The Concorde's windows are very small, much smaller than in other airliners. So when we see the Concorde in a newsreel we immediately equate the window size with which we are familiar with the windows in the Concorde. We assume that the relationship or *proportion* of window size to overall fuselage is conventional, and that assumption gives us a larger-than-actual image of the size of the plane. In terms of architecture, proportion and scale are tools by which the architect can create relationships that may be straightforward or deceptive. We must decide how these elements are used, and to what effect. In addition, proportion in many buildings is mathematical: the relationships of one part to another often is based on ratios of three to two, one to two, one to three, and so on as were the parts of the chest of drawers discussed in Chapter 1. Discovering such relationships in the buildings we see is one of the fascinating ways in which we can respond to architecture.

Context

An architectural design must take into account its context, or environment. In many cases context is essential to the statement made by the design. For example, Chartres Cathedral (Fig. 10.27) sits at the center of and on the highest point in the village of Chartres. Its placement at that particular location had a purpose for the medieval artisans and clerics responsible for its design. The centrality of the cathedral to the community was an essential statement of the centrality of the church to the life of the medieval community. Context also has a psychological bearing on scale. A skyscraper in the midst of skyscrapers has great mass, but does not appear as massive in scale when overshadowed by another, taller skyscraper. A cathedral, when compared with a skyscraper, is relatively small in scale. However, when standing at the center of a community

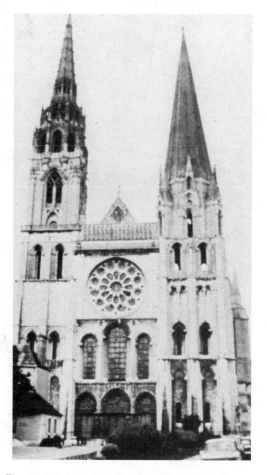

Fig. 10.27. Exterior, Chartres Cathedral, France.

of small houses, it appears quite the opposite.

Two additional aspects of context concern the design of line, form, and texture relative to the physical environment of the building. On one hand, the environment can be shaped according to the compositional qualities of the building. Perhaps the best illustration of that principle is Louis XIV's palace at Versailles, whose formal symmetry is reflected in the design of thousands of acres around it. On a more modest scale, the formal gardens of Hampton Court (Fig. 10.28) reflect the line and form of the palace.

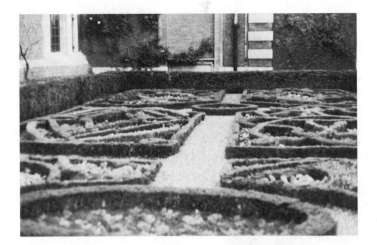

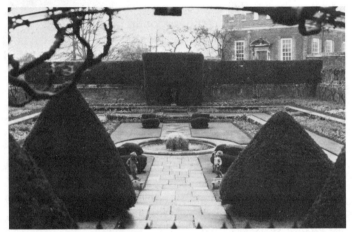

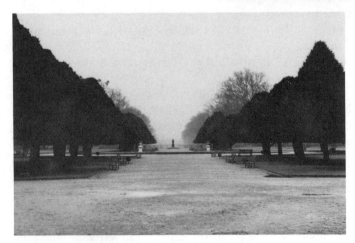

Fig.10.28.   Three views of formal landscaping, Hampton Court Palace, England.

On the other hand, a building may be designed so as to reflect the natural characteristics of its environment. Frank Lloyd Wright's *Falling Water* (Fig. 9.3) illustrates this principle. Such an idea has been advanced by many architects, and can be seen especially in residences in which large expanses of glass allow us to feel a part of the outside while we are inside. The interior decoration of such houses often takes as its theme the colors, textures, lines, and forms of the environment surrounding the home. Natural fibers, earth tones, delicate wooden furniture, pictures that reflect the surroundings, large open spaces—together they form the core of the design, selection, and placement of nearly every item in the home, from walls to furniture to silverware.

Space

It seems so logical as to be absurd to state that architecture must concern space—for what else, by definition, is architecture? However, the world is overwhelmed with examples of architectural design that have not met that need. Design of space essentially means the design and flow of contiguous *spaces* relative to function. Take, for example, a sports arena. Of primary concern is the space necessary for the sports intended to occupy the building. Will it house basketball, hockey, track, football, or baseball? Each of these sports places a design restriction on the architect, and there may be curious results when functions not intended by the design are forced into its parameters. When the Brooklyn Dodgers moved to Los Angeles they played for a time in the Los Angeles Coliseum, a facility designed for the Olympic games and track and field and reasonably suited for the addition of football. However, the imposition of baseball created ridiculous effects—the left-field fence was only slightly over 200 feet from home plate! In addition to the requirements of the game, a sports arena must also accommodate the requirements of the spectators. Pillars that obstruct the spectator's view do not create good will and the purchase of tickets. Likewise, attempting to put more seats in a confined space than ought to be there can create great discomfort. Where to draw the line between more seats and fan comfort is not an easy decision. The Montreal Forum, in which anyone over the height of five feet two inches is forced to sit with the knees under the chin, has not proven to be deleterious to ticket sales for the Montreal Canadiens hockey team. However, such a design of space might be disastrous for a franchise in a less hockey-oriented city.

Finally, the design of space must concern the relationship of various needs peripheral to the primary functions of the building. Again, in a sports arena the sport and its access to the spectator are primary. However, the relationship of access to spaces such as rest rooms and concession stands must also be considered. I once had season basketball tickets in an arena seating 14,000 people in which access to the *two* concession stands required standing in a line that, because of spatial design, intersected the line to the rest rooms! If the effect was not chaotic, it certainly was confusing, especially at half time of an exciting game.

Climate

Climate always has been a factor in architectural design in zones of severe temperature, either hot or cold. As the world's energy supplies diminish, this factor will grow in importance. In the temperate climate of much of the United States, solar systems and designs that make use of the moderating influence of the earth are common. These are passive systems—that is, the design accommodates natural phenomena rather than adding technological devices such as solar collectors. For example, in the colder sections of the

United States a building can be made energy-efficient by designing it with no glass, or minimal glass, on its north-facing side. Windows facing south can be covered or uncovered to catch existing sunlight, which even in midwinter provides considerable warmth. Also, since temperatures at the shallow depth of three feet below the earth's surface rarely exceed or go below fifty degrees, regardless of season, the earth presents a gold mine of potential for design. Houses built into the sides of hills or recessed below the earth's surface require much less heat or cooling than those standing fully exposed—regardless of climate extremes. Even in zones of uniform and moderate temperature climate is a design factor. The "California lifestyle," as it often is known, is responsible for design that accommodates easy access to the out of doors, and large open spaces with free-flowing traffic patterns.

HOW DOES IT STIMULATE THE SENSES?

As should be clear at this point, our sensual response to a form of aesthetic design is a composite experience. To be sure, the individual characteristics we have discussed previously are the stimuli for our response. However, response is a product of the moment and happens because stimuli working in concert affect us in a particular manner. So, since in other chapters we have already considered how particular design considerations might affect us, I wish to make this final chapter's analysis a bit more like our actual experience, that is a spontaneous response to the artwork. My remarks will be brief; much more could be said of each example. However, in the following progression of comparisions, I wish not to be impeded by excessive detail concerning each work.

Chartres Cathedral

The gothic cathedral has been described as the perfect synthesis of intellect, spirituality, and engineering. The upward, striving line of the Gothic arch makes a simple yet powerful statement of medieval people's striving to understand their earthly relation to the spiritual unknown. Even today the simplicity and grace of that design have an effect on most who view a gothic Cathedral. Chartres Cathedral (Figs. 10.27 and 10.29), unlike the symmetry of other gothic churches, has an assymetrical design, arising from the replacement of one of its steeples because of fire. The new steeple reflects a later and more complex gothic style, and as a result impedes the eye as it progresses upward. Only after some

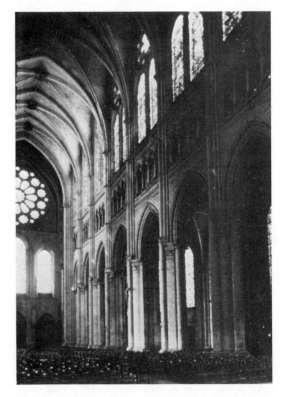

Fig. 10.29. Interior, Chartres Cathedral, France.

pause does the eye reach the tip of the spire, the point of which symbolizes the individual's escape from the earthly known to the unknown.

Included in this grandeur of simple vertical line is an ethereal lightness that defies the material from which the cathedral is constructed. The medieval architect has created in stone not the heavy yet elegant composition of of the early Greeks, which focused upon treatment of stone, but rather a treatment of stone that focuses on space—the ultimate mystery. Inside the cathedral the design of stained glass kept high above the worshipers' heads so controls the light entering the cathedral that the overwhelming effect is, again, one of mystery. Line, form, scale, color, structure, balance, proportion, context, and space all combine to form a un-

ified composition that has stood for seven hundred years as a prototype and symbol of the Christian experience.

Church of the Holy Family

The Christian experience is also the denominator of the design of the Church of the Holy Family (Fig. 10.30). However, despite the clarity of line and the upward striving power of its composition, this church has a modern sophistication, perhaps speaking more of our own conception of space, which to us is less unknowable and more conquerable, than did the churches of our medieval predecessors. The juxtaposing of rectilinear and curvilinear line creates an active and dynamic response, one that prompts in us abruptness rather than mystery. The composition is cool, and its material calls attention

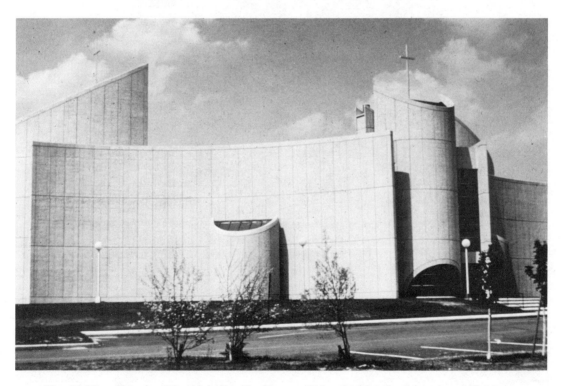

Fig. 10.30. Church of the Holy Family, Parma, Ohio. *Architects:* Conrad and Fleishman.

to itself—to its starkness and to its lack of decoration. The Church of the Holy Family achieves its balance psychologically, by intent, rather than by accident, as was the case with Chartres Cathedral.

Each part of the church is distinct, and is not quite subordinate to the totality of the design. This building perhaps represents a philosophy intermediate between the philosophy underlying the Chartres Cathedral, whose entire design can be reduced to a single motif—the gothic arch—and a philosophy such as the baroque, as seen in the Hall of Mirrors of the Palace of Versailles (Fig.

10.31). No single part of the design of this hall epitomizes the whole, yet each part is subordinate to the whole. Our response to the hall is shaped by its ornate complexity, which calls for detachment and investigation and intends to overwhelm us with its opulence. Here, as in most art, the expression and the stimuli reflect the patron. Chartres Cathedral reflects the medieval church, the Church of the Holy Family, the contemporary church, and Versailles, King Louis XIV. Versailles is complex, highly active, and yet warm. The richness of its textures, the warmth of its colors, and its curvilinear soft-

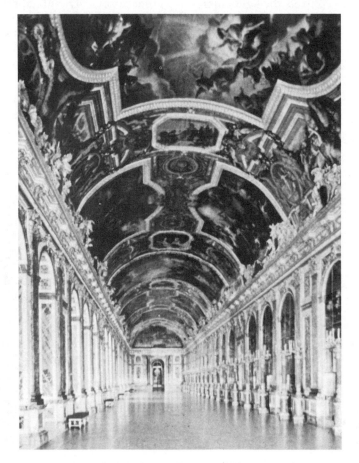

Fig. 10.31. Hall of Mirrors, Palace of Versailles, France.

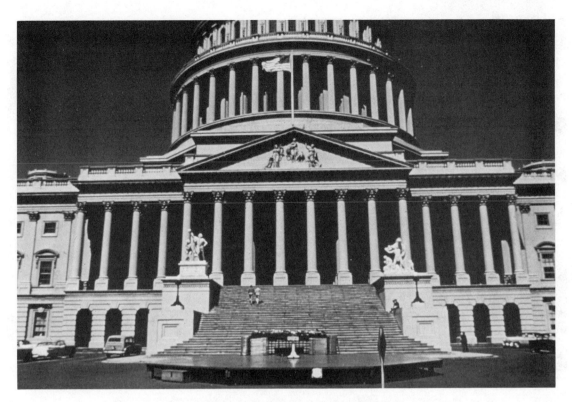

Fig. 10.32. United States Capitol Building.

ness create a certain kind of comfort despite its scale and formality.

United States Capitol Building

In this neoclassic house of government (Fig. 10.32) formality creates a foursquare, solid response. The symmetry of its design, the weight of its material, and its coldness give us a sense of impersonal power, which is heightened by the crushing weight of the dome. Rather than the upward-striving spiritual release of the gothic arch, or even the powerful elegance of the Greek post-and-lintel, the Capitol Building, based on a Roman prototype, elicits a sense of struggle. This is achieved through upward columnar thrust (heightened by the context provided by Capitol Hill) and downward thrust (of the dome) focused toward the interior of the building.

Guggenheim Museum

The architect Louis Sullivan, of whom Frank Lloyd Wright was a pupil, is credited with the concept that form follows function. To a degree we have seen that concept in the previous examples, even though, with the exception of the Church of the Holy Family, they all precede Sullivan in time. A worthy question concerning the Guggenheim Museum (Fig. 10.33) might be how well Wright followed his teacher's philosophy. There is a story that Wright hated New York City because of unpleasant experiences he had had with the city fathers during previous projects. As a result, the Guggenheim,

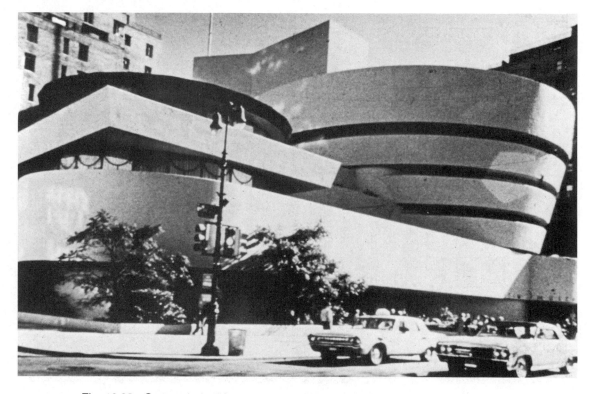

Fig. 10.33. Guggenheim Museum, New York City. *Architect:* Frank Lloyd Wright.

done late in his life, became his final gesture of derision to the city. This center of contemporary culture and art, with its single, circular ramp from street level to roof, was built (so the story goes) from the plans for a parking garage! Be that as it may, the line and form of this building create a simple, smoothly flowing, leisurely, upward movement juxtaposed against a stark and dynamic rectilinear form. The building's line, color, and the feeling they produce are contemporary statements—appropriate to the contemporary art the museum houses. The modern design of the Guggenheim is quite in contrast with the classical proportions of the Metropolitan Museum of Art, just down the street, which houses great works of ancient and modern art. The interior design is outwardly expressed in the ramp, and one can speculate that the slowly curving, unbroken line of the ramp is highly appropriate to the leisurely pace that one should follow when going through a museum.

Zarzuela Race Track

Leisurely progress through the Guggenheim is diametrically opposite the sensation stimulated by the cantilevered roof of the grandstand at Zarzuela Race Track in Spain (Fig. 10.20). Speed, power, and flight are its preeminent concerns. The sense of dynamic instability inherent in the structural form, i.e., cantilever, and this particular application of that form, mirror the dynamic instability and forward power of the race horse at full speed. However, despite the form and the strong diagonals of this design, it is not out of control; the architect has unified the design through repetition of the track-level arcade in the arched line of the cantilevered roof. The design is dynamic, and yet humanized in the softness of its curves and the control of its scale.

Sears Tower

Nothing symbolizes the technological achievement of modern humans more than the skyscraper. Also, nothing symbolizes the subordination of humans to their technology more than the scale of this, the world's tallest building (Fig. 10.34). Designed of rectangular components placed side by side, the Sears Tower is a glass and steel monolith overwhelming in its scale and proportions and cold in its materials. As a point of departure, its appeal to our senses raises the question of what comes next, the conquest of space or a return to respect for its natural mysteries?

CHRONOLOGY OF SELECTED MAJOR PERIODS AND EXAMPLES FOR STUDY IN ARCHITECTURE

C. 4000 B.C.–C. 1000 B.C.
  Ancient Egypt
    pyramids
    tombs

C. 1200 B.C.–C. 300 B.C.
  Ancient Greece
    Parthenon
    Temple of Athena
    Theater of Dionysos

C. 500 B.C.–C. 300 A.D.
  Roman Architecture
    Colosseum
    Pantheon
    Baths of Diocletian
    aqueduct, Segovia, Spain

C. 300 A.D.–C. 1500
  Early Christian and Byzantine Architecture
    Old St. Peter's Basicila, Rome
    Hagia Sophia, Constantinople

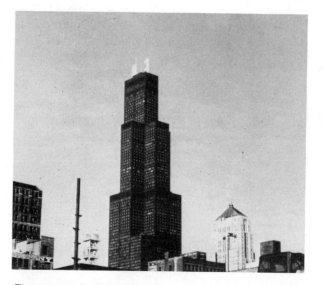

Fig. 10.34. Sears Tower, Chicago. *Architects:* Skidmore, Owings, and Merrill.

c. 900–c. 1200
   Romanesque Europe
      St. Trophime, Arles
      St. Sernin, Toulouse
      St. Pierre, Angoulême
      Leaning Tower, Pisa
      Cathedral of Worms

c. 1200–c. 1400
   Gothic Architecture
      Chartres Cathedral
      Cathedral of Notre Dame de Paris
      Amiens Cathedral
      Exeter Cathedral

c. 1400–c. 1500
   Italy (early Renaissance)
      Cathedral of Florence
      Brunelleschi: Pazzi Chapel
      Michelozzo: Medici-Riccardi Palace

c. 1480–c. 1550
   High Renaissance
      Bramante: Tempietto, Rome
      Framante Palace, Rome
      Michelangelo: apse, St. Peters, Rome

c. 1510–c. 1570
   Mannerism
      Château of Chambord
      Lescot: Lescot Wing of the Louvre

c. 1570–c. 1700
   Baroque Architecture
      Ribera: Hospicio de San Fernando, Madrid

Perrault: East Facade of the Louvre
Le Vau, Hardovin-Mansart: Palace of Versailles

c. 1700–1800
   Classical Architecture
      Jefferson: Rotunda, University of Virginia
      Gabriel: Petit Trianon, Versailles
      Soufflot: Pantheon, Paris
   Rococo Architecture
      Pöppelmann: Zwinger Palace, Dresden
      Zimmermann: Church at Die Weis, Bavaria

c. 1800–c. 1900
   Neoclassical Revival
      La Madeleine, Paris
      Arc de Triomphe de l'etoile, Paris
      Capitol Building, Washington
   Modern Architecture
      Sullivan: Prudential Building, Buffalo, N.Y.

c. 1900–
   Gilbert: Woolworth Building, New York City
   Wright: Robie House, Chicago; *Falling Water,* Bear
      Run, Pennsylvania
   Hood and Howell: Chicago Tribune Tower
   Behrens: Turbine Factory, Berlin
   Gropius: Bauhaus, Dessau, Germany
   Van der Rohe: Tugendhat House, Czechoslovakia
   Le Corbusier: Savoye House Poissy-sur-Seine,
      France
   Skidmore, Owings, and Merrill: Lever House, New
      York City

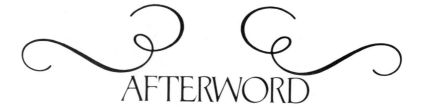

AFTERWORD

There really is little that needs to be said by way of summary to this text, except to draw attention to what has *not* been included. We have not dealt much with philosophy of art; only in passing have we noted art history. Above all, we have not even covered completely the technical information that was our focus. We have covered only the basic skeleton. While I have attempted to remain as neutral as possible in presenting information about each of the arts, there is no denying that subjectivity is present. The method of treatment was arbitrary, as was the choice of information presented. Some readers may find such a cognitive approach sterile and disturbing. As indicated earlier, however, these pages should be viewed only as an introduction. The real life, the enthusiasm, the enjoyment, and the meaning of the arts depend on what happens next. If through the information presented in these pages some-

one has found a new appreciation for an art form that was previously an enigma, or has found a means by which previous knowledge has been enlarged, then this book will have achieved its goal.

Finally, it should be obvious, and it will become obvious, that not every definition of every term is uniformly agreed upon by artists themselves. Words serve only as a convenience for us as we try in some way to cope with what we see and what we hear, how and why we react as we do to those experiences, and how and why we try to share them with others. It may not be possible to understand the whats and the whys of some works of art, such as totally abstract paintings or dance presentations. Sometimes the significance or the meaning must wait until we have passed the time barrier and become historians rather than journalists in our perception.

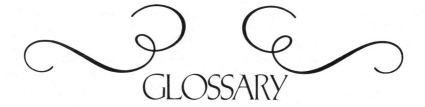

GLOSSARY

a

ABA: In music, a three-part structure that consists of an opening section, a second section, and a return to the first section.

Absolute music: Music that is free from any reference to nonmusical ideas, such as a text or a program—for example, Mozart's Symphony No. 40.

Abstraction: A thing apart; removed from real life.

Accelerando: In music, a gradual increase in tempo.

Accent: In music, a stress that occurs at regular intervals of time. In the visual arts, any device used to highlight or draw attention to a particular area, such as an accent color. See also **focal point.**

Adagio: A musical term meaning slow and graceful.

Additive: In sculpture, those works that are built. In color, the term refers to the mixing of hues of light.

Aereal perspective: The indication of distance in painting through use of light and atmosphere.

Aesthetic distance: The combination of mental and physical factors that provides the proper separation between a viewer and an artwork; it enables the viewer to achieve a desired response. See **detachment.**

Affective: Relating to feelings or emotions, as opposed to facts. See **cognitive.**

Allegretto: A musical term denoting a lively tempo, but one slower than allegro.

Allegro: A musical term meaning brisk or lively.

Alto: In music, the lowest female voice.

Andante: A musical term meaning a medium, leisurely, walking tempo.

Andantino: A musical term meaning a tempo a little faster than andante.

Appoggiatura: In music, an ornamental note or series of notes above and below a tone of a chord.

Aquatint: An intaglio printmaking process in

which the plate is treated with a resin substance to create textured tonal areas.

Arabesque: A classical ballet pose. The body is supported on one leg, and the other leg is extended behind with the knee straight.

Arcade: A series of arches placed side by side.

Arch: In architecture, a structural system in which space is spanned by a curved member supported by two legs.

Aria: In opera or oratorio, a highly dramatic melody for a single voice.

Articulation: The connection of the parts of an artwork.

Art song: A vocal musical composition in which the text is the principal focus. See **song cycle.**

Assemblé: In ballet, a leap with one foot brushing the floor at the moment of the leap and both feet coming together in fifth position at the finish.

b

Balletomane: A term used by ballet enthusiasts to refer to themselves. A combination of *ballet* and *mania.*

Baroque: A seventeenth– and eighteenth–century style of art, architecture, and music that is highly ornamental.

Barre: A wooden railing used by dancers to maintain balance while practicing.

Barrel vault (tunnel vault): A series of arches placed back to back to enclose space.

Battement jeté: A ballet movement using a small brush kick with the toe sliding on the floor until the foot is fully extended about two inches off the floor.

Beats: In music, the equal parts into which a measure is divided.

Binary form: A musical form consisting of two sections.

Biomorphic: Representing life forms, as opposed to geometric forms.

Bridge: In music, transitional material between themes or sections of a composition.

c

Cadence: In music, the specific harmonic arrangement that indicates the closing of a phrase.

Camera pan: The turning of the camera from one side to the other to follow the movement of a subject.

Canon: A musical composition in which each voice imitates the theme in counterpoint.

Cantilever. An architectural structural system in which an overhanging beam is supported only at one end.

Capital: The transition between the top of a column and the lintel.

Chaîné: A series of spinning turns in ballet utilizing a half turn of the body on each step.

Chamber music: Vocal or instrumental music suitable for performance in small rooms.

Changement de pied: In ballet, a small jump in which the positions of the feet are reversed.

Character oxfords: Shoes worn by dancers which look like ordinary street shoes, but which are, in actuality, specially constructed for dance.

Chiaroscuro: Light and shade. In painting, the use of highlight and shadow to give the appearance of three-dimensionality to two-dimensional forms. In theatre, the use of light to enhance the plasticity of the human body or the elements of scenery.

Chord: Three or more musical tones played at the same time.

Choreography: The composition of a dance work; the arrangement of patterns of movement in dance.

Chromatic scale: A musical scale consisting of half steps.

Cinematic motif: In film, a visual image that is repeated either in identical form or in variation.

Cinema verité: Candid camera; a televisionlike technique of recording life and people as they are. The hand-held camera, natural sound, and minimal editing are characteristic.

Classic: Adhering to traditional standards. A specific style embodying those characteristics referring to the ideas and standards of ancient Greece and Rome.

Coda: A passage added to the end of a musical composition to produce a satisfactory close.

Cognitive: Facts and objectivity as opposed to emotions and subjectivity. See **affective.**

Conjunct melody: In music, a melody comprising notes close together in the scale.

Consonance: The feeling of a comfortable relationship between elements of a composition, in pictures, sculpture, music, theatre, dance, or architecture. Consonance may be both physical and cultural in its ramifications.

Conventions: The customs or accepted underlying principles of an art, such as the willing suspension of disbelief in the theatre.

Corinthian: A specific order of Greek columns employing an elaborate leaf motif in the capital.

Corps de ballet: The chorus of a ballet ensemble.

Counterpoint: In music, two or more independent melodies played in opposition to each other at the same time.

Crescendo: An increase in loudness.

Crosscutting: In film, alternation between two independent actions that are related thematically or by plot to give the impression of simultaneous occurrence.

Curvilinear: Formed or characterized by curved line.

Cutting: The trimming and joining that occurs during the process of editing film.

Cutting within the frame: Changing the viewpoint of the camera within a shot by moving from a long or medium shot to a close-up, without cutting the film.

d

Decrescendo: A decrease in loudness.

Demi-hauteur: A ballet pose with the leg positioned at a 45-degree angle to the ground.

Demi-Plié: In ballet, a half bend of the knees in any of the five positions.

Denouement: The section of a play's structure in which events are brought to a conclusion.

Detachment: Intellectual as opposed to emotional involvement. The opposite of *empathy*.

Diatonic minor: The standard musical minor scale achieved by lowering by one half step, the third and sixth of the diatonic or standard major scale.

Disjunct melody: In music, melody characterized by skips or jumps in the scale. The opposite of *conjunct melody*.

Dissonance: The occurrence of inharmonious elements in music or the other arts. The opposite of *consonance*.

Divertissement: A dance, or a portion thereof, intended as a diversion from the idea content of the work.

Documentary: In photography or film, the recording of actual events and relationships using real-life subjects as opposed to professional actors.

Dome: An architectural form based on the principles of the arch in which space is defined by a hemisphere used as a ceiling.

Doric: A Greek order of column having no base and only a simple slab as a capital.

Drypoint: An intaglio process in which the metal plate is scratched with a sharp needlelike tool.

Dynamics: The range and relationship of elements such as volume, intensity, force, and action in an artwork.

e

Eclecticism: A style of design that combines examples of several differing styles in a single composition.

Editing: The composition of a film from various shots and sound tracks.

Elevation: In dance, the height to which a dancer leaps.

Empathy: Emotional-physical involvement in

events to which one is a witness but not a participant.

Engraving: An intaglio process in which sharp, definitive lines are cut into a metal plate.

Entablature: The upper section of a building; it is usually supported by columns, and includes a lintel.

Entrechat: In ballet, a jump beginning from fifth position in which the dancer reverses the legs front and back one or more times before landing in fifth position. Similar to the changement de pied.

Ephemeral: Transitory, not lasting.

Esprit d'escalier: French, meaning "spirit of the stairs." Remarks, thought of after the fact, that could have been *bon mots* had they been thought of at the right moment; witty remarks.

Etching: An intaglio process in which lines are cut in the metal plate by an acid bath.

Etude: A study; a lesson. A composition, usually instrumental, intended mainly for the practice of some point of technique.

f

Farce: A theatrical genre characterized by broad, slapstick humor and implausible plots.

Fenestration: Exterior openings, such as windows and archways, in an architectural facade.

Fluting: The vertical ridges in a column.

Focal point (focal area): A major or minor area of visual attraction in picture, sculpture, dance, play, film, landscape design, or building.

Foreground: The area of a picture, usually at the bottom, that appears to be closest to the respondent.

Form cutting: In film, the framing in a successive shot of an object that has a shape similar to an image in the preceding shot.

Forte: A musical term meaning loud.

Found object: An object taken from life that is presented as an artwork.

Fresco: A method of painting in which pigment is mixed with wet plaster and applied as part of the wall surface.

Fugue: Originated from a Latin word meaning "flight." A conventional musical composition in which a theme is developed by counterpoint.

g

Galliard: A court dance done spiritedly in triple meter.

Genre: A category of artistic composition characterized by a particular style, form, or content.

Geometric: Based on man-made patterns such as triangles, rectangles, circles, ellipses, and so on. The opposite of *biomorphic*.

Gestalt: A whole. The total of all elements in an entity.

Gothic: A style of architecture based on a pointed-arch structure and characterized by simplicity, verticality, elegance, and lightness.

Gouache: A watercolor medium in which gum is added to ground opaque colors mixed with water.

Grande seconde: Ballet pose with the leg in second position in the air.

Grand jeté: In ballet, a leap from one foot to the other, usually with a running start.

Grand plié: In ballet, a full bend of the knees with the heels raised and the knees opened wide toward the toes. May be done in any of the five positions.

Grave: In music, a tempo marking meaning slow.

Groin vault: The ceiling formation created by the intersection of two tunnel or barrel vaults.

h

Harmony: The relationship of like elements, such as musical notes, colors, and repetitional patterns. See **consonance** and **dissonance.**

Homophony: A musical texture characterized by chordal development of one melody. See **monophony** and **polyphony.**

Hue: The spectrum notation of color; a specific, pure color with a measurable wavelength. There are primary hues, secondary hues, and tertiary hues.

i

Icon: An artwork whose subject matter includes idolatry, veneration, or some other religious content.

Identification: See **empathy.**

Impasto: The painting technique of applying pigment so as to create a three-dimensional surface.

Intaglio: The printmaking process in which ink is transferred from the grooves of a metal plate to paper by extreme pressure.

Intensity: The degree of purity of a hue. In music, theater, and dance, that quality of dynamics denoting the amount of force used to create a sound or movement.

Interval: The difference in pitch between two tones.

Ionic: A Greek order of column that employs a scroll-like capital with a circular base.

Iris: In film and photography, the adjustable circular control of the aperture of a lens.

Isolation shot: In film, the isolation of the subject of interest in the center of the frame.

j

Jeté: In ballet, a small jump from one foot to the other, beginning and ending with one foot raised.

Jump cut: In film, the instantaneous cut from one scene to another or from one shot to another; often used for shock effect.

k

Key: A system of tones in music based on and named after a given tone—the tonic.

l

Largo: In music, a tempo notation meaning large, broad, very slow, and stately movement.

Legato: In music, a term indicating that passages are to be played with smoothness and without break between the tones.

Lento: A musical term indicating a slow tempo.

Libretto: The words, or text, of an opera or musical.

Linear perspective: The creation of the illusion of distance in a two-dimensional artwork through the convention of line and foreshortening—that is, the illusion that parallel lines come together in the distance.

Lintel: The horizontal member of a post-and-lintel structure in architecture.

Lithography: A printmaking technique, based on the principle that oil and water do not mix, in which ink is applied to a piece of paper from a specially prepared stone.

m

Magnitude: The scope or universality of the theme in a play or film.

Melodrama: A theatrical genre characterized by sterotyped characters, implausible plots, and emphasis on spectacle.

Melody: In music, a succession of single tones.

Mime: In dance or theatre, actions that imitate human or animal movements.

Mise en scène: The complete visual environment in the theater, dance, and film, including setting, lighting, costumes, properties, and physical structure of the theatre.

Modern dance: A form of concert dancing relying on emotional use of the body, as opposed to formalized or conventional movement, and stressing human emotion and the human condition.

Modulation: A change of key or tonality in music.

Monophony: In music, a musical texture employing a single melody line without harmonic support.

Montage: In the visual arts, the process of making a single composition by combining parts of other pictures so that the parts form a whole, and yet remain distinct. In film, a rapid sequence of shots which bring together associated ideas or images.

Moog synthesizer: See **synthesizer.**

Motive (motif): In music, a short, recurrent melodic or rhythmic pattern. In the other arts, a recurrent element.

n

Nonobjective, nonrepresentational: Lacking identification with real life.

o

Objective camera: A camera position based on a third-person viewpoint.

Objet d'art: A French term meaning "object of art."

Octave: In music, the distance between a specific pitch vibration and its double; for example, concert A equals 440 vibrations per second, one octave above that pitch equals 880, and one octave below equals 220.

On point: In ballet, a specific technique utilizing special shoes in which the dancer dances on the points of the toes.

Opéra bouffe: A comic opera.

Opus: A single work of art.

Overtones (overtone series): The sounds produced by the division of a vibrating body into equal parts. See **sympathetic vibration.**

p

Palette: In the visual arts, the composite use of color, including range and tonality.

Pas: In ballet, a combination of steps forming one dance.

Pas de deux: A dance for two dancers, usually performed by a ballerina and her male partner.

Pavane: A stately court dance in 2/4 time; usually follows a galliard.

Pediment: The typically triangular roof piece characteristic of the Greek and Roman style of post-and-lintel structure.

Pendentives: Curved triangular segments leading from the corners of a rectangular structure to the base of a dome.

Perspective: The representation of distance and three-dimensionality on a two-dimensional surface. See also **linear perspective** and **aereal perspective.**

Photojournalism: Photography of actual events that have sociological significance.

Piano: A musical term meaning soft.

Pirouette: In ballet, a full turn on the toe or ball of one foot.

Plasticity: The capability of being molded or altered. In film, the ability to be cut and shaped. In painting, dance, and theater, the accentuation of three-dimensionality of form through chiaroscuro.

Platemark: The ridged or embossed effect created by the pressure used in transferring ink to paper from a metal plate in the intaglio process.

Polyphony: See **counterpoint.**

Port de bras: The technique of moving the arms correctly in dance.

Post-and-lintel: An architectural structure in which horizontal pieces (lintels) are held up by vertical columns (posts); similar to post-and-beam structure, which usually utilizes wooden posts and beams held together by nails or pegs.

Presto: A musical term signifying a rapid tempo.

Program music: Music that refers to nonmusical ideas through a descriptive title or text. The opposite of *absolute music.*

Prototype: The model on which something is based.

Pyramidal structure: In theatre, film, and dance, the rising of action to a peak, which then tapers to a conclusion.

q

Quadrille: (1) An American square dance. (2) A European ballroom dance of the eighteenth and nineteenth centuries.

r

Realism: The artistic selection and use of elements from life; contrasts with naturalism, in which no artistic selection is utilized.

Recitative: In opera, sung dialogue.

Rectilinear: In the visual arts, the formed use of straight lines and angles.

Relevé: In ballet, the raising of the body to full height or the half height during the execution of a step or movement.

Relief printing: The process in printmaking by which the ink is transferred to the paper from raised areas on a printing block.

Representationalism: The use of objects that are recognizable from real life.

Requiem: A Mass for the dead.

Rhythm: The relationship, either of time or space, between recurring elements of a composition.

Ribbed vault: A structure in which arches are connected by diagonal as well as horizontal members.

Ritardando: In music, a decrease in tempo.

Rondo: A form of musical composition employing a return to an initial theme after the presentation of each new theme.

Ronds de jambe à têrre: In ballet, a rapid semicircular movement of the foot in which the toe remains on the floor and the heel brushes the floor in first position as it completes the semicircle.

Rubato: A style of musical performance in which liberty is taken by the performer with the rhythm of the piece.

s

Saturation: In color, the purity of a hue in terms of whiteness; The whiter the hue, the less saturated it is.

Scale: In music, a graduated series of ascending or descending musical tones. In architecture, the mass of the building in relation to the human body.

Serigraphy: A printmaking process in which ink is forced through a piece of stretched fabric, part of which has been blocked out—for example, silkscreening and stenciling.

Song cycle: A group of art songs combined around a similar text or theme.

Sonority: In music, the characteristic of texture resulting from chordal spacing.

Staccato: In music, the technique of playing so that individual notes are detached and separated from each other.

Static: Devoid of movement or other dynamic qualities.

Stereotype: A standardized concept or image.

Style: The individual characteristics of a work of art that identify it with a particular artist, nationality, historical period, or school of artists.

Stylization: Reliance on conventions, distortions, or theatricality; the exaggeration of characteristics that are fundamentally verisimilar.

Subjective camera: A camera position that gives the audience the impression that they are actual participants in the scene.

Subtractive: In sculpture, referring to works that are carved. In color, referring to the mixing of pigments as opposed to the mixing of colored light.

Symbolism: The suggestion through imagery of something that is invisible or intangible.

Symmetry: The balancing of elements in design by placing physically equal objects on either side of a centerline.

Sympathetic vibration: The physical phenomenon of one vibrating body being set in motion by a second vibrating body. See also **overtone.**

Symphony: A large musical ensemble; a symphony orchestra. Also, a musical composition for orchestra usually consisting of three or four movements.

Syncopation: In a musical composition, the displacement of accent from the normally accented beat to the offbeat.

Synthesizer (also called *Moog synthesizer*): An electronic instrument that produces and combines musical sounds.

t

Tempera: An opaque watercolor medium, referring to ground pigments and their color binders such as gum, glue, or egg.

Tempo: The rate of speed at which a musical composition is performed. In theater, film, or dance, the rate of speed of the overall performance.

Terra cotta: An earth-brown clay used in ceramics and sculpture.

Tessitura: The general musical range of the voice in a particular composition.

Texture: In art, the two-dimensional or three-dimensional quality of the surface of a work. In music, the melodic and harmonic characteristics of the composition.

Theatricality: Exaggeration and artificiality; the opposite of *verisimilitude.*

Theme: The general subject of an artwork, whether melodic or philosophical.

Timbre: The characteristic of a sound that results from the particular source of the sound. The difference between the sound of a violin and the sound of the human voice is a difference in timbre. Also called *tone color.*

Tonality: In music, the specific key in which a composition is written. In the visual arts, the characteristics of value.

Tondo: A circular painting.

Tonic: In music, the root tone (*do*) of a key.

Triad: A chord consisting of three tones.

Tunnel vault: See **barrel vault.**

Tutu: A many-layered bell-shaped crinoline skirt worn by a ballerina.

v

Value scale: In the visual arts, the range of tonalities from white to black.

Variation: Repetition of a theme with minor or major changes.

Verisimilitude: The appearance of reality in any element of the arts.

Virtuoso: Referring to the display of impressive technique or skill by an artist.

Vivace: A musical term denoting a vivacious or lively tempo.

w

Waltz: A ballroom dance in 3/4 time.

Woodcut: A relief printing executed from a design cut in the plank of the grain.

Wood engraving: A relief printing made from a design cut in the butt of the grain.

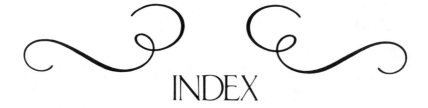

INDEX